The
Politics of Mercantilism

PHILIP W. BUCK

OCTAGON BOOKS

A DIVISION OF FARRAR, STRAUS AND GIROUX

New York   1974

Reprinted 1964
by special arrangement with Holt, Rinehart and Winston, Inc.

Second Octagon printing 1974

OCTAGON BOOKS
A DIVISION OF FARRAR, STRAUS & GIROUX, INC.
19 Union Square West
New York, N. Y. 10003

LIBRARY OF CONGRESS CATALOG CARD NUMBER: 64-24844
ISBN 0-374-91083-9

Manufactured by Braun-Brumfield, Inc.
Ann Arbor, Michigan

Printed in the United States of America

To my Father and Mother

Preface

THE rise of political and economic dictatorship in the twentieth century gives contemporary significance to a discussion of mercantilism; for modern totalitarianism—an awkward word used in this book to include the Soviet, Fascist, and Nazi states and their policies—is in many ways a revival of the ideas and practices of the mercantile system. The primary purpose of this study, however, is to analyze the political doctrines of the English mercantilists, a numerous and various group of men who wrote on economic and political subjects in England during the seventeenth and eighteenth centuries.

Since this subject is of some interest to the general reader, a sketch of the plan of this study may be given for his convenience. The first chapter outlines briefly the conditions which gave rise to mercantilist doctrine and the practices of states in that period. The second summarizes the economic thought of these writers. The third and fourth set forth the political implications of mercantilist economic ideas, and describe the nature of the state which was to carry the program into action. The last chapter criticizes mercantilist political doctrine, and compares it to the theories of present-day dictatorships.

For the student of the subject, the footnotes constitute a fairly extensive bibliography of English mercantilist writings. Longer notes, giving lists of writers, who discussed a particular subject, or presenting discussion of bibliography, are placed at the back of the book. These longer notes, in every case, are indicated by a footnote on the appropriate page of the text.

The analytical table of contents gives, by means of titles and sub-titles, a guide to the presentation of the subject. There is extensive quotation from the works of the writers, in order to allow them to speak for themselves as far as is possible within the compass of a small book.

The author wishes to make acknowledgment to Professor R. G. Gettell of the University of California, under whose direction the study was begun; to Professors B. F. Haley and Maxwell Savelle of Stanford University, who read most of the manuscript and gave much aid by criticism and suggestion; and to his colleagues in the Department of Political Science, who have consistently given him sympathy and encouragement.

The research required for the study would have been impossible without the splendid resources of the Huntington Library at San Marino, California; and the completion of the work was made pleasant by the unfailing courtesy and kindness of its staff.

Responsibility for viewpoints expressed and errors committed must, of course, rest upon the author.

P. W. B.

Stanford University,
November 1, 1941.

Contents

CHAPTER 1

The Historical Background of English Mercantilism

THE economic programs of modern dictatorships—both of the left and of the right—invite comparison with the state controls of the national economy which were advocated by the mercantilist writers of the seventeenth and eighteenth centuries. There are enough important similarities to make such a comparison illuminating. The mercantilist system established and maintained an elaborate regulation of the nation's foreign trade; fascist and communist states either monopolize or strictly manage the amount and the nature of the nation's exports and imports. The mercantilist writers advocated an extensive system of regulation of the internal economy of the community, devised for the purpose of making effective use of all economic resources; the modern dictatorships have set up the complicated machinery of the totalitarian state. Above all, in both cases the purpose is similar; mercantilists, fascists, and communists aim at making the state powerful by directing and controlling the economic activities of the nation.

These are tempting analogies: they suggest that the study of the objectives and techniques proposed and supported by English pamphleteers three centuries ago might give some insight into the economic aspects of twentieth century dictatorship and could conceivably afford some standards for judgment of the value of state direction of the economic activities of the community.

1

Historians themselves, however, have taught us to look with some suspicion at historical analogies; and it would be misleading to press too far any evaluation based upon a comparison of mercantilist practice with that of the totalitarian states.   One aspect, which has been mentioned already, is truly suggestive.   In both cases, however far removed they may be by the lapse of time, the dominant interest of the national state is asserted: the right of the state to regulate economic affairs.   Curiously enough, the political doctrines of mercantilism have had relatively little attention from scholars; it is the historians of economic, not of political thought, who have analyzed mercantilist theory.[1]   The contribution of these early theorists to the development of the science of economics has been carefully examined, and in all such studies the peculiarly nationalist character of the system has been set forth.   But their views of the state, which should exercise such a wide range of powers in the economic sphere, have had little critical examination.   It is proper, therefore, to attempt an evaluation of the political doctrines of the mercantilists; and such is the purpose of this study.

The mercantile system, however, does not readily yield to description or analysis.   To begin with, it can hardly be called a system.   There is no coherent body of theory developed by one writer; there is not even the relatively consistent viewpoint of a group of allied thinkers.   It is necessary, in fact, to review the work of a number of men who wrote without much reference to one another's ideas, and who varied considerably in their approach, in their terminology, and even in their subject matter.   The general family resemblance which their statements exhibit is due more to the similarity of the conditions they discussed than to any consistent agreement on any common body of doctrine.   This arises, in large part, from the

[1] For a discussion of the writings on mercantilism, see p. 195.

significant fact that the men who worked out the theories were often men of action rather than of study; they were not economists, they were merchants.[2]

A second difficulty, and perhaps a greater, follows immediately from what has just been said. These writings are dispersed over a long period. It is justifiable, perhaps, to go back so far in English history as the *Libelle of Englyshe Polycye* written before 1438,[3] and one of the classics is the *Discourse of the Common Weal of this Realm of England*, written in 1549.[4] One of the latest of the writers who could properly claim an important place in this broad ideological kinship is Sir James Steuart, whose *Principles of Political Economy*[5] was published in 1767.

As might be expected, the mercantilist position was never completely stated, nor even supported, by any one of these men who were so widely separated by years or centuries, and whose occupations and experience differed greatly at any given decade. It is true, however, that they all display a common attitude of mind, characterized chiefly by their mutual insistence that the state should control economic organization and practice in the interest of national aggrandizement. This community of attitude sprang from the conditions of the times in which they lived, and from the policies of the kingdom of which they were all loyal subjects. Indeed, the term "Mercantilism" is more often used to describe the policies of states during the sixteenth, seventeenth and eighteenth centuries

[2] Schacht, H. G. H., *Der Theoretische Gehalt des Englischen Merkantilismus*, Berlin, 1900, pp. 100-101.

[3] *The Libelle of Englyshe Polycye*, ed., Sir George Warner, Oxford, 1926. For date and authorship, see the introduction.

[4] *A Discourse of the Common Weal of this Realm of England*, ed., Elizabeth Lamond, Cambridge, 1895. (Hereafter cited as [Hales], *Discourse*.) Miss Lamond carefully discusses authorship and date of publication in her introduction.

[5] Steuart, Sir James, *An Inquiry into the Principles of Political Economy*, London, 1767.

than to identify the theories held by the advocates of those policies.[6]

I. THE GENESIS OF THE MERCANTILIST DOCTRINE

Before any attempt can be made to analyze English mercantilist doctrine, particularly its political aspect, it is necessary to make at least a brief sketch of the historical situation in which it originated and developed. It is impossible to review the period in detail, since it includes the reigns of the Tudors and the Stuarts, and even extends to some time after the Glorious Revolution. During this long period three powerful forces were at work which were of paramount importance to the development of mercantilist theory, and these forces may be stated and described with reasonable succinctness.

The first was the rise of the national state; the intimate relationship of mercantilism with the growing strength of national institutions is apparent—it might even be called one of those institutions. The second factor which contributed to the development of national economic policy and to its statement and defense by the writers of the period is now referred to by historians as the "commercial revolution." The growth of a money and credit economy provided a new economic and commercial environment in which the state developed the new lines of policy. The

[6] This is the meaning of the word "Mercantilism" as employed by Professor Brentano in the title of the second volume of his *Geschichte der Wirtschaftlichen Entwicklung Englands*, Jena, 1927, "Die Zeit des Merkantilismus," and in the title of the short study by J. W. Horrocks, *A Short History of Mercantilism*, New York, 1925.

Professor E. A. J. Johnson complains of the vagueness of the term in the first chapter of his *Predecessors of Adam Smith*, New York, 1937, pp. 3-5. Nevertheless it does identify a group of writers and a body of doctrine, so it is used in this examination of their political doctrines. Its admitted vagueness is a difficulty, but is not completely destructive of any value in the term.

third was the decline of the medieval economy. The state inherited a rich legacy of rights over the economic and commercial structure from decaying feudal institutions and conceptions, by the use of which it was able to assert its claim to control many economic activities; and the community was willing to accept such an exercise of authority.

A. *The Rise of the National State*

The effectiveness of the new national institutions was in large part the result of the strength of the English monarchy; it is no real exaggeration to say that it was an absolute monarchy at the time that national commercial policy was developing. From the time that William the Conqueror imposed a feudal centralization upon the kingdom, laying the foundation of a national tax system and subordinating the power of the towns and the barons alike, the monarchy furnished the driving force for the administration of national affairs. In the thirteenth century, during the reigns of Edward I and Edward III, such medieval obstructions to trade as road and river tolls, local coinages, and town and city dues, all of which had the effect of internal customs barriers, were abolished or reduced. At the same time some characteristic commercial policies made their appearance: Flemish weavers were induced to settle in England in order to stimulate an industry which was already of great importance and later was to have an even larger share in the nation's industrial development; prohibitions were put upon the exportation of raw wool and the importation of foreign cloth; early in the fourteenth century a staple was set up in Flanders for the marketing of English stuffs abroad. National political institutions were growing to make the powers of the state effective in the whole community; the Parliament had been set up before the beginning of the fourteenth century, and the royal courts had begun to build up a body of common law for the kingdom.[7]

It is the age of the Tudors, however, which displays the full panoply of the powers and policies of the state in the economic field. Three powerful and popular monarchs, Henry VII, Henry VIII, and Elizabeth, successfully built up national power and policy, with a careful eye to commercial and industrial strength. The navigation acts gave government encouragement to shipping; the preamble of the act of 1540 clearly states this objective; the commercial treaties with the Netherlands were designed to win favorable opportunities for trade; the privileges of the Hanseatic merchants in England were withdrawn and many of the English trading companies received official support in the effort to establish an active foreign trade.[8] Industry as well as commerce became the concern of the state: there were tariff policies giving protection to native manufacture; the Statute of Artificers and the Poor Law provided the machinery to control conditions of apprentice-

[7] It would be easy to multiply references on the point of the importance of the national state, and its absolutist character; the works of Schmoller, von Heyking, and Haney already cited attest it (see note 1, above). Knight, Barnes, and Flugel, in their *Economic History of Europe in Modern Times*, Boston, 1928, pp. 314-322, give a succinct summary.

It is instructive to read together the accounts of early commercial policy given by Cunningham, *Growth of English Industry and Commerce*, ed., 1905, and Lipson, E., *Economic History of England*, London, 1927, 1931, and Maitland's fine, though early, study of the constitutional development, *The Constitutional History of England*, Cambridge, 1908, reprinted 1920, to note the growth of machinery and policy.

A fine analysis of the importance of the English monarchy in this development of national power is given in Heckscher, *Mercantilism*, trans. M. Shapiro, London, 1935, Vol. I, pp. 46-56, in connection with the early disappearance of tolls and dues.

[8] In addition to Cunningham's great work, two recent histories written on a similar scale must be cited: Lipson, referred to above, and Brentano, L., *Geschichte der Wirtschaftlichen Entwicklung Englands*, Jena, 1927, Vol. II. The whole growth of the national policies is set forth in each, without any fundamental divergence on the general character of the development.

ship and, in effect, to enforce a patriotic duty to labor; agriculture was encouraged with the corn laws.[9]

Equally important was the development of a national administrative machinery. The point of origin for national administration was the organization of national finance, the customs and the excises. In the Tudor reigns the Parliament, by then a national institution, the Council, a central pivot of the enforcement of policy, and the local justices of the peace, agents of the central government for industrial and labor regulation, furnished the means for translating plans into practice. In the days of the Stuarts the Board of Trade and Plantations was added to this armory of weapons for the management of economic affairs, so that mercantilist objectives could still be achieved, though the effective popularity of the monarchs had diminished.[10]

There is no need to emphasize or elaborate the vital importance of the development of the national state and the growth of a national administrative mechanism as one of the most essential conditions for the appearance of the mercantile system. It is true that any brief survey ignores many aspects of this long and exciting period. The Wars of the Roses interposed a period of confusion, with a corresponding decay in the powers of the central

[9] The success of the Tudors in leadership is succinctly put by A. D. Innes, *England under the Tudors*, 6th ed., London, 1921, p. 6: "The note of the period is a practical absolutism tempered by a judicious recognition of forms and precedents, and made possible by an extremely skilful attention to and consideration for popular sentiment. . . . Their principle was to secure their own way by giving it the appearance of being the People's will."

[10] An admirable description in brief compass of the administrative machinery developed by the Tudors is given in Sir William Ashley's *The Economic Organization of England*, London, 1914, reprinted with additional chapter by G. C. Allen, 1935. A much earlier, but very enlightening study is Schanz, G., *Englische Handelspolitik, gegen Ende des Mittelalters*, Leipzig, 1882. Finally, Heckscher gives a penetrating analysis of the whole pattern of the control of industry in England in Ch. VI of his first volume.

government, between the reign of Edward III and the strong leadership of the Tudors. The marital adventures of Henry VIII and the flirtations of Elizabeth gave as much concern to the Crown's ministers during those reigns as did the problems of commercial policy. The Stuarts, partly because they publicly claimed powers which before had been exercised by Henry VIII and Elizabeth without any fanfare of divine right or royal prerogative, precipitated two political and constitutional revolutions. After the Glorious Revolution the growth of political parties and the wars on the continent concern the government and the people fully as much as the economic changes which presage the Industrial Revolution.

But in all this pageant, as in the commercial and industrial policies, the growing power of the national state is displayed. There are conflicts between this state and rivals of its own kind upon the continent; but there is also the steady growth of a constitutional and administrative organization by which the objectives of national aggrandizement are to be compassed under the leadership of able and ambitious monarchs supported by a ruling aristocracy and a wealthy merchant class. The appearance of the national state, then, is one of the indispensable prerequisites to the growth of mercantilist policy and theory.[11]

B. *The Commercial Revolution: Money, Credit, and Prices*

The national state would not have developed this type of policy, however, had not the general economic situation of the European community altered slowly but completely from what it had been during the Middle Ages. This process of change was a powerful force in the growth

---

[11] Heckscher, *op. cit.*, Vol. II, Part II, "Mercantilism as a System of Power." Here the importance of the national state is made clearly manifest.

of the mercantile system; it is usually referred to as the "commercial revolution" and its most conspicuous and important aspect is the growth of a money and credit economy. The commercial revolution is at once a familiar and controversial subject; but only its familiar processes are of significance in the present connection.

European trade increased in volume, widened in geographical scope, and changed in character. More goods of commoner and bulkier kinds changed hands, more efficient means of transport were devised, and a new supply of precious metals flowed in from the new world. Prices rose, and banks and exchanges developed to handle the expanding trade within countries and between nations. "Europe was gradually approaching a real price economy." [12]

For the English government and the English merchant the concrete manifestation of this general European change was a transformation of English trade from a passive to an active participation in the commerce of the time. The first preliminary was to free London and the other trading centers of the domination of the foreign merchants and financiers. The Steelyard of the Hanseatic League lost its privileges; the Italian money lenders were denied the advantages they had formerly possessed at the English court. The English gild merchant, and later the English craft gild, took an active part in pushing the sale of goods abroad, and in the development of trading con-

[12] Knight, Barnes, and Flugel, *Economic History of Europe in Modern Times*, Boston, 1928, p. 300. See pp. 299-300 for an excellent summarizing paragraph. The significance of the change to a money economy is brilliantly stated by Professor Tawney in *Religion and the Rise of Capitalism*, New York, 1926, Ch. II, Sec. 1.

The historians of theory are all in agreement on this point; there might be noted Haney, L. H., *op. cit.*, pp. 104-106; Gettell, R. G., *History of Political Thought*, New York, 1924, Ch. VII; Gonnard, R., *op. cit.*, pp. 92-96. The importance of money to the state in England is set forth by Cunningham, *op. cit.*, Vol. II, Part I, pp. 2-11; and Brentano, *op. cit.*, Vol. II, Ch. 19.

nections. The Merchant Adventurers, and the establishment of the Staple, all contributed to the growing trade.[13]

In the fifteenth and sixteenth centuries the growth of commerce was reflected in a change in the organization of trading and manufacture. The gild system, once an effective means for carrying on trade and manufacture, showed itself to be too rigid for the expanding opportunities. It was displaced by the domestic system of industry, and the capitalist entrepreneur appeared in the woolen industry. This merchant draper, as he was called, became a dealer in goods, and employed people in the villages and the country to work up the raw materials which he brought them; and then he called for the finished product and sold it either at the markets in England, or, if he possessed the necessary connections, in some market abroad.[14]

During this period, while the form of English commercial and industrial organization was changing, the gilds lost their power as a means of enforcing regulation of conditions of labor, of standards of manufacture, of prices of goods. The national state seemed then to be the appropriate agency for directing and regulating this expanding manufacture and commerce, and the new merchant class were eager, even vociferous, in demanding that protective and regulatory action should be set up to safeguard their interests and adjust their difficulties. The state, recogniz-

[13] For these changes in commercial policy see Schanz, *Englische Handelspolitik*, Vol. I, Part I, Ch. II; Brentano, *op. cit.*, Vol. II, p. 164, and Ch. XXVII; Lipson, *op. cit.*, Vol. I, pp. 452-471; Ashley, Sir William, *An Introduction to English Economic History and Theory*, 3rd ed., London, 1906, Vol. I, Part I, pp. 96-113. (Referred to hereafter as Ashley, *Economic History*.)

For the development of the gilds: Gross, Charles, *The Gild Merchant*, Oxford, 1890; Lipson, *op. cit.*, Vol. II, Ch. VII.

[14] For the change in organization from gild master to merchant draper see Ashley, *Economic History*, Vol. I, Part II, Ch. III; Brentano, *op. cit.*, Vol. II, Ch. 24; Lipson, *op. cit.*, Vol. I, pp. 414-423. Unwin, G., *Industrial Organization in the Sixteenth and Seventeenth Centuries*, Oxford, 1904, gives a brilliant analysis of this change in English industrial organization.

ing its own interest in the development of commerce, manufacture and shipping, was ready to assume these new tasks in order to increase its power and authority.

C. *The Decline of the Medieval Economy*

The success of the new national authority depended to a large extent upon the measure of assent which the community was willing to accord to it as it broadened its powers over economic activity. The people were prepared to accept such regulation, because of the traditions which were carried over from the teachings of the church, and the traditions of medieval economic relationships.

The economic teaching of the church fathers had stressed the conception of a just price; the idea that a moral duty lay upon both buyer and seller to arrive at a bargain which fairly took into account the real need for the commodity sold, and the fair costs of producing it. Canonist doctrine on the paying of interest is also illuminating. Here again is the conception that there must be a moral justification underlying economic relationships; interest as mere usury was condemned, though payment for the loss of benefit from money loaned or for the injury arising from not having it at hand was allowable.

The canonist teachings were often avoided by various ingenious subterfuges; but nevertheless the medieval economy, through the regulatory power of the craft and merchant gilds and the courts merchant of the towns, was really subjected to a certain amount of orderly control, aimed at safeguarding the welfare of the community as a whole.

It was a natural development, then, for the relatively new and energetic national administration to avail itself of these characteristic ideas and institutions in carrying out a mercantilist policy. Sometimes the institutions themselves were mobilized for the new service, as when the Tudor government at one time nationalized the gilds;

oftener familiar types of regulation were vested in the
hands of the justices of the peace or the privy council.
The religious conception of society, which had justified
the ordering of economic activities in the interest of the
Kingdom of God and the salvation of men's souls, gave
way to a nationalist conception of society which justified
regulation of industrial and commercial relationships in
the interest of the Kingdom of England and the profit of
her merchant classes.[15]

In summary, it is possible to say that the rise of the
national state, the appearance of a money economy, and
the decay of medieval economic institutions, gave rise to
the mercantile system. If the complicated history can be
stated simply, the story is that of a vigorous institution
seizing the heritage of rights and customs which had
grown up in the feudal economy, and adapting them to
the new opportunities for national strength which were
afforded by the changes of the commercial revolution.
It is true that many other factors operated in this long
span of centuries from the fifteenth to the eighteenth;
and it is also true that the pattern of policy and administration varied greatly during the period. Nevertheless it
is still possible to assign to the combination of these three
general factors—the national state, the exchange economy,
and the declining economic ideas and institutions of the

---

[15] Ashley, *Economic History*, Vol. I, Part I, Ch. III, and Part II, Ch. VI.
Lipson, *op. cit.*, Vol. I, Chs. VII and VIII, give a good description of the
range and content of gild and municipal regulation. The relation of
medieval regulations and teachings to the development of national authority is brought out in Heckscher, *op. cit.*, Vol. I, Ch. VI, and in the
last section of that chapter he makes a penetrating analysis of the later
decline of this industrial regulation. The influence of municipal regulation upon national policy is also analyzed in his second volume, Part III,
Ch. III, dealing with the "policy of provision," and in Part V, Ch. II, he
points out the contrast between the "amoral" ends of mercantilist policy
and the religious conceptions in canonist economics. Finally, there is an
admirable brief treatment of English canonist doctrine, and of the transition to mercantilist ideas in Beer, M., *Early British Economics*, London,
1938, Chs. I-VI.

Middle Ages—the establishment of the conditions which led to the objectives and practices of the mercantilist states, and to the theories of the mercantilist writers.

II. THE MERCANTILIST PRACTICE

The policies of the English state, when it undertook to guide the national economy, showed two chief aspects. The first, and most familiar, includes the external policies designed to make the nation strong against the other states of Europe; the second exhibits a set of domestic or internal regulations.

A. *The External Policies of Mercantilism*

The guiding principle behind the management of foreign trade relations and, for that matter, a great part of foreign policy as well, was the doctrine of the favorable balance of trade. One of the most succinct statements of it was given by one of its early advocates:

> The ordinary means therefore to encrease our wealth and treasure is by Forraign Trade, wherein we must ever observe this rule; to sell more to strangers yearly than wee consume of theirs in value. . . . That part of our stock which is not returned to us in wares must necessarily be brought home in treasure.[16]

Almost exactly a century after Thomas Mun asserted this doctrine, Bishop Berkeley was demanding in *The Querist,* "Whether that trade should not be accounted most pernicious, wherein the Balance is most against us?"[17] The doctrine antedates Mun's famous statement of it by well over a century, and the persistent reiteration of the idea

[16] Mun, Thomas, *England's Treasure by Forraign Trade*, ed., Sir William Ashley, New York, 1895, pp. 7-8. (Written in 1630 probably, but first published in 1664.)

[17] Berkeley, George, *The Querist*, ed. by J. H. Hollander, Baltimore, 1910, question no. 167. (Written and published about 1734-36.)

was matched by a remarkably consistent tariff policy. Towns and gilds had already pursued protectionist lines of action, so the government could have claimed respectable precedents, had it been necessary. The powerful driving force, however, was the desire for national aggrandizement by securing treasure and increasing shipping. All the states of Europe were dazzled by the flow of precious metals into Spain and Portugal, and while some Elizabethan gentlemen secured a share of it by the direct method of robbing the galleons as they crossed the Spanish Main, the English monarchs inclined to the advice of the merchants in and out of Parliament, who counseled the use of a tariff policy which would secure a favorable balance of trade.

The full panoply of protective tariffs came early and quickly into existence—prohibitions on the export of bullion, wool, and naval stores, bounties upon the export of corn and some manufactured goods, duties upon the import of foreign textiles and exotic luxuries. It was not till the time of Gladstone in the nineteenth century that this elaborate mechanism of customs duties was completely swept away.

Fully as important as the tariff policy was the steady effort to increase English shipping, embodied in the long series of the navigation acts. Privileges were given to English ships in English ports, and in the colonial and Eastern trades. The materials of shipbuilding were jealously guarded both at home and in the colonies. Care was taken that English seamen should man the mercantile marine; this led to the encouragement of fish days in Elizabeth's reign, the whole community eating fish in order to maintain the hardy race of British mariners. The navy and the merchant marine were almost the same thing in those times, so that armament and commercial strength were intimately linked. Taken as a whole, the navigation laws were an excellent illustration of the constancy of mercantile policy; they were not actually repealed till 1849—a sufficiently startling date—though the enforcement of them had been gradually allowed to lapse long before that time.

The old colonial system was an important part of the external policies of mercantilism. England was eager to participate in the wealth that came from colonial enterprise and the trading opportunities that accompanied the establishment of plantations abroad; and the Elizabethan adventurers were more than willing to run the risks that such schemes involved. The state began to encourage colonization—the motives of national gain are clearly declared in the charters granted by the crown. The political rivalry with other imperial powers is obvious enough, but there were economic objectives to be secured as well. The colonial trade was reserved to English ships and English merchants by the navigation laws and a system of customs duties. The colonies were also to be the sources of essential raw materials like naval stores, and were to yield exotic goods like tobacco so that home demand might be satisfied without prejudicing the balance of trade, or better still, were to produce enough so that such goods might be re-exported to the other states of Europe. Population policy was also involved. In the seventeenth century, confronted with the problem of poverty it seemed to many of the mercantilists that England was overpopulated, and so the colonies offered an opportunity to set the surplus of people to work in the plantations. In the eighteenth century, though many writers worried over a shortage of hands, the incorporation of the new world into an imperial economy was well established, and there was general agreement that labor in the overseas territories was productively employed in the national interest. One of the reasons that the hands in the New World were engaged in furthering the strength of the nation was that a fairly consistent policy had been followed in discouraging colonial manufactures that competed with home industries.   The old colonial system, with its monopoly of the trade from colonies, the assignment of manufactures in the new world to a subordinate and supplementary place, and the tariffs designed to monopolize the colonial market, was one of the most characteristic of the external policies of mercantilism.

National diplomacy, as might be expected, was frequently aimed at the achievement of commercial and economic strength.   The trade treaties with the countries of the continent, the war with the Dutch in Cromwell's time, the constant urging of the pamphleteers that France or the Netherlands or both should be regarded as dangerous rivals, all these are reflections of the drive toward establishing and maintaining the power of Great Britain against the competing states of Europe.[18]

B. *The Internal Policies of Mercantilism*

Such were the external policies of mercantilism; but it had its internal or domestic aspect as well.   The same interest in national strength that laid out the lines of imperial and foreign policy justified the discipline and direction of the economic activities of the home community.   The experience and the traditions of medieval institutions prepared both governors and governed for extensive programs of regulation.

Prices and qualities of goods had been regulated since

[18] On tariff policy the works of Cunningham, Lipson, and Brentano must be referred to. Heckscher, in the work so often cited because of its authoritative treatment, devotes all of Part III in the second volume to "Mercantilism as a System of Protection," making an especially acute analysis of the "fear of goods" (pp. 112-129).

On the colonial system the works of G. L. Beer, *Origins of the British Colonial System, 1578-1660*, New York, 1908, and *The Old Colonial System*, 2 vols., New York, 1912, are classic. There is no fundamental modification of the analysis made there in the more recent general histories of Lipson and Brentano.

the Tudor times; and even when the rise of the domestic form of manufacture made administration exceedingly difficult if not impossible, there was still frequent demand that the justices be more active in this duty, and that the officers of search and inspection be brought into full performance of their ancient tasks.

Labor, recognized as one of the essential factors of production, was subjected to careful control. The Statute of Artificers had set up a machinery for the regulation of wages which was quite actively exercised. The Elizabethan Poor Law had declared the obligation of the able-bodied members of the community to engage in productive labor. The training of the laborer was established in the acts which governed apprenticeship. The origin of this pattern of administration runs back to a medieval situation, the scarcity of laborers after the Black Death; but its maintenance was part of a general attitude which sanctioned the use of government authority to ensure the effective use of the skill and industry of the working classes.[19]

Finally, the state made spasmodic efforts to control consumption. It was only logical that a government which was regulating industry with regard to standards and prices, and fixing wage levels and conditions of apprenticeship for the laborers, should also attempt, at least, to impose some control on the consumption of goods. The mercantilists were constantly demanding sumptuary legislation: "If we were not too much affected to Pride, monstrous fashions, and Riot, above all other nations, one million and a half of pounds might plentifully supply our wants," Mun lamented. He felt, indeed, that the English had been "of late years besotting themselves in a beastly manner, sucking smoak, and drinking healths, until death

---

[19] An admirable treatment of the labor theories of the mercantilists is to be found in Furniss, E. S., *The Position of the Laborer in a System of Nationalism*, Boston, 1920.

stares many in the face." [20]   There had been sumptuary laws in the reign of Edward III; and there were fish days re-established by Burleigh while Elizabeth was queen. The tariff legislation was often aimed at restraining the taste for foreign luxuries which might overbalance the trade and inflict a loss of treasure on the realm.   In the seventeenth and eighteenth centuries foreign buttons and buttonholes, French lawns and cambrics were prohibited in order to establish such trades in England.   However logical the effort to control consumption might be, the difficulties of administering such legislation were very great, and so it never achieved much prominence as a part of the mercantile policies.

This brief sketch of the origin and nature of the policies and practices of mercantilism must serve as an introduction to an analysis of the theories put forth by its advocates.   To them the growing power of the national government—made manifest in the authority of the monarchy despite the revolutions which ended two of the Stuart reigns—offered the promise of effective economic as well as political leadership.   Moreover, trade was expanding and business organization changing; and since many of the mercantilists were businessmen turned pamphleteers, they constantly demanded that the power of the state should be put forth to make England and English merchants more prosperous and powerful in the rivalry of European commerce.   The sanctions for the exercise of government authority lay in the extensive and detailed pattern of regulation of economic activity which had been established in the medieval economy of the towns, and which had been given moral approbation in the economic teachings of the church.

In this forcing environment, then, the twofold aspect of mercantilist policy made its appearance.   The external

---

[20] Mun, Thomas, *England's Treasure by Forraign Trade*, ed., Sir William Ashley, New York, 1895, pp. 98 and 99.

policies—tariffs, bounties, prohibitions, the navigation acts, the old colonial system, diplomatic bargaining, and even war—were knit together by the guiding idea of the favorable balance of trade. The internal regulations—the elaborate controls of industry, labor, and even at times the consumption of goods—were the product of a scheme to strengthen the domestic economy of the realm, though the doctrine of the favorable balance often entered into these also as a motivating force.

The period in which these forces operated and in which the theories were developed is a long one, extending from the fourteenth century, perhaps even earlier, to the middle of the eighteenth century and the beginning of the Industrial Revolution. There is, then, a host of writers expressing various views, but they do partake of a common attitude springing from the persistent underlying factors which gave rise to mercantilism, and which sustained its general policies. This historical background must be kept in mind while the economic theories of the mercantilists are examined. The political doctrines, which are closely linked to the economic ideas, can then be analyzed.

CHAPTER II

Mercantilist Economic Doctrine

THE English mercantilists thought and wrote of the economic and political problems of their time. They saw these problems as national problems; for the rise of the national state under the aggressive leadership of the Tudors, and despite the arbitrary claims of the Stuarts, was one of the most pervasive influences in the community of which they were members. Their doctrines were predicated upon the action, and depended upon the sanctions, of this vigorous institution. The titles of their books and pamphlets constantly assert this viewpoint, from Clement Armstrong's *How to Reforme the Realme in Settyng them to Werke and to Restore Tillage* [1] and John Hales' *A Discourse of the Common Weal of this Realm of England* [2] both written in the first half of the sixteenth century, to James Anderson's curious blend of nationalism and free trade, *Observations on the Means of Exciting a Spirit of National Industry, chiefly intended to promote the Agriculture, Commerce, Manufacturies and Fisheries of Scotland,* [3] published in 1777. The national economy was the subject of their study; they constructed a system of *politi-*

[1] *How to Reforme the Realme in Settyng them to Werke and to Restore Tillage.* Probably written by Clement Armstrong in 1535 or 1536. Goldsmith's Library, University of London, MSS no. 10. (In Tawney and Power, *Tudor Economic Documents*, Vol. III, pp. 115-129, London, Longmans, Green, 1924.)

[2] [Hales, John], *A Discourse of the Common Weal of This Realm of England,* edited by Elizabeth Lamond, Cambridge, 1893.

[3] Anderson, James, *Observations on the Means of Exciting a Spirit of National Industry, chiefly intended to promote the Agriculture, Commerce, Manufacturies and Fisheries of Scotland.* In a series of letters to a friend. Edinburgh, 1777.

cal economics, if the term may be used. No one mercantilist writer puts forward a complete system, but through more than two centuries most of them steadily insisted upon the right and the duty of the state to assume control of the economic activities of the nation. It would be easy to suggest that the control of the internal economy was a logical consequence of the desire to win treasure by foreign trade; but as a matter of fact their proposals in this field rested also upon the idea that the state should exercise control over these matters—as had been the case in English medieval society—in the interests of a well-balanced social and economic structure. A third set of relationships held equal importance for them with the foreign trade and the domestic economy—the encouragement and regulation of the colonies and the colonial trade. The plantations were to be fitted into an imperial economic scheme; the territories in the new world and the trading connections in the Orient were to minister to the strength of the mother country. Probably ghosts of mercantilist writers hovered in the Parliament Hall at Ottawa and applauded the negotiation of the treaties of imperial preference! That chorus of ghostly applause, however, contained some dissenting voices—there were practical critics of the mercantilist point of view and some writers, the Tory Free Traders, who put forward a cosmopolitan economic theory. If Gladstone and Cobden turned in their graves when the Ottawa treaties were finally ratified, so also did Nicholas Barbon and Dudley North.

To appreciate the true significance of the mercantilists' economic doctrines, then, it is necessary to analyze their proposals for controlling Britain's foreign trade, their schemes for regulating her domestic economy, and their plans for managing her colonial empire. Finally, the few protagonists of cosmopolitanism and the practical critics of the prevailing point of view cannot be ignored.

I. THE CONTROL OF FOREIGN TRADE: THE DOCTRINE OF THE FAVORABLE BALANCE OF TRADE

The earliest, and crudest, statement of the doctrine of the favorable balance of trade was put exclusively in terms of money or treasure by the bullionist school of writers in the sixteenth and seventeenth centuries. The English government in the reign of Henry VI had required merchants to bring gold to the mint whenever they received payment for a sale abroad. The enforcement of such a balance of bargains was designed to avoid the drain of gold to foreign countries. Loss of treasure by foreign trade had been perceived and condemned very early by writers on England's policies. In 1436 the author of the *Libelle of Englyshe Polycye* had devoted all of his seventh "chapitle" to an attack on the "Venicyans and the Florentynes" because they brought luxuries to the English, encouraged them in extravagant living, and bore away the English gold.[4] Both the increase in vice and the decrease in gold seemed extremely prejudicial to the welfare of the nation. John Hales, in his *Discourse of the Common Weal of This Realm* of England written before the middle of the sixteenth century, studies the various kinds of artificers of the kingdom and reckons as "only tollorable" those who "sell wares growinge beyonde the seas, and doe fetch out oure treasure of the same" while "clothiars, tannars, cappers and worsted makers" should be cherished as the only ones which "by their misteries and faculties doe bringe in anie treasour." [5]

At the end of the sixteenth century an increasing number of transactions were carried on by exchange, and the

[4] *The Libelle of Englyshe Polycye*, edited by Sir George Warner, Oxford, 1926.

[5] [Hales], *Discourse*, pp. 91-93.

phenomenon of the rise and fall of the exchange introduced a new complication into the calculation of how the kingdom stood by its foreign trade. A series of three pamphlets published between 1599 and 1608, probably written by Thomas Milles, analyzed this new problem, and pointed out how important was the work of the customs officials in controlling trade which, if left uncontrolled, might draw treasure out of the kingdom.[6] Gerard de Malynes made the foreign exchanges, and the urgent necessity of management of them by the state, the subject of a number of pamphlets, the most famous being *A Treatise of the Canker of Englands Commonwealth* printed in 1601.[7] He carried on an acrimonious, even abusive, controversy with Edward Misselden, who had in 1622 and 1623 set forth the view the kingdom should manage the general balance of trade, but should not interfere with the exchanges.[8]

The warfare of these two redoubtable pamphleteers, in which ink was shed like water, was fought over a practical, as well as theoretical, issue. The British East India Company was carrying on a very profitable trade in eastern commodities which were bought by exporting gold and silver bullion and coin. The defenders of the Company, and Misselden was one of them, strove to establish the view that what mattered to England's welfare was that the *general* balance of trade should be favorable, not that each

[6] [Milles, Thomas], *The Customers Apology*, London, 1599, *The Customers Replie*, London, 1601, and *The Customers Alphabet and Primer*, London [1608]. The "customer" in each one of these titles is the customs and port official, and all of these pamphlets emphasize how important is his function to the welfare of the kingdom.

[7] Malynes, Gerard de, *A Treatise of the Canker of Englands Commonwealth*, London, 1601.

[8] Misselden, Edward, *Free Trade, or the means to make trade florish*, London, 1622 and *The Circle of Commerce, of the Balance of Trade, in defence of Free Trade*, London, 1623. This controversy between Malynes and Misselden is admirably summarized by E. A. J. Johnson, *Predecessors of Adam Smith*, New York, Prentice-Hall, 1937, pp. 45-54 and 66-69.

particular trade should bring in more treasure than it exported. The talents of Thomas Mun were also exerted in the Company's behalf, and his *Discourse of Trade from England unto the East Indies,*[9] published in 1621, is one of the best defenses for the trade in bullion. A little more than ten years later he wrote one of the most succinct statements of the doctrine of the general balance of trade in the famous pamphlet, *England's Treasure by Forraign Trade:* "The ordinary means therefore to encrease our wealth and treasure is by Forraign Trade, wherein wee must ever observe this rule: to sell more to strangers yearly than we consume of theirs in value." [10]

This debate over bullion exports and the risks of the East India trade ran on through the century; in 1697 John Pollexfen asserted that "nothing but Bullion Imported, can make amends for Bullion Exported. Which if not observed we may Trade away our Riches, but not get Riches by Trade." [11] There is no need, however, to review this long debate, for government policy was accommodated to the view of the adherents of the doctrine of the general balance, which "in the seventeenth and eighteenth centuries became the cornerstone of the mercantilist theory of foreign commerce." [12]

Throughout this long period the theory was upheld by a series of distinguished writers, and was maintained unchanged in its essential tenets. Sir William Temple put it thus in 1672:

[9] Mun, Thomas, *A Discourse of Trade from England unto the East Indies,* London, 1621. (Reprinted in McCulloch, J. R., *Early English Tracts on Commerce,* pp. 1-47, London, printed for the Political Economy Club, 1856.)

[10] Mun, Thomas, *England's Treasure by Forraign Trade,* edited by Sir William Ashley, London, 1903, p. 7. This tract was published by Mun's son in 1664, but was written some thirty years before.

[11] Pollexfen, John, *England and East India inconsistent in their Manufactures,* London, 1697, p. 19.

[12] Lipson, E., *The Economic History of England,* London, A. and C. Black, 1927, 1931, Vol. III, pp. 24-25.

It is no constant rule, that trade makes riches; for there may be a trade that impoverishes a nation: as it is not going often to market that enriches the countryman; but on the contrary, if every time he comes there, he buys to a greater value than he sells, he grows the poorer the oftener he goes: but the only certain scale of riches, arising from trade in a nation, is the proportion of what is exported for the consumption of others, to what is imported for their own.[13]

Nearly a century later Sir James Steuart is singing sophisticated variations upon the same theme:

If the value of matter imported, be greater than the value of what is exported, the country gains. If a greater value of labour be imported, than exported, the country loses. Why? Because in the first case, strangers must have paid, in matter, the surplus of labour exported; and in the second case, because the country must have paid to strangers, in matter, the surplus of labour imported. It is therefore a general maxim, to discourage the importation of work, and to encourage the exportation of it.[14]

In the intervening time a host of more and less distinguished writers kept the chorus going.[15]

The nationalist character of the doctrine is apparent in any one of its numerous statements. Its supporters advocated extensive control of the foreign trade of the nation by tariffs, bounties, and prohibitions, in order to secure the favorable balance. The author of a memorandum prepared for the Royal Commission on the Exchanges in 1564 thought this could

. . . esely be brought to pass if wee wold tempere and forbeare the superfluous delycasye of our Expences of Strange

[13] Temple, Sir William, *Observations upon the United Provinces of the Netherlands,* in *Works,* Vol. I, London, 1814, p. 175.

[14] Steuart, Sir James, *Principles of Political Economy,* London, 1767, Vol. I, p. 336.

[15] For a list of the writers who discuss the favorable balance of trade doctrine, see p. 197.

wares, and of strange victualles, and withall yf our Englishe
wares weare caused to be brought to the beste value before
they be vented, and also yf Necessary wares of strange Con-
treyes were caused to be made here more plentifully; . . . [16]

This calls for extensive control of both foreign trade and
domestic manufacture; but it is no more ambitious a program than that which Sir James Steuart outlined toward
the end of the eighteenth century for his ideal statesman
to pursue in regulating the price level of the raw materials which were indispensable to a country engaged in
foreign trade:

> The whole purport of this plan is to point out the opera-
> tion of three very easy principles. The first, That in a coun-
> try entirely taken up with the objects of promoting foreign
> trade, no competition should be allowed to come from abroad
> for articles of the first necessity, and principally for food,
> so as to raise prices beyond a certain standard. The second,
> That no domestic competition should be allowed upon articles
> of superfluity, so as to raise prices beyond a certain standard.
> The third, That when these standards cannot be preserved,
> and that from natural causes, prices get above them, public
> money must be thrown into the scale to bring prices to the
> level of those for exportation.[17]

Steuart is referring here to competition among purchasers,
but the implications of extensive state control of production, as well as prices, are apparent enough in his last sentence.

The favorable balance, then, yields wealth itself for the
society. The rise and fall of the balance, however, tells
more than the mere gain in treasure; it is a barometer of

---

[16] *Memorandum prepared for the Royal Commission on the Exchanges,*
1564, Harleian MSS., 660, 38 *ff.*, 107 seq. (in Tawney and Power, *op. cit.*,
Vol. III, p. 353.)

[17] Steuart, *op. cit.*, Vol. I, p. 270. The whole of Chapter XV outlines a
mercantilist program, modified somewhat by the greater economic knowledge of the latter eighteenth century.

general prosperity. All these writers believed that a continuing favorable balance was the best possible assurance that the nation's hands could be employed, that the purity of the coinage could be maintained, and that commerce and shipping were active. Continuing the passage from the *Discourse of the Common Weal* cited above, John Hales states the various values of the favorable balance through the mouth of his character, the learned Doctor:

> . . . townes and Cities would be replenished with all kinds of artificers . . . so as we should not only have enowghe of such thinges to serve our realme, and save an infinite treasour that goeth now over for so manie of the same, but also might spare of such things redie wroughte to be sold over, whearby we should fetch againe other necessarie commodities and treasours. And thus shoulde be both replenished the Realme of people able to defende it, and also winne much treasour to the same.[18]

By 1640 Ralph Maddison was stating the barometer or index use of the general balance more directly, in *Englands Looking In and Out*:

> And if we do not carry an even hand with forrainers in preserving and encreasing our moneys, as forrainers do, we shall in time undervalue our commodities, for want of money, and consequently overbalance our Trade in price or qualitie, and continuing the same course, send out our monyes in change for commodities, and have no more commodities than we had before; which course will infallibly impoverish the Realme exceedingly: when there is a want of money or wasting of bullion, the commodities of the Realme Wooll and Woollen manufactures, will fall in price; the commodities falling, rents will fall accordingly; when rents do fall by such a necessitie, the necessitie spreads itselfe over the land: And (Tenants haveing taken leases) at enhanced prices of the Countrey commodities, not knowing the efficient cause of this

18 [Hales], *Discourse*, pp. 92-93.

change, will lay the cause upon the Landlords and grow in hatred towards them, not knowing how to hold their farmes, nor what to doe if they give them over; this is a fearefull effect that followeth the want of a convenient stocke of money to maintaine the price. . . . [19]

In the eighteenth century William Wood states the same ideas more succinctly, but no more effectively:

That therefore the *Balance,* which is either paid or received by Means of our *Trade* with any particular Country, is one certain medium to judge of the value of that *Trade;* for every particular *Trade* contributes so much to the subsistence of *our* People, and the improvement of *our* Lands, as the *Balance* it pays to us . . . [20]

If it be remembered that in that period treasure was an important national resource, for it furnished the chief realizable asset in the event of war, and that in times of peace gold and silver constituted a much larger proportion of the circulating medium of the country than they do today, the mercantilists were not far out when they regarded treasure as highly valuable for its own sake, and useful as an index of the economic welfare of the community.

Every meaning of the doctrine was sharpened for these seventeenth- and eighteenth-century observers by the impression that there existed only a fixed amount of trade in the world, and that it behooved each nation to compete as fiercely and successfully as possible for as large a share of that amount as it could secure. Sir William Temple

[19] Maddison or Maddestone, Ralph, *Englands Looking In and Out,* London, 1640, pp. 11-12.

[20] Wood, William, *A Survey of Trade,* second edition, London, 1719, p. 85. This is a substantial work. For a careful analysis of the balance of trade doctrine, and a defense of it against some criticisms, see E. Lipson, *op. cit.,* Vol. III, pp. 89-98; and for a masterly analysis of all its implications, E. F. Heckscher, *Mercantilism* (trans. by Mendel Shapiro), London, 1935, Vol. II, Part IV, especially pp. 238-261.

phrased this idea with his customary elegance: ". . . it seems to be with trade, as with the sea (its element) that has a certain pitch above which it never rises in the highest tides, and begins to ebb, as soon as ever it ceases to flow; and ever loses ground in one place, proportionable to what it gains in another." [21] The argument could be given a specious air of complete certainty if put in terms of a single commodity, as Richard Haines put it:

That if all the Wooll, not only of England, Scotland and Ireland, but France and Spain also, could be Manufactur'd in England; yet there would be no more Cloth in the World, than now there is, for what is not made in England is made elsewhere; since it is certain Wool is neither Burnt, rotted, nor any wise willfully destroyed in any Nation . . . but is either converted at Home or abroad. Therefore, the more we convert in England, the less in other Nations; and the more they Decrease in their Manufactory, the more shall we Increase in Wealth, Trade, Seamen, and Navies of Ships, for the Strength and Safety of our nation.[22]

The same sentiments are echoed in the works of Postlethwayt, writing in the eighteenth century,[23] and even Petty, despite the shrewdness of his analysis, fell at least once into this error.[24]

Small wonder, then, that the mercantilists steadily urged the need of controlling the foreign trade of the nation, for

[21] Temple, Sir William, *op. cit.*, in *Works*, Vol. I, pp. 184-185.

[22] Haines, Richard, *A Breviat of Some Proposals*, London, 1679, p. 4.

[23] Postlethwayt, Malachy, *Dictionary of Commerce*, London edition of 1774, under title "Labour": "There seems to be but a limited quantity of trade in Europe. . . . That England is in the channel of exporting and supplying to the value of fifteen millions; if it should in any year supply twenty millions it must be at the expense and diminution of the sales of others. . . ."

[24] Petty, Sir William, *Economic Writings*, edited by C. H. Hull, Cambridge, 1899, Vol. II, p. 354: "this little hint is the model of the greatest work in the world, which is the making of England as considerable for trade as *Holland;* for there is but a certain proportion of trade in the world . . ." As the editor points out, these words may be Graunt's.

it was the only true source of wealth, the chief index of
the community's economic welfare, and since the trade of
the world was limited in amount, each nation must steadily strive to gain the largest part of it.   Indeed, the mechanisms of tariffs, bounties, prohibitions and even management of the exchanges were not enough to guarantee the
community's success; the wider implications of the subject
reached into the internal economy of the kingdom.

II. THE CONTROL OF DOMESTIC ECONOMY

The regulation of the domestic economy of the realm
was much more complicated a task than the control of
foreign trade, and therefore cannot be so compactly reviewed.   A wide variety of schemes were proposed by different writers; they all expressed, however, the concern of
the nation with its industry, its labor force, its agriculture,
and its habits of consumption, in order that it might be
economically strong within itself, and capable of competing successfully with other national states of Europe, all
of which were pursuing similar policies for similar ends.

A. *The Control of Industry*

The tariff policies which were to secure a favorable balance of trade were also to serve as a means of directing and
assisting industry.   Home manufactures were to receive
the benefits of protective duties, which often went the
length of complete prohibitions upon the import of particular commodities.   The raw materials which were
worked up by these industries were to be secured upon
the most advantageous terms possible, and preferably were
to be produced at home.   John Hales set forth the underlying idea of the whole program when he said of the trades
which brought in treasure: "Therfore these artes ar to be
cherishede wheras they be used; and wheare they be not

they shoulde be set up." [25]   He outlined the policies to
secure this object:

First by stayinge of wares wrought beyond the sea, which
might be wrought within, and from comminge in to be sold;
Secondarilie by restrayninge of our wooles, tinne, and felles,
and other commodities passinge over unwrought; and thirdly
by bringinge in, undernethe the protection of good townes,
artificers dwellinge in the countries makinge wares to be sold
outwarde, and these wares to be vewed and sealed by the
towne seale before they be sold; I think our townes might be
brought soune to their aunciente wealthe againe, or better. [26]

The woolen manufacture furnished one of the staples
of English export during these times, and the program for
industry may be revealed in terms of wool and woolen
goods.   Hales considered the woolen trades as one of the
chief of those to be cherished in the manner described
above; John Wheeler in 1601 defended the society of Merchant Adventurers because they increased this essential
manufacture. [27]   Twenty years later Malynes attacked the
Merchant Adventurers because in his opinion they were
not doing what Wheeler had claimed for them; but both
he and the company's defender had the same program for
the woolen manufacture. [28]   In 1669 the anonymous author
of *England's Glory by the Benefit of Wool*, after advocating the usual restraints upon the exportation of raw wool,
and the usual encouragements to the manufacture and
sale of cloth, expatiated upon the widespread benefits to
everyone of this important industry:

Next then to his Majestyes loss [if the nation fails to regulate the trade] is that of the Merchant and Cloathier; after

[25] [Hales], *Discourse*, p. 127.
[26] *Ibid.*, pp. 130-131.
[27] Wheeler, John, *A Treatise of Commerce*, London, 1601, pp. 21-22, 55-58.
[28] Malynes, Gerard de, *The Maintenance of Free Trade, according to
the three essential parts of Traffique* . . . London, 1622, pp. 50-55.

which must follow detriment to all other persons depending upon Trade, there being such a connexion of Trades one to another. . . . Those supply the Farmers and Graziers with money, for you to supply the Gentry. They again scatter it amongst the Tradesmen, as may be witnessed by the building of the City of London, how Provision and all Consumptive goods are advanced by it: by which circulation all degrees are either imployed, enriched, or both; and hence naturally comes Content, Harmony, and Pleasure, one in another; the Poor being by Imployment delivered from fear of want, the Gentry, Merchant, and Tradesmen, by the establishment of trade therein . . . Nobility, Gentry, Lawyers, Physicians, Scholars of all sorts; shop-keepers are they that receive from these and distribute it again, and all are consequently concerned in this rich Treasure of Wool, because this being a Manufacture at Home, sets more hands at work than half of the Nation . . . [29]

Two years later William Carter stole this passage and incorporated it for emphasis in a pamphlet of his in which he pleaded for more effective enforcement of the prohibitions upon the export of raw wool.[30]   He published at least two other pleas, in which he set forth his own griefs as a customs official, and urged improvement of the laws and the machinery of enforcement.[31]   Within the same decade John Collins urged the same sort of control for Irish wool, so that it would be monopolized for the benefit of the English manufacture.[32]

Besides reserving the native raw material, and encourag-

[29] *England's Glory. By the Benefit of Wool* . . . London, 1669, pp. 14-15.

[30] Carter, William, *England's Interest by Trade Asserted*, London, 1671. The whole pamphlet deals with his difficulties in enforcing the prohibitions on the shipment of wool; the passage which he plagiarized is found on pp. 12-13.

[31] Carter, William, *An Abstract of Proceedings to Prevent Exportation of Wooll Unmanufactured*, London, 1688, and *A Brief Advertisement to the Merchant and Clothier*, London, 1672.

[32] Collins, John, *A Plea for the bringing in of Irish Cattel*, London, 1680. He extends his argument to tin, and to linen.

ing the export of the finished article, these writers wished to reserve the home market, and protect the clothiers from the competition of exotic foreign stuffs. In a pamphlet attributed to Daniel Defoe—it might be said that Defoe must really have been a propaganda organization, for his output surely exceeded that of a single pen, even in his long lifetime—the entrance of Indian "printed and painted Callicoes" into Britain was condemned, and the general rule of safeguarding the home market stated:

That the Woollen and Silk Manufactures of the Kingdom being the Staple of our Trade, and the most considerable and essential part of our Wealth, the Fund of our Exportation, the Support of our Navigation, and the only Means we have for the Employing and Subsisting our Poor; it is therefore the common Interest of the Whole Kingdom to discourage every other Manufacture, whether foreign or assum'd, so far as those manufactures are ruinous to, and inconsistent with the Prosperity of the said British Manufactures of Wooll and Silk.[33]

These views endured throughout the period. They were persistently repeated for wool and silk, and often declared for leather, tin, and other commodities.[34] As late as the fourth decade of the eighteenth century a group of pamphlets appeared in a discussion of a scheme for registering raw wool exports in order to restrain them,[35] and in

[33] [Defoe, Daniel], *A Brief State of the Question, between the Printed and Painted Callicoes and the Woollen and Silk Manufacture*, London, 1719, pp. 3-4, unnumbered, of the preface.

[34] For a list of works by other authors advocating schemes to encourage various manufactures, see p. 199.

[35] [Webber, Samuel], *A Short Account of the State of our Woolen Manufactures*, London, 1739, proposes a registry scheme. Anon., *Remarks upon Mr. Webber's Scheme*, London, 1741, criticizes the method, but agrees on the need of some control of wool [Webster, William], *The Consequences of Trade*, London, 1740, and *Draper Confuted*, London, 1740, and *Draper's Reply*, London, 1741, are defenses. [Webb, Daniel], *An Essay presented, or a Method*, London, 1744, presents the registry scheme once more.

1765 Sir William Mildmay was still declaring the orthodox mercantilist position with regard to manufactures in general:

> . . . all our laws and policies ought to be subservient to the following ends and purposes—First, to encourage the EX-PORTATION of all our *wrought manufactures* and superfluous *unimproveable* commodities; but on the other hand, to prevent the *exportation* of all our *raw* products, capable of being *improved* or *manufactured*—Secondly, to allow the IMPORTA-TION of such *foreign materials* as are either *necessary, useful,* or *convenient;* but, on the contrary, to discourage the bringing in of *such products* or *manufactures* which *we* can raise or make ourselves—And lastly, to admit the RE-EXPORTATION of what is *foreign,* so as not to *interrupt* nor *anticipate* the sale of *our native* commodities.[36]

Sir William's italics and capitals convey no greater degree of earnestness than does the sober print of his predecessors.

The woolen manufacture furnishes an instance of a general program to protect existing industries; but the mercantilist writers demanded more. New industries were to be set up; and to achieve this end monopolies were granted, bounties were offered upon export, workmen were attracted from foreign lands, and inventions were encouraged. The state was to undertake the task of initiating new activities, for the interest of the state seemed to be clearly involved.

The fishing industry was a subject of grave concern for three centuries. The woolen manufacture was clearly an established industry; but the fishing trade was never established to the satisfaction of the pamphleteers. It is hard to tell which grieved them most, the British failure to fish, or the Dutch success in catching them. As early as 1580 Robert Hitchcock proposed a publicly financed and man-

---

[36] Mildmay, Sir William, *The Laws and Policy of England, relating to Trade*, London, 1765, p. 73.

aged scheme to encourage fishing, by which the idle were to be employed, and the loss of gold for purchases abroad was to be remedied.[37]   Before the end of the century *A Briefe note of the Benefits that grow to this Realme by the Observation of Fish Daies* offered arguments to uphold government action of another kind to encourage the trade.[38]   Henry Maydman in 1691 linked such schemes to the development of the navy,[39] and in the early seventeenth century Tobias Gentleman and Edward Sharpe had offered details of technique and management.[40]   J. B. states the full import of all these proposals in 1679:

> But, Sir, you must not expect that the fishery is to be carried on by any private persons; it must be the publick act of the State, the Laws, Powers, and management thereof must be settled by Act of Parliament, a good *Fundus* and Bank of Money must be raised for its advance and encouragement, otherwise it will return to no account, and every small loss which shall fall upon it, will be the overthrow and dissolution of the whole, as it hath been heretofore found by experience.[41]

Rare indeed is the author, like the anonymous one who published *The Dutch Barrier Our's* in 1712,[42] who is willing to let the Dutch have the fish; well into the eighteenth

---

[37] Hitchcock, Robert, *A Pollitique Platt, for the Honour of the Prince,* London, 1580.

[38] *A Briefe Note of the Benefits that grow to this Realme by the Observation of Fish Daies,* London, 1595.   This defends the laws which require the eating of fish, on the theory that the catching of them will be thus encouraged.

[39] Maydman, Henry, *Naval Speculations and Maritime Politicks,* London, 1691, pp. 251-265.

[40] Gentleman, Tobias, *England's Way to Win Wealth,* London, 1614; Sharpe, Edward, *Britaine's Busse, or a computation of the charge of a Busse or herring ship,* London, 1615.

[41] [B., J.], *An Account of the French Usurpation upon the Trade of England,* London, 1679, p. 13.

[42] *The Dutch Barrier Our's: or the Interests of England and Holland Inseparable,* London, 1712.

century the trail of the herring lies through all their writings.[43]

Direct government encouragement of a new industry was an accepted part of the creed; but frequently it was proposed that a monopoly be granted to set up essential enterprises. Fortrey put the case for the monopolistic companies, even though they might raise prices, though he considered this unlikely:

The whole commodity being in their hands, they will make the most that can be made of it; none having the like commodities to undersell them: and the like advantage they have again in what they buy; whereby in truth, our own commodities are sold the dearer to strangers, and foreign commodities bought much the cheaper; when both would happen contrary in a free trade.[44]

The monopolies were, however, the subject of a very considerable controversy, both in their simple commercial aspect and in the ugly character they presented as part of the fiscal maneuvers of the Stuart kings. The dispute has important political implications, which must be examined later when an analysis is made of the political doctrines of these authors; at the moment the fact of importance is that the grant of monopoly was often suggested as a means of initiating new enterprises.

There were a variety of other proposals for the establishment of new industries. John Hales' recommendation that foreign artisans be brought in has already been cited; it was repeated by J. B., and William Petyt.[45] Malachy Postlethwayt proposed an extensive scheme which in-

[43] For other recommendations for establishing the fishing trade, see p. 200.

[44] Fortrey, Samuel, *England's Interest and Improvement*, London, 1673 (in McCulloch, J. R., *Early English Tracts on Commerce*, p. 245).

[45] [Hales], *Discourse*, p. 127; [B., J.], *An Account of the French Usurpation upon the Trade of England*, London, 1679, p. 6 et seq.; [Petyt, William], *Britannia Languens*, London, 1680, p. 30.

cluded the careful study of methods of manufacture used abroad, the encouragement of inventions, and subsidies to bring both methods and inventions into active use.[46] The use of government funds in this way was advocated as late as 1767 by Sir James Steuart.[47] It is unnecessary to multiply instances; the significant feature that is common to all these proposals is the constant demand for the exercise of state authority, and for the spending of government funds. "Without these primary Encouragements and Superintendence of the Government, it will be hard to nourish up any new Manufactures, or to enlarge any old ones, at least, suddenly, to any degree." [48]

These views committed the state to large obligations in aid of industry, but the favors had strings to them. The government, so to speak, purchased the rights of control, and exercised supervision over the prices and the qualities of the goods produced. The chief object to be achieved was the establishment of a reputation for form and quality in British commodities which would find them a ready market abroad, and so improve the favorable balance of trade, but the interests of the home consumer were also to be protected. The kinship of such regulation with the standards imposed in a medieval economy is immediately recognizable but the motives are different; the national interest was at stake, and private enterprise was forced to accept public control. The real difference in purpose can be stated briefly. In the medieval economy regulation was justified by ethical and religious conceptions of just price and equitable dealing designed to protect the interests of the members and classes of the community; mercantilism, imposing a like control upon prices and standards of qual-

46 Postlethwayt, Malachy, *Great Britain's Commercial Interest Explained and Improved*, London, 2nd ed., 1759, dissertations vii, viii, and xxxiii.

47 Steuart, Sir James, *Political Economy*, Vol. I, p. 304.

48 [Petyt, William], *Britannia Languens, or a Discourse of Trade*, London, 1680, p. 30.

ity, argued the need of the state for economic strength as the justification for the exercise of authority. Proposals of this sort appear in the literature of the sixteenth century; they are one of the means to "Reforme the Realme in Settyng them to Werke . . ." [49] Malynes asked for regulation of the standards of quality of goods as well as the management of the foreign exchanges.[50] Regulation was demanded most of the time in the interest of the foreign trade, as the author of *Britannia Languens* expressed the view in 1680:

'Tis confessed, Manufactures may be made *deceitfully,* which may disgrace and prejudice our vent abroad; but this fraud is an act of Skill, which cannot be discovered or prevented, without the daily scrutinies of Judicious persons, for which our other former Statutes have already made *some provision,* but *defective;* it were to be wished, there was a constant Judicature of Men knowing in Trade in every County to supervise the sufficiency of Manufactures: . . . [51]

An anonymous writer two years earlier, while he had an eye on the foreign trade, was also concerned with what might be called the domestic relations of the woolen industry. He recited a long list of the grievances suffered from the manipulations of the factors who had assumed charge of the sale, but not the making of cloth; and demanded that the office of alnager be revived to regularize the marketing of the goods, in the interest of both buyer and seller.[52] Even when the demand for the direct exer-

---

[49] *How to Reforme the Realme in Settyng them to Werke and to Restore Tillage,* 1535 or 1536 (in Tawney and Power, *Tudor Economic Documents,* Vol. III, pp. 115-129).

[50] Malynes, Gerard de, *England's View, in the unmasking of two Paradoxes,* London, 1603, p. 138; and *The Maintenance of Free Trade,* London, 1622, pp. 46-54.

[51] [Petyt, William], *op. cit.,* pp. 198-199.

[52] *The Ancient Trades Decayed, Repaired Again,* London, 1678, pp. 10-11 of Sec. VI. This item was issued again in 1681 by the same printer, under the title, *The Trade of England Revived.*

cise of government authority is not put explicitly by these writers, it is clearly implied in all their ambitious schemes for the increase of national power and welfare. In 1747 George Coade looks back at the record, and remarks with satisfaction:

I now come to demonstrate, that the Trade of England in particular owes also its Origin, its very Existence, to the Care and Protection of our Government; and that the great Progress it made at different Periods of Time, has always been owing to the prudent and seasonable Interposition of the Legislature.[53]

Sir William Mildmay, a score of years later, perhaps marks the conclusion of this steady demand for state supervision which had been reiterated by many writers for more than two hundred years.[54]

The mercantilist program for domestic industry has so far been stated in terms of commodities and the methods of making and selling them. But it is clear that in all this care for goods, the real concern was with *enterprise* and the means of fostering and maintaining its activity. Since many of these men, like Thomas Mun, were merchants turned theorists and propagandists, they fully realized the importance of capital and investment; in fact, to many of them the favorable balance of trade was important chiefly as a means of securing trading capital; treasure was significant only when it was put to work. Their omnipotent and omnipresent state was therefore required to extend its functions into this field. As in the case of the regulation of standards and prices of goods, the arguments for such an extension of power had the benefit of highly respectable medieval ancestry. The medieval church had long

[53] Coade, George, *A Letter to the Honourable the Lords Commissioners of Trade and Plantations,* London, 1747, p. 28.
[54] Mildmay, Sir William, *The Laws and Policy of England, Relating to Trade,* London, 1765, pp. 23, 45-46. For other works demanding controls of standards and prices see p. 201.

condemned usury as a sin; nevertheless in the sixteenth century the usurer, so-called, was one of the chief agents for furnishing capital to small traders and manufacturers.

The mercantilist attitude toward regulation of the rate of interest, then, furnishes another example of how a medieval prohibition was transformed into one of the supervisory powers of the national state. The church in the middle ages had condemned the taking of usury as a sin; the mercantilists, anxious to stimulate commercial and industrial enterprise, wanted to control the interest rate, keeping it low enough to make capital available to the merchants and manufacturers who were building England's economic strength. It would be extremely interesting to trace this delicate transformation from moral sin to political offense, with the accompanying change from the sanctions of religious condemnation to the demand for government control, but here it is sufficient to recognize that the transition was accomplished.[55]   Many of the mercantilist writers from the sixteenth century onward demanded that the state intervene in order to make operating capital available to the merchants and manufacturers who were driving England's domestic and foreign trade, and they had benefit of clergy, so to speak, for their program.

A very considerable literature centers around the possibility of government regulation of the rate of interest. Malynes and Robinson, writing in the first half of the seventeenth century, have no doubts at all of the usefulness of limiting the interest rate to six per cent or less by government fiat.[56]   Sir Josiah Child was equally positive:

[55] The development is brilliantly analyzed by R. H. Tawney in his introduction to Wilson's *Discourse upon Usury*, ed., Tawney, London, 1925, and the analysis is carried further in the Holland Memorial Lectures, published under the title, *Religion and the Rise of Capitalism*, New York, 1926.

[56] Malynes, Gerard de, *St. George for England*, London, 1601; Robinson, Henry, *England's Safety in Trade's Encrease*, London, 1641, pp. 6-8.

There is nothing in the world will engage our merchants to spend less and trade more, but the abatement of interest; for the subduing of interest will bring in a multitude of traders, as it hath in Holland to such a degree, that almost all of their people of both sexes are traders.[57]

The two Thomas Culpeppers, father and son, published each a number of pamphlets, demonstrating the evil effects of *excessive* usury, that is, an exorbitant rate of interest, upon the trade, the agriculture, the labor, and the morals, of England.[58] The son in 1670 reprinted his father's treatise of 1621 upon the occasion of an attack upon its arguments by Thomas Manly.[59] Judged by modern economic theory, Manly had the better of the argument, for he held to the point that the high interest rate was due to a shortage of capital and a plenty of borrowers. Other writers continued the debate, the most famous being John Locke; [60] but the controversy never went beyond a dispute over methods, for all the disputants wanted to guarantee that England should not suffer from a lack of funds for trade and manufacture.

Differences as to the possibility of controlling the interest rate by law were resolved, in a fashion, by almost unanimous agreement upon the necessity for a national bank, and on various schemes for mobilizing public credit to make it available to the commercial community. A great

[57] Child, Sir Josiah, *A Discourse of Trade*, London, 1690, edition of 1775 cited here at pp. xii-xiii of the preface; he states the same views in *Brief Observations Concerning Trade*, London, 1668, and *A Short Addition to the Observations*, London, 1668.

[58] Culpepper, Sir Thomas, Sr., *A Tract against the High Rate of Usury*, London, 1621; Culpepper, Sir Thomas, Jr., *The Necessity of Abating Usury Re-asserted*, London, 1670; and *A Discourse shewing the many Advantages which will accrue to this Kingdom by the Abatement of Usury*, London, 1668.

[59] Manly, Thomas, *Usury at Six Per Cent. Examined*, London, 1668.

[60] Locke, John, *Considerations of the Consequences of the Lowering of Interest and Raising the Value of Money*, London, 1691; and *Further Considerations*, London, 1695 (both in *Works*, 9th edition, London, 1794, Vol. IV, pp. 1-130 and 130-206, respectively).

many plans were offered during the seventeenth and eighteenth centuries, for what would now be called nationalization of banks, or making credit a public utility. John Benbrigge proposed the establishment of a bank as a means of controlling usury, in fact, of making "usury" a means to national economic strength.[61] John Cary thought that England, by virtue of her parliamentary government, was particularly well situated to set up a bank, "for as an easy government is its own Security, so that Security encourages Trade, and these two accompanied with the Profits offered to a running Cash, will make all Europe desire to settle their Monies here." [62] It is unnecessary to devote much space to the controls of finance, because the proposals were simple. A passage from Steuart in which he defines the relation of the state—represented by his "statesman"—to the matters of borrowing and interest shows an eighteenth century economist asking for an extensive program:

He should set out by such steps of administration as will discourage borrowing, in those who employ their money in prodigality and dissipation, as far as may be consistent with the interest of the lower classes employed in supplying home consumption. . . . He should abstain from borrowing himself, and even from creating new outlets for money, except for the most cogent motives. By this he will, in a short time, greatly reduce the rate of interest.[63]

This continuous concern with the interest rate, and the persistent proposals for the creation of banks arose from the mercantilists' recognition of the importance of trading

[61] Benbrigge, John, *Usura Accommadata*, London, 1646.
[62] Cary, John, *An Essay Toward Settling National Credit* (in the 1745 edition of his *Discourse of Trade*, pp. 173-190).
[63] Steuart, Sir James, *Principles of Political Economy*, Vol. II, p. 124.
Other proposals for the establishment of banks, and for controlling the interest rate, are dealt with in the following chapters, where an analysis is made of the administrative machineries suggested by the mercantilists.

capital. One of the chief concerns of the bullionists, when they demanded policies to bring treasure into the kingdom and keep it there, was to provide the money or bullion which they believed to constitute in large part the liquid capital for commercial operations. Similarly seventeenth- and eighteenth-century writers demanding credit policies, banks, and sometimes regulation of the interest rate, were animated by their recognition of the need for financing manufacturing and commerce. Thomas Mun wanted treasure to drive England's foreign trade; James Steuart wanted a low interest rate in order to stimulate domestic manufacture; and their ideas were of a piece with all the others.[64]

Mercantilism, then, involved a comprehensive program of state control and encouragement of industry. Tariffs and prohibitions afforded protection; monopolies, bounties on exports, the attraction of skilled artisans from other countries, and the encouragement of inventions were means of setting up new industries. The state was called upon to control prices and standards; and medieval tradition made the demand seem a natural one. These writers wanted England to be busy and active, for it was by making things and selling things that she could be strong.

B. *The Control of Labor: Mercantilist Population Doctrines*

A busy England in the seventeenth and eighteenth centuries was possible only if a large number of laborers and craftsmen were hard at work. The labor force, therefore, needed regulation fully as much as did the processes of production or the financing of industry and trade. The mercantilist view on these matters arose in large part from

---

[64] Beer, M., *Early British Economics from the XIIIth to the Middle of the XVIIIth Century*, London, 1938, pp. 187-192. The whole book is an admirable succinct summary of the development of economic ideas during the period, done by a very learned writer.

the conviction that labor was one of the most productive of all the resources of the nation; but the arguments used to justify the regulation of prices and quality of goods enforced the labor doctrines. If it was important for the foreign trade to regulate the standards of quality of commodities and—so far as possible—their exchange value, it was equally important to regulate the labor expended in producing them. Indeed, since industry had not reached a factory type of organization, regulation of labor was practically tantamount to regulation of the whole process of production.

The argument was carried even farther. Because the labor process constituted most of the whole process of manufacture, and because manufactured goods were the most valuable export the nation had to offer in competition with other nations in the international market, it was imperative that England should possess a large employed population, for in numbers of people at work lay the chief source of economic power. This conclusion was further supported by the political consideration that manpower was of tremendous importance in war.

The learned doctor in John Hales' *Discourse* complained that the purchase of wares from abroad was injuring the realm, and urged that all such manufactures be set up at home, and "thus should be both replenished the Realme of people able to defende it, and also winne much treasour to the same." [65] Malynes repeated the same sentiments just over fifty years later:

The third [means of wealth in a commonwealth] depends upon the trade and trafficke of merchandise, and upon the

---

[65] [Hales], *Discourse*, pp. 92-93.

E. S. Furniss has analyzed the mercantilist doctrines on population and labor in an admirable study, *The Position of the Laborer in a System of Nationalism*, Boston, 1920. The doctrines of population, employment, wages, and state control of labor in general are subjected to searching study, and the interpretation is supported with a wealth of citation.

persons of men according to their degree and quality. Which meanes are increased by the inhabiting of countries and multitude of people: which causeth Princes to study to make their countries populous, and to increase the commerce and trafficke, by the gaines whereof, the wealth is increased. For albeit, that the multitude of people maketh the price of lands to rise, and victuals to become dearer: yet the Prince and the subjects meanes of maintenance do increase, and one doth live by another, alwayes so as there be had a singular care to set poore men on work, and the idle droane do not consume the sweete honey.[66]

Roger Coke, who was far from being a convinced mercantilist, nevertheless completely concurred with his contemporaries in the seventeenth century when he insisted upon the importance of population and employment.[67]

In the sixteenth and seventeenth centuries the writers express a naïve confidence in the direct relationship between population and national riches; they believe that if the kingdom has plenty of people, the people can take care of themselves and the kingdom too. Samuel Fortrey stated it when he said: "People and plenty are commonly the begetters the one of the other, if rightly ordered." [68] Even the sophisticated Sir William Temple echoed the same belief:

The true and natural ground of trade and riches is number of people in proportion to the compass of ground they inhabit . . . People are multiplied in a country by the temper of the climate favorable to generation, to health, and to long life; or else by the circumstances of safety and ease under the

66 Malynes, Gerard de, *England's View, in the Unmasking of two Paradoxes* . . . London, 1603, p. 133.

67 Coke, Roger, *A Detection of the Court and State of England.* . . . London, 1694, pp. 47-48, unnumbered, of the Introduction.

68 Fortrey, Samuel, *England's Interest and Improvement,* London, 1673. (In McCulloch, J. R., *Early English Tracts on Commerce,* London, 1856, p. 219.)

government, the credit whereof invites men to it, when they cannot be either safe or easy at home. When things are once in motion, trade begets trade, as fire does fire; and people go where much people are already gone.[69]

This view persisted for another century, and in the middle of the eighteenth century Roger North, criticizing the poor laws because they restricted the opportunities of the poor to make a living, insisted upon the benefits of a large population:

It is a strange Blindness to Esteem Numbers of People a Burthen, when so much Good comes from them; their very Eating and Drinking is a profitable Consumption of our Country's Product, and their Labour is sowing Riches for the Public to Reap. . . .[70]

At about the same time Josiah Tucker, then rector of St. Stephens in Bristol, was asking, "Was a Country *thinly* inhabited ever *rich?*—Was a populous Country ever *poor?*" [71]

However great the faith might be in the numbers of people, all the mercantilists agreed that no benefit arose from great multitudes of idle people. If the population was to be employed, it was necessary for the state to provide training for the manufacturing crafts, force the ablebodied poor to work and care for the impotent, and regulate the wages of the laborers. Roger Coke proposed, near the end of the seventeenth century,

That in every Village a Work-house be erected, or at least, every Village contribute to the Erecting of one in another Village, for to instruct the Youth of both Sexes, in such Arts or Mysteries as are more proper in them, whereby the Nation may reap the benefit of their Employments, and the poorer

[69] Temple, Sir William, *An Essay Upon the Advancement of Trade in Ireland,* 1673. (In His *Works,* London, 1814, Vol. III, pp. 2-3.)

[70] North, Roger, *A Discourse of the Poor,* London, 1753, p. 78.

[71] Tucker, Josiah, *Reflections on the Expediency of a Law for the Naturalization of Foreign Protestants,* London, 1751, p. 19.

sort of People be not forced to flee out of their Country, or become a burden to it.[72]

This is only one of the many proposals to train the working force of the nation; there will be opportunity in a later chapter to examine these schemes carefully. Joshua Gee devoted a whole chapter to the necessity of putting the poor to work.[73] The pamphlets teem with suggestions for workhouses, for compelling apprenticeship, and like devices designed to insure that the laborers should really labor.

Coupled with the idea that the population should be employed was a doctrine of low wages, related to the theories of the favorable balance of trade. The author of *The Grand Concern of England Explained* put the case succinctly in 1673:

As for the loss of the Foreign Trade we had, and the want of the consumption that used to be of our Manufacturies in Foreign parts, no other reason can be given, but that Foreigners are able to make their work cheaper than we do, and thereby are able to undersell us where-ever we come; . . . the more reason there is then . . . to endeavour the reducing the wages of our Manufacturers, and themselves to a more sober and less expansive way of living . . . and nothing can be more conducing to this end, than to enjoyn all English men not to wear anything but what is of our own Growth and Manufacturies; which will increase Consumption at home, and set those at work who now live idle, and by giving them full work, would bring down their wages: so that then we having our Wool and Leather cheaper than Foreigners have, and being able to manufacture them at as easie rates as they do, it will then necessarily follow, that we may undersell them in Foreign markets . . .[74]

[72] Coke, *op. cit.*, p. 495.
[73] Gee, Joshua, *Trade and Navigation of Great Britain Considered*, 3rd edition, London, 1731, Ch. XXIII.
[74] *The Grand Concern of England Explained* . . . London, 1673, pp. 54-55.

This is representative of the prevailing doctrine throughout three centuries, though there were a few advocates of high wages. Like many other doctrines of the time, it owed some of its force to the earlier ideas of a medieval society, in which the regulation of wages by government authority was as familiar as the establishment of just prices.

The laboring poor, then, constituted one of the most important sources of wealth to the kingdom. They must be many, they must be trained to useful trades, they must not be over-paid; and all this must be achieved by the steady exercise of the authority of the state. "The Labours of the People bestowed this way, must necessarily glomerate the Riches of the World, and must render any Nation a prodigy of Wealth . . ." [75]

C. *The Encouragement of Agriculture: the Defense of Enclosure and the Corn Laws*

Manufacturing seemed to offer the best means of making any nation a prodigy of wealth because it combined the value of the labor embodied in the goods with the value of the raw materials. While the mercantilists were concerned chiefly with manufacture, they gave their attention to agriculture as well. Adam Smith's criticism of the mercantile system, condemning its disregard for farms and farmers, has been revised by economic historians; and it is now clear that the mercantilists had a real regard for the importance of agriculture, and some ideas as to how it should be made to contribute to the economy of the kingdom.

Their first concern was with the use of land. They hoped that the total area under tillage could be increased,

[75] [Petyt, William], *Britannia Languens,* London, 1680, p. 25.
For a brilliantly incisive summary of the whole labor doctrine see E. S. Furniss, *The Position of the Laborer Under a System of Nationalism,* Boston, 1920, pp. 195-200.

so that the kingdom would be self-sustaining so far as food supplies were concerned. This had more than a wartime significance; in peace time it was important to feed the laboring population on home-grown food, and to furnish wool and flax for the textile trades. Many of the writers were convinced that land was lying idle, they hoped that heath and marsh could be reclaimed and put into production. More important to all of them, however, was the need for improving methods of farming, so that land under cultivation could be made more productive.

During the sixteenth, seventeenth and eighteenth centuries English agriculture was changing from medieval to modern organization and methods. The typical manor, with its tenants tending strips in two or three common fields, and running their stock on the common and waste land, offered little possibility for the improvement of tillage. In the fifteenth and sixteenth centuries the fields were enclosed in some parts of England, mainly for the pasturage of sheep. In the two succeeding centuries a true revolution in agriculture began, and enclosure was a means by which it was possible for the enterprising farmer to introduce new methods of cultivation. The chief feature of medieval agriculture was its communal character, so far as the techniques of farming were concerned. The individual farmer, or landlord, could change methods, crops, or livestock only if he could get his land into a field with a hedge or fence around it (i.e., enclosed) instead of having control of small holdings in two or three large fields with all the other cultivators of the manor. This was the great agrarian issue of these centuries; and since the mercantilists wanted an increase in the output of English agriculture, they were predominantly on the side of the enclosers.

John Hales, writing in the middle of the sixteenth century and fresh from experience on a royal commission of investigation, was doubtful of the equity and the social consequences of enclosure; but he was sure that the remedy for the agrarian difficulties lay in the improvement of agriculture, and the encouragement of the consumption of domestic products and manufactures.[76]   Adam Moore, more than a century later, had no qualms; in fact, he thought that besides the national advantage to be gained from the introduction of improved methods there was a further merit in the discipline of the poor and idle which would result from the changes in the organization of agriculture.[77]   In the succeeding twenty years the same view was set forth by the anonymous author of *England's Great Happiness, or a Dialogue between Content and Complaint,*[78] and by Samuel Fortrey, in *England's Interest and Improvement.*   Fortrey's statement is very succinct and explicit:

> . . . much land is tilled with great labour, and small profit; and much land fed to the starving of the cattel, and the impoverishing of the inhabitants; to the increase of nothing but beggery in this nation; all which inconveniences would by enclosure be prevented.[79]

The same arguments for enclosure and the same interest in the improvements in agricultural methods were stated during the seventeenth century by Postlethwayt.[80]

The state policy quite consistently supported by most of the mercantilists was embodied in the corn laws.   During Elizabeth's reign, restrictions on the export of corn

[76] [Hales], *Discourse,* the third dialogue.

[77] Moore, Adam, *Bread for the Poor,* London, 1653.

[78] *England's Great Happiness, or a Dialogue between Content and Complaint,* London, 1677 (in McCulloch, J. R., *Early English Tracts on Commerce,* London, 1856, pp. 250-274).

[79] Fortrey, Samuel, *England's Interest and Improvement,* London, 1673 (in McCulloch, *op. cit.,* p. 228).

[80] Postlethwayt, Malachy, *Great Britain's Commercial Interest Explained and Improved,* 2nd ed., London, 1759, dissertations i, iii, iv, ix, and x. See also his *Dictionary of Trade and Commerce,* 4th ed., London, 1774, under the title "Landed Interest."

were lifted; and Charles I offered a modest bounty on that sent abroad. The corn laws of the seventeenth and eighteenth centuries combined restrictions on imports with encouragement to exports, so that the English farmer could benefit from the policies of the state. The English consumer's interest was safeguarded to a limited extent by giving the clerks of the market some powers over the sale prices and practices in the corn trade. Postlethwayt argued for these policies, particularly for the restrictions on import of corn designed to protect the home producer; [81] and Defoe pointed with pride to the fact that England had really become a corn exporting country.[82] James Anderson, writing a year after the publication of *The Wealth of Nations,* proposed that the legislature should regulate agriculture and the corn trade sufficiently to guarantee a steady price, and stubbornly defended the corn laws against Adam Smith's criticisms by arguing that bounties were offered on export only when prices were low and duties charged when prices were high.[83]

The mercantilists' concern with agriculture, and their willingness to support state action which would increase production and improve methods of cultivation, was linked to the theories of trade and wages. Sometimes it was stated in the form of a general dogma, which was taken to be self-evident, as George Coade enunciated it in the middle of the eighteenth century:

Between the Landed and Trading Interest in this Kingdom there ever has been, and ever will be an inseparable Affinity. They mutually furnish each other with all the Conveniences of Life, and no real Preference can be given either to the one

[81] Postlethwayt, Malachy, *Great Britain's Commercial Interest Explained and Improved,* dissertations iv and v. See also Gee, Joshua, *Trade and Navigation of Great Britain Considered,* 3rd ed., London, 1731, Ch. XXIV.

[82] Defoe, Daniel, *A Plan of the English Commerce,* London, 1738 (reprinted at Oxford, 1928, Ch. VII).

[83] Anderson, James, *Observations on the Means of Exciting a Spirit of National Industry,* Edinburgh, 1777, pp. 294-304.

or to the other. It is demonstrably true, that it can never go ill with Trade but Land will fall nor ill with Land but Trade will feel it.[84]

More often a careful argument was advanced, as Postlethwayt presented it a little more than a decade later:

If this general improvement of old lands, and cultivation of fresh, be extended to the due political degree it will admit of in this nation, the universal plenty of all things will be so magnified, as to render the price of the necessaries of life no more than one half, or even one third what it is at present. This will inevitably reduce the general price of labour, that being regulated by the price of the necessaries of life: and will not this render all our fabrics and manufactures cheaper . . . ? Hereby we cannot fail being enabled continually to augment the value of our exports beyond that of our imports; this will gradually increase the balances of our trade with many particular nations, and the general balance in like proportion; which will be brought into the realm in hard money. From which additional plenty of money, the people in general will become greater consumers of the productions of the land, and manufactures, the state grow more and more populous, as things grow cheaper and money more plentiful.[85]

Encouragement to enclosure and stabilization of prices by the use of the corn laws were the means of linking agricultural activity to the general economic system. As in the fields of industry and trade, the power of the state was to assist, and sometimes to guide and direct, the nation's farmers. It is true that the mercantilists emphasized manufacture and foreign trade, but they did not ignore the importance of the land and its cultivators in their plans for developing the national economy.

[84] Coade, George, *A Letter to the Honourable Lords Commissioners of Trade and Plantations*, London, 1747, p. 21.

[85] Postlethwayt, Malachy, *Great Britain's Commercial Interest Explained and Improved*, pp. 2-3.

For similar statements of interest in improving the condition of agriculture, see p. 201.

D. *The Control of Consumption: the Sumptuary Laws*

The mercantilists continually compared the state to a family; national economy was only domestic economy writ large. Every family in every century knows two ways of accumulating a surplus: one is, of course, to increase the family income; the second is to curtail the family expenditures. The mercantilists adhered closely to the analogy and proposed that the state should use both means: they wished to see England increase her foreign trade and gain a surplus of wealth and treasure; at the same time they insisted that the nation must not squander that hard-earned surplus.

Logically the system required that control of consumption be added to the regulation of industry and agriculture; but it is important to remember that this was not a single coherent scheme; it was a set of practical proposals made by practical men. Having a regard for realities, these men of business could see that while rationing of the nation might be an admirable way of achieving their purposes, it would be difficult to enforce such plans. Nevertheless they hoped to restrain the most immoral extravagances of their fellow citizens, and proposed a considerable measure of regulation of consumption by sumptuary legislation. In securing acceptance of their proposals they were aided, as they had been in other fields, by the inheritance of the traditions of a medieval economy. The doctrines of the canonists and the practice of the feudal state had included the regulation of the expenditure of the classes and the masses; the mercantile rules for consumption could trace a respectable genealogy back to the reigns of the two Edwards.

Expressions of pious hope—all the pleas for sumptuary laws have an extremely high moral tone—were much more frequent than precise suggestions for government action.

The writer of the *Libelle of Englyshe Polycye* deplored the purchases from the Italian cities:

> All spicerye and other grocers ware,
> Wyth swete wynes, all manere of chaffare,
> Apes and japes and marmusettes taylede,
> Nifles, trifles, that litell have availed . . . [86]

Thomas Mun was echoing these sentiments two centuries later.[87] "Whether if drunkenness be a necessary evil," Bishop Berkeley acidly inquired in the early part of the eighteenth century, "men may not as well get drunk with the growth of their own country?" In an earlier essay he had urged, "Frugality of manners is the nourishment and strength of bodies politic . . . Men are apt to measure national prosperity by riches. It would be righter to measure it by the use of them." [88]

These exhortations were readily converted into proposals for legislation. "It is evident," the worthy bishop continued, "that old taxes may be better borne, as well as new ones raised, by sumptuary laws judiciously framed, not to damage our trade, but to retrench our luxury." He asked, "whether nations as wise and opulent as ours, have not made sumptuary laws, and what hinders us from doing the same?" [89] His contemporaries advanced programs of the same kind. "To banish luxury quite, by a long series of steady government and wisdom, is certainly most advisable," Davenant declared, "but if the people is not to be reformed, and if this spending humour is not to be cured, care must be taken to entail on the prodigal a vast

---

[86] *The Libelle of Englyshe Polycye*, "vij chapitle," lines 346-349.

[87] Mun, Thomas, *England's Treasure by Forraign Trade*, pp. 88-89.

[88] Berkeley, George, *The Querist*, 1734-1736, edited by J. H. Hollander, Baltimore, 1910, Part I, question 119, and *Essay Toward Preventing the Ruin of Great Britain*, 1721 (in *Works*, edited by Alexander Campbell Fraser, Oxford, 1871, p. 200).

[89] Berkeley, *The Querist*, Part I, question 109; and *Essay Toward preventing the Ruin of Great Britain*, p. 200.

estate . . ." [90] This was the cautious statement of a public official, conscious of the difficulties of enforcement. Many men of business were willing to be less cautious: "what is of the utmost consequence to us, is, that by laying high duties we are always able to check the Vanity of our people in their extream fondness of wearing exotick Manufactures. . . ." [91]

The control of consumption completed, more logically and symmetrically than any one of its many supporters intended, the regulations which the mercantile system imposed upon the domestic economy. Their own analogy of the household is the truest metaphor that can be used to characterize their program. The king was the father of a national family; he should take care that he provided well for it. Manufacture and agriculture were the sources of the family income; and that income should always more than cover the expenditures so that a reserve of treasure might be stored in the counting house. So far as possible the family should produce the goods which it consumed; the customs officers were the father's watchful eyes. Within the household the operations of manufactures were carefully supervised, both as to price and quality. The servants were the nation's laboring classes; they were to be trained, disciplined, cared for in adversity, and rewarded with a bare but secure subsistence. Frugal and careful expenditure must be the rule, from motives of economy and decent respectability. Behold here a happy nation in this well-ordered household; secure within its walls, successful in the marts of trade outside its gates!

This family discipline could not be relaxed even if some

[90] Davenant, Charles, *Discourses of the Public Revenues and on Trade,* 1698 (in *Works,* London, 1771, Vol. I, p. 392).

[91] Gee, Joshua, *Trade and Navigation of Great Britain Considered,* 3rd edition, London, 1731, p. 113.

For additional bibliography on the proposals for sumptuary legislation see below in the notes on Chapter III, where the duties of the classes are discussed.

of the adventurous sons crossed the seas, and took up a residence in the New World. The economy of empire was but an extension of the national economy; the household might grow to imperial dimensions but the family was to hold together as closely as ever.

III. THE ECONOMICS OF EMPIRE: THE NAVIGATION LAWS AND THE COLONIAL SYSTEM

It was the firm conviction of the mercantilists that the essential doctrines of their system would apply as well to the British Empire—though the term was not in use in their time they would have welcomed it—as to the British Isles. The control of foreign trade was just as necessary for the mother country and her plantations as for the mother country alone; and it was quite as practicable to control the economy of the empire as it was to control the domestic economy of the kingdom. It was only necessary to adjust the relationship of the new territories to the old—to fit the plantations neatly into the scheme. The navigation policy was already at hand and had been used to encourage shipping before the British dominions had extended beyond the seas; it was an easy task to adapt this well-established practice to the new situation. The management of trade and manufacture in the colonies presented problems of some novelty; but solutions could be found by applying familiar mercantilist principles.

A. *The Defense of the Navigation Laws*

The first and simplest argument for the navigation laws was frankly political. In 1436 the guiding maxim for English maritime policy had been stated:

> Cheryche marchandyse, kepe thamyralte,
> That we bee maysteres of the narowe see,[92]

[92] *The Libelle of Englyshe Polycye,* lines 6-7.

and in the latter part of the eighteenth century Adam Smith grudgingly admitted, in an oft-quoted sentence, "As defence, however, is of much more importance than opulence, the act of navigation is perhaps, the wisest of all the commercial regulations of England." [93] The maxim and the admission both arose from the logic of England's geographical position, and from the glorious tradition of the English navy. Since there was little difference between a merchantman and a man-of-war even as late as the eighteenth century, the general agreement among the various writers on the political importance of the navigation acts was not surprising.[94]

An economic defense for the policy was also developed, but it did not achieve the wide acceptance that was won by the political considerations. Fortrey stated the analysis which others repeated or elaborated slightly:

It is true, that the same commodity brought hither in any of our own vessels, cannot be afforded so cheap as what might be brought by others; by reason indeed, that our shipping is much more chargeable, and better manned than any other: but this being rightly considered, it is rather an advantage than a prejudice to the publick: for if commodities be thereby anything the dearer, here at home, yet we buy them as cheap abroad as any other; and all that other should have gained of us by the carriage will now be earned by our own people; and whatever it costs the purchaser here, is no prejudice to the publick, when our own nation receives the profit of it; especially it being the increase of that, in which consists the greatest honour and safety of the kingdom.[95]

The political argument rings out in the last sentence, but the rest of the passage states clearly the mercantilist posi-

---

[93] Smith, Adam, *The Wealth of Nations*, Everyman edition, Vol. I, p. 408.

[94] For the statement of the political argument for the navigation laws by a number of authors, see p. 202.

[95] Fortrey, Samuel, *England's Interest*, London, 1673 (in McCulloch, J. R., *Early English Tracts on Commerce*, London, pp. 242-243).

tion that it is worth a little hardship to some consumers if the economic welfare of the nation and its surplus of wealth can be protected.   Child defended the acts of navigation because they aided England in competing with the Dutch; Mun pointed out the gain the nation's trade balance received from freights; and many others supported some or all of the economic claims for the policy.[96]

Upon both economic and political grounds the laws were justified; in addition they possessed a special significance for the management of the colonial trade.

B. *The Old Colonial System*

The easy and natural approach which the English mercantilists made to the problem of defining the relationship of the colonies to the mother country was to apply their fundamental concept of British self-sufficiency. "This desire to free England from the necessity of purchasing from foreigners formed the underlying basis of English commercial and colonial expansion; it led directly to the formation of the East India company and to the colonization of America." [97]   Dalby Thomas put this succinctly at the turn of the seventeenth century:

By the hands employed in those colonies, foreign commodities become native, to the great enriching of England, as aforesaid; and to the lessening the riches and strength of all other European nations, that produce the like commodities.[98]

His general argument gained in point when he stated it in terms of a particular commodity:

[96] Child, Sir Josiah, *Trade and the Interest of Money Considered,* London, 1775, Ch. IV.

For other statements of the economic argument for the navigation laws, see p. 203.

[97] Beer, G. L., *Origins of the British Colonial System,* New York, 1908, p. 57.

[98] Thomas, Dalby, *An Historical Account of the West Indies,* London, 1690 (in *Harleian Miscellany,* ed. 1809, Vol. II, p. 373).

Consider, too, that, before sugars were produced in our own colonies, it bore three times the price it doth now; so that, by the same consumption, at the same price, except we made it ourselves, we should be forced to give in money, or money's worth, (as native commodities or labour) two millions four hundred thousand pounds for the sugar we spend, or be without it to such a degree of disadvantage of well-living, as that retrenchment would amount to.[99]

This was an argument for practical men, stated in terms of pounds, shillings, and pence. Many practical men were found who agreed with it; in fact, it had been advanced long before Thomas wrote, and was repeated throughout the eighteenth century. It was put most eloquently, perhaps, by John Cary:

I take England and its Plantations to be one great Body, those being so many Limbs or Counties belonging to it, therefore when we consume their growth we do as it were spend the fruits of our own Land, and what thereof we sell to our Neighbours for Bullion, or such Commodities as we must pay for therein, brings a second profit to the nation.[100]

However often the point was made, it still seemed necessary to reiterate it during the course of the years:

In short, whatever we have from our own Plantations costs us nothing, but the Labour of manufacturing Goods for them, and that of bringing theirs here, while to other Countries we are weak enough to continue paying those very Sums of Money which we get from those plantations.[101]

This concept of national self-sufficiency which would result from the raw materials and exotic goods obtained

[99] Thomas, Dalby, *op. cit.*, p. 363.

[100] Cary, John, *An Essay on the State of England, in Relation to Its Trade*, Bristol, 1695, pp. 67-68.

[101] [Hall, F.], *The Importance of the British Plantations in America*, London, 1731, pp. 5-6.

For other statements of the general argument for colonies as an extension of the realm, see p. 203.

from the colonies encountered one difficulty. There was
the danger in the minds of some Englishmen that the new
dominions might rob the mother country of one of its
most important sources of national strength: its people.
Fear of depopulation, however, carried no weight until
after the last decade of the seventeenth century. Indeed,
the earlier defenders of the empire welcomed the prospect
of emigration as a solution for the pressing problems of
poor relief. John Hagthorpe in 1625 advocated raising a
public stock to assist the poor to go out to the plantations:

> How great a benefit it might produce in twenty to thirty
> years, by unburthening this land, of a million of poore peo-
> ple, whose labour, and imployment there, might bring as
> much profit to this Commonwealth, as here their idleness
> doth prejudice, I submit to each judicious censure.[102]

Hagthorpe's viewpoint would not have received much support by the end of the century, but by that time the argument for the plantations had been modified to meet any
fears of a drain of people from the mother country. This
was achieved by extending the mercantilist conception of
a controlled domestic economy to the new boundaries of
the empire. Dalby Thomas had to meet the fear of depopulation, and he had the answer ready in 1690:

> From what has been said of the nature and managing of
> plantations, is demonstrated, beyond all scruple, that those
> hands employed in our colonies are, for their number, the
> most profitable subjects of these dominions, as well to the
> ends of consumption and delight, as for increasing the wealth,
> power, and glory of the nation.[103]

In 1767 this same argument, more elaborately stated, was
still being put forward; and by a writer who had been in-

---

102 Hagthorpe, John, *England's Exchequer*, London, 1625, p. 26. For
other statements of the advantage of colonies as a means of taking care of
population, see p. 204.

103 Thomas, Dalby, *An Historical Account of the West Indies*, London,
1690 (in *Harleian Miscellany*, ed., 1809, Vol. II, p. 374).

dulging a dismal hypothesis that it was quite possible that Britain faced decay of her economic strength:

if we only suppose, that every person there employs one at home, the three millions of people we have in America, with Asia and Africa, will almost maintain as many in Britain, which are nigh half the people. And as the colonies increase so fast, if you find employments for them, to support the nation at home, and make them mutually supply one another, the manner of doing which was the first design of this discourse, you might have twice as many people in Britain, as the land would maintain. By that means Britain might vye with all its enemies and rivals, and maintain more people than France.[104]

The productiveness of the plantations was the answer to any risk of loss of people from the mother country. The mercantilists expected more from the colonies, however, than exotic goods like tobacco, or substantial necessities like foodstuffs, naval stores, and raw materials. The value of the colonial market for the sale of home manufactures was clearly realized and repeatedly stated. Thomas worked out a highly optimistic calculation: "each white man, woman, and child, residing in the sugar-plantations, occasions the consumption of more of our native commodities, and manufactures, than ten at home do." He proceeded to itemize their purchases, and arrived at the satisfactory total of eighteen pounds per person per annum, "a far greater consumption . . . than labourers at home make." [105] Defoe, who can be taken as a gauge of public opinion as well as an advocate for imperial economics, wrote in 1729: "It is evident, that by the Increase of our Colonies, the Consumption of our Manufactures

---

[104] [Mitchell, John], *The Present State of Great Britain and North America*, London, 1767, pp. 127-128.

For further discussion of the arguments against fear of depopulation, see p. 204.

[105] Thomas, *op. cit.*, pp. 364, 368.

has been exceedingly increased; not only experience proves it, but the Nature of the Thing makes it impossible otherwise." [106]   This was a trade worth monopolizing; so the power of the state was invoked to exclude foreigners from the colonial commerce by the use of the navigation laws and the customs duties.

One more control was necessary to secure the full benefits of the plantations to the mother country.   Industry and manufacture in the colonies required regulation and management to prevent unwelcome competition with similar employments at home.   New England was regarded with disfavor because her products competed with those of the English manufacturers.   Thomas put it very delicately:

> Thus began that numerous colony in New England, where, under frugal laws . . . they live without applying themselves to planting any tobacco, or other American commodities . . . They, to all intents and purposes, imitate Old England . . . and do now supply the other colonies with provisions . . . how conveniently for the nation's interest I shall not determine, being no enemy to any kind of honest industry.   But this cannot chuse but be allowed; that if any hands in the Indies [i.e., the New World] be wrong employed for domestic interest, it must be theirs, and those other colonies, which settle with no other prospect than the like way of living.[107]

Other writers were less tactful in expressing this viewpoint, and Postlethwayt stated the propositions bluntly:

> Let the British Plantations follow the same maxims: Let them gradually strive to interfere as little as possible in their productions and manufactures with those of their mother

[106] [Defoe, Daniel], *An Humble Proposal to the People of England*, London, 1729, p. 43.
  For other statements of the value of the colonial market, see p. 205.
  [107] Thomas, *op. cit.*, p. 377.

country . . . and let their agriculture and their arts be lev-
elled as much as possible against those of rival nations . . .[108]

The mercantilist colonial policy was repeated throughout
the course of the eighteenth century, despite the rising
chorus of protest in the colonies themselves.

Regarded closely, the old colonial policy was merely
the familiar doctrines of mercantilist economics applied
to the new imperial situation. To sanction the regulation
of the colonial trade there stood the ancient precedents
of the tariff controls over the English mercantile activity
which had existed long before the Pilgrim Fathers thought
of chartering the Mayflower; to justify the restriction of
colonial industries to certain fields there were the traditions of careful supervision of English manufactures since
the time of the Tudors; small wonder that when at last
the American colonies revolted the mercantilists felt that
such conduct was ungrateful, unconventional, and un-
English.

There were a few writers during this period who, had
they been alive when the Declaration of Independence was
signed, would have heartily sympathized with the colonists'
side of the argument. These were the isolated, unorthodox individuals who had criticized the mercantile system
in various of its details, and sometimes in its fundamental
doctrines.

IV. HERETICS AND DISSENTERS: THE TORY FREE-TRADERS AND THE PRACTICAL CRITICS

Some exceptional men of the late seventeenth century
held views which ran fundamentally counter to the main

[108] Postlethwayt, Malachy, *Great Britain's Commercial Interest Explained and Improved*, 2nd ed., London, 1759, Vol. I, p. 71.
For other statements of the necessity for controlling colonial manufactures, and for conflicts of interest in the empire, see p. 205.

current of the economic thought of their time.   Indeed, they advanced a cosmopolitan economics which was completely at variance with the views of their contemporaries. These were the heretics—if a theological term may be borrowed to describe them—the unrepentant sinners who never came forward to the mourner's bench, nor even joined in the amen chorus which rose from the congregation.

One of the earliest among these was Roger Coke, who published his *Treatise* in 1671 and 1675.[109]   The most striking feature of the work is its effort to analyze economic phenomena objectively and mathematically; Coke was a great admirer of Euclid's geometry, and modeled his work upon its logical symmetry.   Having set up in his introduction a series of "Axioms" and "Petitions" which had for him the character of self-evident truth possessed by the propositions of Euclidean geometry, he applied the analysis to practical situations in the following manner:

The Law against Naturalization, before the Crown of England had the accession of the American Plantations, did hinder the improvement of the valuable Trades of England, and the Fishing Trade.

Act. The Law against Naturalization.

Question. Whether, etc. it hindered the improvement of the valuable Trades of England, and the Fishing Trade.   I say it did.   [This last is a momentary lapse from the manner of Euclid.]

[109] Coke, Roger, *A Treatise wherein is demonstrated, that the Church and State of England are in equal danger with the Trade of it,* London, 1671.   (Hereafter cited as *"Treatise."*)   Four years later he published *England's Improvements* (London, 1671), the title page of which declared it to be the two remaining parts of the *Treatise.*   Both these works had been preceded by a shorter one, *A Discourse of Trade,* London, 1670, which is only distinguishable from the *Treatise* by a long and poetic introduction, describing Trade as a coy lady who must be wooed at sea. Finally he published a two-volume work, *A Detection of the Court and State of England, during the Four Last Reigns, and the Inter-Regnum,* London, 1694.   (Hereafter cited as *"A Detection."*)

Axiom 1. For every business will be so much hindered as the means are excluded.

Petition 2. But greater numbers of People, are a mean to improve Trade.

Petition 1. And the Law against Naturalization, before the Crown of England had the accession of the American Plantations, did exclude great numbers of People from inhabiting and trading with us.

Therefore it hindered the improvement of the valuable trades of England, and the Fishing Trade, which was to be demonstrated.[110]

While this has more the aspect than the true substance of the relentless logic of mathematics, it does present Coke's striving for objective analysis. His approach yielded him results which were genuinely contrary to the conclusions of his contemporaries, who started with the initial intention of stating the national interest in economic affairs. He criticized the navigation laws: "the Act of Navigation debars us of the greatest part of the World from Trading with us" [111] and condemned the prohibitions on the Scottish and Irish trade, because these restrictions reduced commercial and industrial activity.[112] He attacked the monopolies and the trading corporations possessing special privileges, including the manufacturing guilds.[113] He even went the length of arguing for free importation of goods into England:

By this free Importation of Goods into the Ports of England, we may infinitely improve the benefits which will accrue to all sort of Artificers by the plenty and cheapness of all things they need, and to the forrein Trades of our Woollen and other Manufacturers, by their Returns into the Ports of England; the multitude of Shipping and Traders, will excite

110 Coke, *Treatise*, pp. 1-2.

111 *Ibid.*, p. 36. See also *A Detection*, Vol. I, pp. 16-17.

112 *Ibid.*, p. 59.

113 *Ibid.*, pp. 69 *ff*. See also *A Detection*, Vol. I, pp. 43-46 of the Introduction, unnumbered.

them to seek employment for their Shipping in all sorts of Commodities we can supply them with, and they the World.[114]

It is important to notice that these criticisms arise from the author's fundamental attitude, which is closely akin to the thinking of the laisser-faire economists of the nineteenth century. He declared this position in the introduction to his *Treatise:*

What is Trade? Trade is the act of getting, preparing, and exchanging things commodious for Humane convenience and necessity. So as Trade happens in three ways: First, by getting things which may be made commodious for men; which are termed the Growths of any place. Secondly, by preparing them to be commodious; which are termed Manufactures. Thirdly, by exchanging these for others, or mony; which is termed Merchandizing. The end of Trade is three fold, viz. Strength, Wealth, and Imployment for all sorts of People.[115]

Despite this philosophical attitude and the mathematical method employed to set it forth, Coke lapsed into many mercantilist views on various subjects. He thought, for example, that it would be wise to control and supervise the retail trades, and restrict the number of people who might enter them; [116] he wanted a Council of Trade to supervise and direct trading activities, and admired the Dutch policies and the Dutch government's concern with commerce; [117] he set a high value on a large employed population, and linked it to a favorable trade balance in the mercantilist manner; [118] and he wanted to reserve the colonial trade and the coasting trade to the English ship-

[114] Coke, *England's Improvements,* Epilogue, p. 114.
[115] Coke, *Treatise,* Introduction, p. 15, unnumbered.
[116] *Ibid.,* p. 69.
[117] *Ibid.,* pp. 129-137. See also *England's Improvement,* Epilogue.
[118] Coke, *A Detection,* Vol. I, pp. 47-48 of the Introduction, unnumbered.

pers.[119]   That he occasionally yielded to the ideas of his time, however, is not surprising; his divergence from his contemporaries in the underlying pattern of his thought is really remarkable.

Some twenty years later another distinguished heretic, Nicholas Barbon, published his *Discourse of Trade*. This compact little work repays analysis as an example of opposition to the prevailing opinions.

Barbon began, as Coke had begun, by defining the true nature of trade: "Trade is the Making, and Selling of one sort of good for another. . . . The chief end of the Business of Trade, is to make a profitable Bargain." [120]   He paid scant attention to the patriotic jargon about the interest of the nation and the prince, but came immediately to hard, commonsense, individualist economics.   "The Value of all Wares arise from their Use; things of no use have no value. . . . The Price of Wares is the present Value; and ariseth by computing the occasions or use for them, with the Quantity to serve that occasion . . . so that Plenty, in respect of the Occasion, makes things cheap; and Scarcity, dear." [121]   He made no sentimental valuation of goods upon any consideration of national necessity: "The Market is the best judge of Value." "Money," he continued, "is a Value made by Law," [122] a gold piece by the river's brim a yellow gold piece was to him, and it was not an evidence of national strength, or increasing national prosperity.   He then went on to analyze credit with equal clarity, and compared interest to rent in terms which orthodox laisser-faire economists could, and do, approve.[123]

119 Coke, *A Detection,* Vol. II, p. 486.

120 Barbon, Nicholas, *A Discourse of Trade,* London, 1690, reprinted and edited by J. H. Hollander, Baltimore, Johns Hopkins University Press, 1905, p. 9 (all citations are to this reprint).

121 *Ibid.,* pp. 13, 15.

122 *Ibid.,* p. 16.

123 *Ibid.,* pp. 19-20.

The benefits of trade arose from its essential nature as he had defined it; it provided the nation with the goods necessary for the support of life and the ease of living. Thus he was able to conclude: "The Chief Causes that promote Trade (not to mention Good Government, Peace, and Situation, with other Advantages) are Industry in the Poor, and Liberality in the Rich." [124]   By virtue of the whole analysis he gave his judgment that "the prohibition of Trade, is the Cause of its Decay; for all foreign wares are brought in by the Exchange of the Native; So that the prohibiting of any Foreign Commodity, doth hinder the Making and Exportation of so much of the Native, as used to be made and exchanged for it." [125]   This may not be quite what the German scholars have called "Smithianismus," but it is certainly not mercantilism.   Perhaps selected statements of this kind make his economics seem more cosmopolitan than they really were—he did concede that it was better to export manufactured goods than raw materials, and did propose lowering of the interest rate by law, two favorite dogmas of his contemporaries.   He also valued the large employed population as fervently as did Samuel Fortrey or Sir William Temple; but even this summary sketch of his *Discourse* reveals that he, like Coke, was really at odds with the prevailing doctrines of his time.   Dudley North and Sir William Petty may be classed with Coke and Barbon to make up a select group of heretics.[126]

Besides these few heretics there were a considerable number of dissenters; most of them members of the con-

---

[124] Barbon, Nicholas, *A Discourse of Trade*, pp. 31-32.

[125] *Ibid.*, p. 35.

[126] North, Dudley, *Discourses upon Trade*, London, 1691, reprinted and edited by J. H. Hollander, Baltimore, Johns Hopkins University Press, 1907; and Petty, Sir William, *Economic Writings*, edited by Charles Henry Hull, Cambridge University Press, 1899, 2 vols.

gregation with good standing, but willing occasionally to criticize the sermon, or to dispute about points of detail in the creed. Such men were the practical critics; they saw difficulties in parts of the mercantilist program, and their views can be summarized with reference to those difficulties.

Quite a number of otherwise orthodox mercantilists criticized high duties, bounties, and the prohibitions upon export. They subscribed, in the main, to the doctrine of the favorable balance of trade, but they felt that trade would be improved by moderation in tariff policies.[127] They often differed from each other in the arguments they offered; some came very close to arguing for free trade, more of them objected to prohibitions on export, or to a very high level of customs duties, on grounds of political and economic expediency.

The dissenters likewise picked flaws in the controls of the domestic economy. The monopolistic companies came in for a good deal of criticism from several of the practical men of business, for they viewed such privileges as likely to limit the volume of trade and production, and thus to injure the favorable balance. Their views on monopolies were of significance in the pattern of their political opinions, and so will be reviewed carefully later. The controls of standards of price and quality of goods, and the proposals to regulate the level of wages came in for relatively little criticism; Child is one of the few who raised objections to such domestic policies, though there were a few others like him.[128] Probably the reason for

[127] For the principal critics of duties, bounties, and prohibitions, see p. 207.

[128] Child, Sir Josiah, *Trade and the Interest of Money Considered*, London, 1669, Chs. I and III, especially pp. 139-40 (paging from the edition of 1775); T. T., *Some General Considerations offered relating to our present Trade*, London, 1698; Paxton, P., *A Discourse concerning the Nature, Advantage, and Improvement of Trade*, London, 1704, especially pp. 13-14, 90.

this silence on the part of the critics with regard to regulations of the domestic economy was due in large part to the fact that the justices of the peace were steadily and continuously performing many of these functions, and familiarity had bred consent.

Finally there were the critics of the imperial policies. The navigation laws did not secure unanimous approval; some ardent advocates of the favorable balance of trade feared that the laws, despite their long standing, restricted rather than expanded the English merchant marine.[129] The regulation of the colonial trade and manufacture did not escape criticism; control seemed to carry political risks and the dangers of extinguishing some of the most advantageous aspects of the economic activity of the plantations.[130]

It must be repeated, however, that these objections had always the character of practical criticism of details of policy; save in the case of the truly unorthodox, like Coke and Barbon, the strictures did not arise from a fundamental divergence from prevailing opinion.

If a final use of the theological metaphor may be permitted, there must be set against the heretics and dissenters those devout worshipers at the shrine of national greatness who tried to defend the doctrine by amending the creed to meet the heresy of cosmopolitanism and the criticisms of the dissenters. It is possible to say that in the eighteenth century there arose a phase of mercantilism which made adaptation to the changing times by, so to speak, substituting paper for gold. Mandeville, Law, and Berkeley might be pointed out as representatives of this

[129] The critics of the navigation laws are relatively few in number: [Petyt, William], *Britannia Languens*, London, 1680, sections V and VI, pp. 281-283; Decker, Sir Matthew, *Essay on the Decline of the Foreign Trade*, London, 1739, Part III; Perrin, William, *Present State of the British and French Sugar Colonies*, London, 1740; [Whately, George], *Principles of Trade*, London, 1774.

[130] For the critics of the restrictive colonial policy, see p. 208.

school of thought. They recognized the importance of economic and commercial activity to the development of national strength, and so proposed an extension of credit through the establishment of a national bank and the issue of a paper currency. They hoped that such devices would achieve a large part of the objectives which the more rigorous controls of industry and commerce had been designed to secure.[131]

Such a viewpoint was not unprecedented in the annals of mercantilist writing. In 1694, after a period of financial difficulties for the English commercial community, and of fiscal problems for the government, the Bank of England was created by parliamentary enactment. Two years later an extensive recoinage, especially of the silver coins, was undertaken by the government with the aid of the Bank. These two important policies were the subject of extensive discussion, and at that time the importance of credit to expanding industry and commerce led to the proposal of many banking and currency schemes, and much controversy about the founding of the Bank. The chief alternative proposed was the establishment of a land bank, a scheme very like the one which John Law managed to institute in France some years later. In all this debate—there is a flood of pamphlet literature at this time—the accepted objectives of stimulating trade and industry in the interest of national strength are continually put forward.[132]

Two other individuals might be mentioned who mark the period of transition from mercantilism to laisser-faire

[131] Professor Espinas pointed out this interesting aspect in *La Troisième Phase et la Dissolution du Mercantilisme*, Paris, 1902. (Extrait de la *Revue Internationale de Sociologie*.) He cites Law, Mandeville, and Berkeley as representative of this transition in thought, together with some French theorists of like convictions. See also Heckscher, E., *Mercantilism*, London, 1935, Vol. II, pp. 231 *ff.*

[132] For the advocates of a national bank, and the proponents of land-bank schemes, see p. 209.

economics. James Steuart is the more important, his two volumes present a mixture of viewpoints; the other is James Anderson, who had read Adam Smith, but presented some criticism of the *Wealth of Nations* in terms that are often reminiscent of mercantilist doctrines.[133]

V. SUMMARY

It must be remembered that any brief review of these ideas, even though notice is given to the divergent viewpoints expressed by some of the writers, imparts an artificial and fictitious unity and coherence to the doctrines. The mercantile system was not really a system; no one writer expressed at one time the balance of trade formula, the insistence on the control of the domestic economy, and the defense of the navigation and colonial policies. It is legitimate, however, to interpret the body of thought which was predominant during the sixteenth and seventeenth centuries, and for a good part of the eighteenth, by describing these viewpoints on trade, industry, and empire. The nationalist character of these fundamental teachings was repeatedly displayed in all the statements. The state was always entitled, frequently obligated, and generally invited to exercise control over most of the economic activities of the nation. It is the breadth of this interest, coupled with the wide extent of power—reaching even to proposals for the control of consumption—which distinguishes the mercantilist doctrines from those, for example, of the advocates of protective tariffs in the nineteenth century.

Malynes used very early a favorite analogy, the metaphor of the nation being like a household: "Neverthelesse (as a commonwealth is nothing else but a great household

---

[133] Steuart, Sir James, *Principles*, London, 1767; Anderson, James, *Observations on the Means of Exciting a Spirit of National Industry* . . . Edinburgh, 1777.

or family:) yet the Prince (being as it were the father of the family) ought to keep a certaine equality in the trade or trafficke between his realme and other countries. . . ." [134] This parable characterizes aptly the import of the position adopted by all the writers. The interests of the members of the household were subordinated to the dominant interest of the family; unequal treatment of them was justifiable, the servants had to accept a scantier living and perform unpleasant tasks. The state was a parent possessing great authority, disciplining the tastes, the labors, the investments of the whole clan.

Obviously the identity and the character of this father and the justification of the vast powers he possessed were questions of the gravest import. Who was he—king, or Parliament, or possibly all the people? By what right had he these powers—through the prerogative of uncritical patriotism and the ideal of national aggrandizement, or by virtue of the social and economic needs of the nation? And what was he—a staff of trained officials capable of exercising expert control and direction of the family budget and employments, or a capricious sovereign or legislature whose ear was inclined at one time to the landed gentry, and at another to the merchant princes?

The mercantilist system, approaching as it did a planned national economy, inevitably involved these political implications. It is important to see if they were recognized and provided for in the mercantilists' conception of the state.

[134] Malynes, Gerard de, *A Treatise of the Canker of Englands Commonwealth,* London, 1601, pp. 2-3.

CHAPTER III

The Political Implications of Mercantilist Economics

ANY planned or regulated economy requires more than establishment of an authority with power to do the planning; there must also be general acceptance of that authority by the community. Otherwise the plan is very likely to remain merely a blueprint and the building projected will never be constructed. A large proportion of the mercantilists were practical men interested in securing real and immediate results; and a good share of their proposals actually went into operation. The economic system they advocated was, in the strictest sense of the words, a *political* economy. It would have been impossible for them to devise it, much less put it to work —if but in part—without taking cognizance of its political implications.

In 1656 the author of *The Golden Fleece* pleaded for better regulation of the woolen industry. He complained of the abuses which had grown up in the making of cloth, and the injury which the nation suffered from the loss of reputation by English manufacturers and traders. The remedy for these evils lay in more rigid supervision of the industry by the state; the alnager's office should be restored to its ancient authority and importance, and its powers should be enlarged and extended. He hoped also that the societies and companies would take their responsibilities to the nation more seriously, and thus safeguard the national interest in the vitally important activities of manufacture and commerce: "For nothing doth more prejudice the publique utility, than that every man should exercise his own fancey, nor is anything a greater Bane to a well governed Common-wealth, than ill-governed and disorderly trade." The preface to his pamphlet set forth the general need for authority in an eloquent passage:

There is neither House, nor City, nor Country . . . nor the Worlde itselfe, which can subsist without Government, saith Cicero . . . which government intends and includes these two Fundamentals or corner stones, Power and Obedience, by which as the Regiment of every Common-wealth doth stand, so the flourishing Trade of England (under Societies and Companies) doth manifest the same to the whole world. . . . The regulated trade of Merchandice performeth all this, by which it beautifies the Earth and Seas, giving intercourse and combination, supplies and riches to each industrious part of the world.[1]

The subject's duty to obey this government was declared by another writer at about the same time:

No man is so void of reason as to deny that he is born for the service of God, his Prince, and Country. God requires it for our good; a Prince out of duty derived out of the Command of God; and Our Country out of the Law of Nature, next unto our Parents. God directs us out of his written word, how to serve him; a Prince out of his humane laws how to serve and to obey him; and our Country out of an instinct of Nature, how to reverence her.[2]

A dialogue published at the beginning of the eighteenth century repeated the same injunctions for the use of state action, this time in maintaining standards of manufacture of goods:

[1] S., W. Gent, *The Golden Fleece, wherein is related the Riches of England's Wools in its Manufactures,* London, 1656, p. 119 (for the sentence quoted first) and the preface, passim (for the longer passage quoted).

[2] Anon., ΙΧΘΥΟΘΗΡΑ, *or, The Royal-Trade of Fishing,* London, 1661, p. 1.

M. Ragouse: . . . you are rightly informed of the care of the French government in this particular; no Ingenuity of any kind, but was rewarded by the French King; which was the ready way to bring Fabricks to their perfection, and thereby to render them acceptable in Foreign Parts. . . .

Mr. Smith: Where a Government is unmindful of their Manufactures, and doth neither encourage Ingenuity, nor discourage deceitful making, Private Interest doth too often prevail, to the debasing of their Commodities; as is notoriously our Case at present in England.[3]

Malachy Postlethwayt gave a more general statement of the same idea in his last published work in 1757; and it is worth noting that this journalist's phrases written in the latter half of the eighteenth century, still ring with the insistence upon the need of state power over commercial and industrial activity:

The effect of commerce is, to give a body politic all the weight and strength, influence and dignity it is capable of receiving. These consist in the number of the inhabitants attracted by its political riches, which are at the same time both real and relative. The real riches of a state are its superior degree of *independence on other states* for necessaries, and the greater quantity of superfluities it has to export. Its relative riches depend on the quantity its trade procures of what men have agreed to call riches, compared with the quantity of the same kind of riches brought into neighbouring states by their trade. A combination of these real and relative riches is what constitutes the art and science of the administration of *political commerce.*[4]

Put thus compactly in a few sentences, and read in conjunction with earlier statements, the emphasis on govern-

---

[3] Anon., *A Dialogue between Mr. Smith, Monsieur Ragouse, Menheir Dorveil, and Mr. Manoel Texiera, in a Walk to Newington,* London, 1701, pp. 3-4.

[4] Postlethwayt, Malachy, *Great-Britain's Commercial Interest Explained and Improved,* 2nd ed., London, 1759, Vol. II, p. 368. (The first edition appeared in 1757.)

ment action is impressive. The necessity for every one of these writers to consider both "the art and science of the administration" and the nature of the administering authority should have been inescapable.

Nevertheless, the mercantilists did in part escape it. Because they were almost always concerned with particular problems, because they were forever devising ways and means of dealing with particular situations, they frequently left unstated the underlying political assumptions upon which their proposals rested. This is a habit of the man of business. But even if they did concentrate their attention upon the trees—and usually one tree at a time—it would be a grave mistake to think they did not know a forest stood there. They were aware of the implications of their economic doctrines; and sometimes they gave them explicit statement.

A still better reason for leaving the political presuppositions unstated was that there seemed to be little occasion to declare and defend them. The mercantilists did not need, for example, to justify the right of the state to regulate the habits of consumption of its citizens—a feature of their proposals which probably seems most extreme to the modern student despite present-day German and Russian rationing of goods—because they were not yet very far away from the doctrines of the canonists. As for the successful assertion of government power, many of them lived under a popular Tudor absolutism, or under a Stuart kingship which either had not been destroyed or had been recently restored with considerable enthusiasm. A good share of the time it doubtless seemed to them superfluous to waste words in stating carefully the justification for vesting these great powers in the state; the rights of the state and its government, for all practical purposes, could be taken for granted. They would have had a little difficulty, so far as the exercise of authority in the field of economic affairs was concerned, in finding opponents with whom to conduct a debate on such a subject.

Nevertheless, the modern student must investigate the assumptions which they failed to make completely explicit if he is to comprehend the nature of their attitude, or even the full meaning of any of their theories. Their share in the development of economic thought has been carefully assessed by the historians of economic theory; but the state which they constantly invited to control and direct economic activity has never received the close attention it deserves from the mercantilists themselves or from their commentators. It may seem a work of supererogation—this wrenching of a political theory from the reluctant text of writers who did not see fit to declare it for themselves. If, however, the task is honestly performed, it should reveal the full nature of the mercantile system; for in that system economics and politics were inseparably joined.

The first and most important presumption is clearly the wide range of state power, and whatever justification for it the mercantilists offered. The second is the obverse of the first, the obligation of obedience of the subject to the state, an obligation which was expressed in terms of the duties of the classes of the community. The third and last to be reviewed is the rivalry between states, for these writers realized the international scene could not be peaceful, occupied as it was by predatory nations devoted to the end of gaining the advantage over one another.

I. THE ASSERTION OF POWER AND THE PRESUMPTION OF RIGHT

The willingness of the mercantilists to vest tremendous economic powers in the state affords a striking contrast with their laisser-faire successors. Their approach to most economic problems was "there ought to be a law"—and in a remarkable number of instances there was one. A political question which constantly engaged the attention of English economists after Adam Smith was the limit to state action in commercial and industrial affairs; the predecessors of Adam Smith cheerfully invoked government power whenever they thought the interest of the nation was at stake. Fundamentally, of course, both groups of thinkers treasured the same goal, England's strength and power; the difference between them lay in the fact that one used government policy to achieve results, the other relied upon the operation of immutable economic laws. The remark may be permitted that with the latter economics became a dismal science.

The review of mercantilist economic doctrines in the preceding chapter pictures the range and the variety of state action in economic affairs. The favorable balance of foreign trade was defended and maintained by an armory of bounties, customs duties and prohibitions; domestic industry was supervised with regard to the quality and price of goods, the management of the wages, training, and perchance the numbers of the working population; agriculture was subjected to regulation by the corn laws and the extension of enclosure was advocated; even the consuming habits of the nation were to be regimented; and the American plantations were knit into a system of imperial economics. While there is hardly need to press this point, some of the expressions of the writers are worth examination.

Sometimes the nation's interest was put generally and broadly, as did Postlethwayt and his predecessors quoted above. Thomas Mun devoted the concluding paragraph of his most famous work to a burst of eloquence on the subject:

Behold then the true form and worth of Forraign Trade, which is, the great Revenue of the King, the Honour of the

Kingdom, the noble profession of Merchant, the school of our arts, the supply of our wants, the employment of our poor, the improvement of our lands, the nurcery of our mariners, the walls of the Kingdom, the means of our treasure, the sinews of our wars, the terror of our enemies. For all so great and weighty reasons do so many well governed States highly countenance the profession, and carefully cherish the action, not only with policy to encrease it, but also with power to protect it from all foreign injuries; because they know it is a principal in reason of State to maintain and defend that which doth support them and their estates.[5]

This vigorous statement may be read again, so to speak, in the words of Sir James Steuart when he discusses the duty of his statesman in fostering infant industries. It is true that the forthright directness of the seventeenth century has been sicklied o'er with the pale cast of relative costs and competitive values, but the demand for extensive state action is still there, and it is well to remember that this statesman must also judge which are the infant industries:

The ruling principle, therefore, which ought to direct a statesman in this first species of trade is to encourage the manufacturing of every branch of natural productions, by extending the home-consumption of them; by excluding all competition with strangers, by permitting the rise of profits, so far as to promote dexterity and emulation in invention and improvement; by relieving the industrious of their work, as often as demand for it falls short. And until it can be exported to advantage, it may be exported with loss at the expence of the public. To spare no expence in procuring the ablest masters in every branch of industry; and so soon as he finds that the real value of the manufactures comes so low as to render it exportable, to employ the hands, as above, and to put an end to these profits he had permitted only as a means of bringing the manufactures to perfection. In pro-

[5] Mun, Thomas, *England's Treasure by Forraign Trade,* London, 1664, ed. Sir William Ashley, New York, 1895, p. 119.

portion as the prices of every species of industry are brought down to the standard of exportation, in such proportion does this species of trade lose its original character, and adopt the second.[6]

Steuart reflected here the struggle in his mind between conceptions approaching laisser-faire, and his unbounded confidence in his "statesman"; it is perfectly clear, however, that he was willing to confide extensive powers of management of commerce and industry to political authority. Perhaps one other eighteenth century statement, published some thirty years earlier than Steuart's *Principles,* should be quoted to show that others hesitated less than he did. Sir William Keith, dealing with the place of the colonies, began his book by declaring trade to be a matter of public interest:

As soon as the Increase of Mankind gave Rise to Society, whereby they became subjected to the Laws of a Civil Government, the Interest of the particular Members was made subservient on all Occasions to that of the Public . . . Trade was regulated according to the Advantages or Disadvantages that accrued to the Community . . . it is inconsistent with the Nature of Things to suppose, that a Civil Government ought to permit, much less to encourage, any Traffick or private Gain to be carried on, which evidently appears to be prejudicial to the Public Interest and Prosperity of the Commonwealth.[7]

All these general statements, though they are scattered through writings published during the course of two centuries, repeat the prevailing viewpoint with considerable fidelity.

The assertion of state authority was more often and more characteristically made with relation to a specific

[6] Steuart, Sir James, *Principles of Political Economy,* London, 1767, Vol. I, p. 304.

[7] Keith, Sir William, Bart., *The History of the British Plantations in America,* London, 1738, p. 3. For other examples of the assertion of the power of the state, see p. 210.

problem or a practical situation. The mercantilist literature bristles with demands for the use of government power and policy in dealing with particular activities in the nation's economy. *The British Merchant,* for example, stated in its first issue a number of maxims of trade which set forth the importance to the nation of the exportation of commodities, the manufacture of native goods, the maintenance of a favorable balance, and a number of similar mercantilist principles. The succeeding issues examined all the important trading connections of England, judged them in terms of national advantage by these touchstones of policy, and asked for state action to guide these trades for the benefit of the nation.[8] Bishop Berkeley put the whole matter with his usual forcefulness of phrase:

Whether Trade be not then on a right foot, when foreign Commodities are imported only in exchange for domestic superfluities? . . . Whether it would not be wise to so order our trade as to export Manufactures rather than provisions, and of those such as employ most hands? Whether she would not be a very vile Matron, and justly thought either mad or foolish that should give away the Necessaries of Life, from her naked and famished children, in Exchange for Pearls to stick in her Hair, and Sweet Meats to please her own palate? [9]

These are specific instances of the assertion of government authority; the nation needed treasure, employment, or goods; it should regulate its foreign trade accordingly.

Proposals of the same nature were continually made for the supervision of industry at home:

[8] King, Charles, compiler, *The British Merchant,* 2nd ed., London, 1743, 3 Vols., passim. This work was first issued as a biweekly answer to Defoe's *Mercator,* and was issued during 1713 and 1714, and Charles King, one of the chief organizers and author of many of the articles, finally collected many of them into these volumes.

[9] Berkeley, George, *The Querist,* 1734-1736, ed. J. H. Hollander, Baltimore, 1910, questions 167, 178, 179.

Seeing trade then is the Fund of Wealth and Power, we cannot wonder that we see the wisest Princes and States anxious and concerned for the Encrease of the Commerce and trade of their Subjects, and of the Growth of the Country; anxious to propagate the Sale of such Goods as are the Manufacture of their own Subjects, and that employes their own People; especially, of such as keep the money of their Dominions at Home, and on the contrary, for prohibiting the Importations from Abroad, of such Things as are the product of other Countries, and of the Labour of other People, as which carry Money back in return, and not Merchandise in Exchange. Nor can we wonder that we see such Princes and States endeavouring to set up such Manufactures in their own countries, which they see successfully and profitably carried on by their Neighbours, and to endeavour to procure the Materials proper for setting up those Manufactures by all just and possible Methods from other Countries.[10]

These were the words of Defoe, who served as a poll of prevailing opinion as well as an advocate. Joshua Gee's arguments for the establishment of new enterprises might well be a continuation of the same passage:

. . . after all, it will be hardly possible to bring any of those Improvements to the desired Perfection, without a steady Resolution in the Government to sustain and support them, and as it were to carry them in their Arms; for new Enterprises will alway be subject to Accidents and Discouragements too difficult for private Persons to surmount them without the assistance of the public, as occasion may require.[11]

Further citation of such proposals would be easy, but unnecessary; reference to the review of economic theories in the preceding chapter reveals the unhesitating acceptance of state authority, always and everywhere.

One further bit of evidence is peculiarly interesting,

[10] Defoe, Daniel, *Plan of the English Commerce*, 1728, reprinted, Oxford, 1928, p. 41.

[11] Gee, Joshua, *Trade and Navigation of Great Britain Considered*, 3rd ed., London, 1731, p. 144. First published London, 1729.

however, and is worth brief examination.   Even the discordant voices of the occasional heretics and dissenters were often in tune with this chorus of national power and national interest.   Roger Coke, despite his mathematical methods and his objective viewpoint toward economic activity, wanted regulation of the retail trade, supervision of the manufacture of wool and the encouragement of the silk industry, and the establishment of a council of trade. The concluding pages of his *Detection* put forward a number of proposals exhibiting a curious mixture of the exercise of state power with demands for freedom of activity.[12]   Much the same thing can be said of Barbon and North.   Paxton, a much less famous writer, did express a consistent viewpoint, but did it by clinging closely to one characteristic doctrine, the need of a large population.   Having made an analysis of the gain by foreign trade in orthodox mercantilist terms, he then arrived at the conclusion that "cheapness and goodness" of manufactures were the only means of maintaining the vitally important favorable balance.   This would be most certainly secured by pursuing policies which would increase the population:

And I am apprehensive these our Misfortunes will not admit of any Remedy, unless we multiply our People; for by that our Consumptions being increased the Value of Land must rise, and our Methods of Living must alter: Our Necessities then, would oblige our People to Parsimony, and our Numbers to Industry; by which Forein Trade would Flourish, and our Poor thence being able to subsist by their own labours in our Manufactures, our Enclosures would be no injury to us: as for all other Methods they seem unnatural, and have hitherto been ineffectual, and, as I apprehend, will for ever be so.[13]

12 Coke, Roger, *A Detection*, Vol. II, pp. 485 et. seq.; *Treatise*, pp. 69, 87-90, 136-137.

13 Paxton, P. (M.D.), *A Discourse concerning the Nature, Advantage, and Improvement of Trade*, London, 1704, p. 90.

The natural process of procreation is here the chief specific for the nation's ills; it will provide the conditions for national greatness, and the care of the state should be directed toward this end. Most of the critics, however, were ready to admit without hesitation the wide range of government authority; only the methods and purposes of its exercise were really open for discussion. Pollexfen, thoroughly orthodox in his viewpoints, expressed this in an extremely interesting paragraph:

It is agreed that the best way to incourage Trade, and make it advantageous to a Nation and useful to afford a livelihood to the vast Number of People that have their sole dependence thereon, is in general to allow all the liberty imaginable. . . .

This might well be a preparation for a laissez-faire policy, but mark how he continues:

But as most general Rules may be liable to some exceptions, so this especially to these two: First, that no Trade ought to be incouraged that is carried on by the exportation of our Bullion, unless to purchase what we absolutely want for our Defence, or support of life. . . . Secondly, that no Wooll be carried out raw or unwrought. Other Laws may be found necessary to prevent abuses in the manufacturing of Goods, keeping the People to Work, and for the incouraging and increasing of Trade, which should be applied as Occasions and Exigencies may require, but none appear necessary (upon these sudden thoughts) contrary to the freedom insisted on, but what may be comprehended under these two exceptions mentioned.[14]

These two exceptions are surely important enough to curtail extensively "all the liberty imaginable"; and later his "sudden thoughts" gave way to the suggestion of other uses of policy to safeguard the national interest in its trade and industry.

[14] Pollexfen, John, *England and East India inconsistent in their Manufactures*, London, 1697, p. 52.

Behind all these assertions of state authority lay the presumption of right. Readiness to propose the use of power and policy is a mark of the mercantilists' willingness to assume that the government clearly had the right to control all these economic activities. To the modern student it seems extraordinary that such extensive domination of the domestic economy and foreign trade could have been proposed without some attempt to set a reasoned justification for it on ethical and philosophical grounds. A Plato, a Bodin, or a Hegel would surely have derived a claim based upon the nature of the institution, or perhaps the character of mankind. A Hitler would devise sanctions based upon Aryan racial needs; a Roosevelt would put forward the humanitarian argument of social necessity.

The key to the mercantilists' position lies in their pragmatic attitude; they did not trouble to reason why; they simply took the right of the state for granted. Patriotism was ample justification for regimentation of the domestic economy; nationalism was the unquestioned foundation for the management of foreign relations and foreign trade. Most of them assumed that the welfare of the community would follow from the pursuit of national strength and power. Davenant came as close as any of them to giving any reasoned justification for the use of state authority:

If such as represent the People are Uncorrupt, Unbyassed etc. and if in this Manner *Private Persons perform their Duty to the Publick,* we shall not fail in all succeeding Times to see a *steddy course of Honesty and Wisdom in such as are trusted with the Administration of Affairs.* And where things are well administer'd, *that Country will always increase in Wealth and Power.* . . . Where men have a prospect of all this, Strangers resort thither with their Wealth and Stocks, whereas Merchants and other cautious Persons abandon Countries, whose Follies and Corruptions subject 'em to continual Changes and frequent Revolutions, so that peradventure upon solid Reasons, and very just Grounds, we may lay down, that nothing more contributes to make a Nation gainers in the general Ballance of Trade, than good Laws well observ'd, and a constant Course of honest and steddy Government.[15]

This may seem a slender and incomplete statement of a case for the great range of authority which these writers advocated. Most of the time, however, the practical program for building up the strength and power of the kingdom was at once the object of their thought and its justification. A majority of these men were often merchants or administrators, interested in practical problems and untroubled by the ethical or philosophical implications of their proposals.

II. THE DUTIES OF THE CLASSES AND THE HARMONY OF INTERESTS

The right to command implied the subject's duty to obey. The mercantilists stated this obligation in terms of the classes of the population. The laborers, the rich, the landlords, and the merchants were all expected to fulfill certain obligations to the body politic. A beneficent harmony of interests assured them all of rewards suited to their station in the community. Though there might be occasional discords, the mercantilists resolutely tuned their ears to disregard them.

[15] Davenant, Charles, *An Essay on the Probable Methods of making a People Gainers in the Balance of Trade,* 2nd ed., London, 1700, pp. 202-203. First published London, 1699. For a similar passage see Postlethwayt, Malachy, *Great-Britain's Commercial Interest Explained and Improved,* 2nd ed., London, 1759, Vol. II, pp. 385-386. First published, London, 1757.

A. *The Laborer's Lot*

The duties of the laboring classes were stated in rigorous terms. It was the fate of the workers to be poor that the nation might be rich, and to be ceaselessly diligent that the nation might be powerful. The economic importance of the labor force of the nation has been analyzed in the preceding chapter where a brief review was made of the labor theories. A good summary statement is furnished by one of the writers in 1753:

> Herein consists the Marrow of that Maxim, *that Numbers of People are the Wealth of a Nation:* as where they are plenty, they must work cheap, and so Manufactures are encouraged for a foreign Market, and their Returns is the Wealth of a Nation, which numbers thus procure.[16]

The author then went on to urge encouragements to marriage, for clearly the ideal representative of the laboring class, for all the mercantilists, was a poor man with a large family—by definition, then, a hard-working man as well. This concern with numbers runs through all their writings and led Steuart into a really extraordinary proposal:

> In order to have a flourishing state, which Sir William Temple beautifully compared to a pyramid, we must form a large and solid basis of the lower classes of mankind . . . But where every one lives by his own industry, a competition comes in, and he who works cheapest gains the preference. . . . I have therefore proposed, that a statesman, well informed of the situation of his people, the state of every class, the number of marriages found in each, should say, let there be so many marriages authorized in every class, distributed in a certain proportion for every parish, city, burrow, etc. in the country; let rules be laid down to direct a preference, in case of competition, between different couples; and let the

16 [Horsley, William], *The Universal Merchant,* London, 1753, preface, p. xv.

consequence of this approbation be, to relieve the parents of all children above a certain number . . .[17]

This is regimentation which fully matches the Hitler government's bonuses to young married couples, or the Mussolini taxes on bachelors; and it can be found expressed in varying degrees by many of Steuart's predecessors. A curious aspect of this faith in numbers is that it was a faith in an unknown number. All estimates of population were the merest guesses; and demands for an accurate census did not appear until well on in the eighteenth century.[18]

Besides the injunction to increase and multiply, there was laid upon the poor the command to labor. The phrases used were those of moral obligation to the community and the state. The author of *The Golden Fleece* put the matter thus in 1656:

It is utterly against reason that a nation can be poor, whose people are numerous, if their industries be compelled and encouraged, and their idlenesse be punished and reformed; it is not the barrennesse of a Country which can forbid this maxim. . . . The Dutch are a numerous Nation, daily multiplying in a Country which hath in comparison, nothing of its own growth to support them either in food or clothing, yet they want nothing in necessaries or wealth, because they are industrious. . . . Now a great encrease of people rests upon the regulation of Trade; for it is not the number of workmen, but the number of good workmen which increas-

[17] Steuart, Sir James, *Principles of Political Economy*, London, 1767, Vol. I, pp. 73-75.
For other statements of the faith in numbers of people, and proposals of state action to increase population, see p. 211.
[18] [Massie, J.], *Calculations of Taxes for a Family of Each Class for One Year*, London, 1756; [Young, Arthur], *Proposals to the Legislature for Numbering the People*, London, 1771, are two well-reasoned pleas for a census of the population. Petty, Sir William, *An Essay in Political Arithmetick*, London, 1682, furnishes some attempts at estimates of the population.

eth Families: and it is Families which encrease and spread good people; . . . Of principal importance therefore is the regulation of Apprentiships, both towards the best encrease of people, and to the honest, creditable, and wealthy manufacture of wools, and especially of clothing . . . [19]

A score of years later another writer coined the sense of this paragraph into an epigram: "The Labours of the Poor, are the Mines of the Rich; Manufacturies and Commerce, the Springs of Wealth to every Nation, whence flow Power at Home, and (the effect of that) Reputation abroad . . ." [20]

Naturally, since it was the duty of the poor to labor, idleness and sloth were roundly condemned:

. . . Henry the Great of France caused all vagrants and idle persons to be sent to serve in his gallies, to oblige them perforce to work; for idle persons who take not care to employ themselves seriously in some thing, are unprofitable to themselves, and pernicious to the Publick: Therefore that State must necessarily be rich and prosperous, which hath Argus eyes to foresee advantages, and Briareus hands, and those imployed. [21]

The duty of the worker was thus described in the seventeenth century; the eighteenth century reiterated the idea, for William Wood wanted

some such Law enacted, as that such of the Poor, as are able, when they have not Work, or cannot find it, the Parish where they are settled should have Power to provide it for them, and they be compelled to work, all Hands might be easily employed, one way or other; and so many new ones might thereby be brought to work, as would make our *Manufac-*

[19] S., W. Gent, *The Golden Fleece*, London, 1656, pp. 79-78, misnumbered.

[20] Philo-Anglicus, Gent., *Bread for the Poor*, London, 1678, p. 3.

[21] [B., J.], *An Account of the French Usurpation upon the Trade of England*, London, 1679, p. 15.

tures, as well flourish, as ease many Parishes of a very great
Charge . . . [22]

There was more at stake than the industry of the laborer;
these quotations show that the mercantilists were anxious
to devise some feasible method of reducing the burden of
poor relief. Their desire for full employment was based
upon mixed motives; labor was one of the essential resources of the national community, and at the same time
the maintenance of the poor was one of the most oner-
ous charges on the local governments. The workhouse
schemes, therefore, continually reflect the two aims: the
first, that of mobilizing the labor force of the nation and
insisting that the duty to labor be fulfilled; the second,
that of freeing the local communities, so far as possible, of
the heavy burden of caring for the unemployed.

But the ideal working man had more to perform for
his country than rearing a large family, and pursuing a
life of persevering toil. He was further required to live
sparely and work cheaply. Thomas Manley put this
bluntly and brutally in the latter half of the seventeenth
century:

> Overvaluing our wages then . . . to maintain good eating
> and drinking, is the capital reason that all forraigners under-
> sell us, and ever will . . .
> The general conspiracy amongst Artificers and Labourers
> is so apparent, that within these twenty-five years the wages
> of Joyners, Bricklayers, Carpenters are increased, I mean
> within fourty miles of London, (against all reason and good
> government) from eighteen and twenty pence a day to 2s. 6d.
> and 3s. and meer Labourers from ten and twelve pence a day
> unto sixteen and twenty pence . . .
> Nor has the increase of wages amongst us been occasioned
> by quickness of Trade, and want of hands (as some suppose)

---

[22] Wood, William, *A Survey of Trade,* London, 1719, p. 256.
For similar condemnations of idleness, and desire for a machinery to
enforce industry, see p. 212.

which are indeed justifiable reasons, but through an exacting humour, and evil disposition of our people . . . so that they may live the better above their station, and work so much the fewer days by how much the more they exact in their wages . . .

I know we have thousands of people miserably poor, yet will not work on such moderate terms the imployers can cheerfully afford them, nor honestly earne sixpence, because they fondly imagine their labour worth ninepence, and so sit idle, without considering that something is better than nothing. . . .

And now whilest our mechanicks . . . thus frequently raise the rates of their wages, Usury has been reduc'd, provisions grow cheaper, vent for our Manufactures dayly less'd through the excessive wages of our Artificers; and they with the whole Nation dwindle into greater poverty, which sufficiently proves encrease of wages to be a notorious prejudice to the Commonwealth, not to be cured by subduction of interest.[23]

Manley's harshness was more than matched in two pamphlets attributed to Daniel Defoe which appeared at the end of the first quarter of the eighteenth century, in which he complained that "the advance of Wages . . . is the support of all the Insolence of Servants, as their ruin'd manners is the Spring of it. . . . The Lab'ring Poor, in spight of double pay, are saucy, mutinous, and beggarly."[24]

In the eighteenth century the argument for cheap wages lost some of its moral character, however, and acquired some economic sophistication:

[23] Manley, Thomas, Gent., *Usury at Six Per Cent. Examined,* London, 1669, pp. 17-20, passim.

[24] [Defoe, Daniel], *The Great Law of Subordination Consider'd,* London, 1724, pp. 79-80; see also two other pamphlets also attributed to him: *Every-Body's Business is No-Body's Business,* London, 1725, and *Giving no Alms to Charity* (in *A Second Volume of the Writings of the Author of the True Born Englishman,* London, 1705, pp. 417-450).

For other statements of the sin of idleness and the obligation to work for low wages, see p. 212.

As the increase both of the stock and revenue of the nation, depends entirely upon the poor labouring People; therefore all measures ought to be taken to make everything cheap, that is necessary for their support and maintenance; for the cheaper they are able to live, the less their wages will be, and consequently our merchants will buy our manufactures the cheaper, and so will be able to sell them in foreign markets at a lower price, which is the only way to keep foreigners from encroaching upon our trade.[25]

In whichever form the argument was advanced, the workman's wage was still to be low; a parsimonious and industrious laboring class was necessary for the kingdom's strength in commerce.

The picture must not be painted in these gloomy colors unrelieved; there were some advocates of high wages and humanitarian treatment. Sir Thomas Culpepper, Jr., writing in direct refutation of Manley on the question of reducing the interest rate, differed with him as strongly on the question of low wages:

. . . if any disproportion there be in wages, (as some in everything may there be, where the Ballance itself is faulty, and the main wheel out of frame,) the remedy falls in of course, and wages will, without more adoe, recover and keep their due Standard; otherwise to dream of augmenting trade by stinting wages, too much resembles the judicious contrivance of that worthy Squire, whom nothing would please but to let his meadow for forty shillings the acre, and buy his Hay at ten shillings the load.[26]

John Cary, writing just at the turn of the seventeenth century, put the same point more carefully; and warned the manufacturer that he must cut costs by improving processes:

[25] Anon., *An Honest Scheme, for Improving the Trade and Credit of the Nation*, London, 1729, pp. 8-9.

[26] Culpepper, Sir Thomas, Jr., *The Necessity of Abating Usury Re-Asserted*, London, 1670, p. 24.

. . . both our Product and Manufactures may be carried on
to advantage without running down the labor of the poor.
. . . Wages must bear a Rate in all Nations according to the
prices of provisions . . . this price of Wheat must arise from
the Rates of Land. . . . This is the case of England, whose
Lands yielding great Rents require good Prices for their Product . . . and you cannot fall Wages unless you fall product,
and if you fall Product, you must necessarily fall Land. . . .

But then the question will be, how is this to be done? I
answer, it proceeds from the Ingenuity of the Manufacturer,
and the Improvements he makes in his ways of working; thus
the Refiner of Sugars goes through that operation in a month,
which our Forefathers required four months to effect. . . .[27]

Despite this endorsement of high wages, however, Cary
agreed with his contemporaries that idleness was a great
evil, and proposed a system of workhouses to enforce the
duty to labor.[28]

Sometimes an argument was advanced for high wages
based upon the idea that the more high-priced labor
there was embodied in a product, the more foreign gold
would bring into the country when sold abroad. John
London of Tiverton wrote in 1740:

Evident it is, that the higher Wages our Workers can earn
in our Manufactures, the more Money from Foreigners will be
brought in among us, and the more it will circulate to the
benefit of all Ranks, Degrees, and Professions among us.[29]

[27] Cary, John, *An Essay on the State of England*, Bristol, 1695, pp. 144-
147.

[28] *Ibid.*, pp. 157-162.

[29] London, John of Tiverton, Merchant, *Some Considerations on the
Importance of the Woollen Manufactures*, London, 1740, p. 8. For
similar statements on the export of labor, see [Harris, Joseph], *An Essay
upon Money and Coins*, London, 1757, p. 24; and many of the writers on
workhouse schemes.

A careful discussion of the "Export of Work and Foreign-Paid In-
comes" is given by E. A. J. Johnson in Ch. XV of his *Predecessors of
Adam Smith*, New York, 1937.

Sir Matthew Hale, among all the authors of workhouse schemes, hoped that they might safeguard the wage level of the poor, and protect them from the unscrupulous employer:

. . . by this means [the establishment of workhouses] there will be a reasonable gage set to wages of Workmen: It is not unknown how that some covetous Masters in hard times . . . will set on work many Poor, but they must take such Wages as they are not able to live upon. . . . But by this means there would be a refuge for the Poor to be imployed at reasonable wages. . . . [30]

Sir Matthew was cautious, however; he advocated no more than a reasonable wage; and it must be remembered that his workhouses were to be managed, and persons committed to them, by magistrates chosen from the landowners and the employers.

There was, then, some division of opinion about the duty of the laborer to accept a low wage. But the words of the few authors who advocated high wages or even "reasonable" wages shone like good deeds in a gloomy world of sparse living and steady toil. The overwhelming weight of opinion was stated by advocates of various workhouse schemes; and in all those proposals the lot of the worker was stated in rigorous terms.[31] Labor was an immensely important resource of the nation which should be devoted to the achievement of national strength. This could be effected by insisting that the working class be numerous, and willing to work hard for modest wages. The establishment of workhouses and the strict enforcement of the poor laws would assure the accomplishment of the end desired. The administration of both was carried on by the gentry, either the landowners or the manu-

[30] Hale, Sir Matthew, *A Discourse touching Provision for the Poor,* London, 1683, pp. 54-55.

For other statements of a high wage doctrine, see p. 213.

[31] For the many workhouse schemes proposed, see p. 213.

facturers, and the laborers themselves were not represented either in the national Parliament or the local quarter sessions.

Nevertheless, the harshness of the doctrine was mitigated by a real concern that all should be employed, and that the really impotent poor should have decent care. The relationship between wages and the cost of provisions was frequently stated; the wage, though low, was to assure a sufficient livelihood. The laboring class furnished one of the most essential elements in England's commercial strength, the production of the manufactures which brought in treasure to the realm. More than this, manpower was an indispensable adjunct to the political power of the kingdom. Though the price set on the services of the working class was low, the value to the nation of the laboring poor was high.

B. *The Responsibilities of the Rich*

The upper classes had a more congenial task; they were to spend while the poor labored. They were not, however, to spend wantonly, carelessly, or prodigally. One of the earliest rules for private spending in the public interest arose from the mercantilists' persistent preoccupation with the favorable balance of trade:

. . . this wante and scarcitie growes from the decaye of the home trades, clothing and exported commodities, these being over-balanced farre, by the commodities imported, and then the private rule holds good for the publique . . . I thinke your wise ancestors knewe very well what they did when they ordained these penall Lawes against the weare of cloth of silver, tissue, laces, and silks by the meaner sort; for if these good and most necessarie laws were executed, then should 200000 of the Kings people, which now live on the charity and benevolence of others, live well and merrily, without burthening the Commonweale . . . A case of conscience not to be neglected by those that have any, that our pride should set so many thousand Turkes, infidels and heretickes at worke, whilest our bretheren here at home, perish for want of imploiment. . . . By these ways without question there goes out of this land in money, and valewable commodities, 2 or 3 millions yearely, to speake nothing of smoake, and other toyes as bad . . . [32]

These were the words of John Hagthorpe, addressed to "the meaner sort," by which he probably meant the lesser gentry, in 1625. Forty years later Thomas Manley expressed the idea much more cynically, for the "men of estates":

Again, I do not at all argue against unnecessary consumptions but against consumptions of forraign commodities, unless they be brought in by our native growths, or manufactures: I say, (speaking as a man) 'tis no wrong to the Commonwealth, if men of estates drink, drab, live profusely, and dye beggars, as long as every penny comes to the natives . . . The mischief only is, when forraigners are the better for this disorder, for that does insensibly ruine the Commonwealth.[33]

The writings of Defoe, and the views expressed in a weekly periodical, *The Craftsman,* show how these opinions maintained themselves well into the eighteenth century.[34]

The advocates of sumptuary laws were not often willing, as Manley was, to condone immoral spending so long as the raw material of sin had a domestic origin. The rich had more to answer for to the community; they had to set an example of proper living. The mercantilists

[32] Hagthorpe, John, Gent., *England's-Exchequer,* London, 1625, pp. 17-19, passim.

[33] Manley, Thomas, *Usury at Six Per Cent. Examined,* London, 1669, p. 10 of the preface, unnumbered.

[34] Defoe, Daniel, *The Compleat English Tradesman,* reprinted, Oxford, 1841, Vol. II, pp. 232-234, first published in London, 1725-1728; *The Craftsman,* issue of November 29, 1729. This periodical was collected in 14 volumes, London, 1731-1737, with the authorship given as that of Caleb D'Anvers of Grays-Inn. The reference given is to Vol. V, pp. 200-201.

understood the social significance of what Veblen was to label "conspicuous spending" centuries later. The example of the gentry could and should be used to restrain the appetites of the poor. The author of the *French Usurpation upon the Trade of England* wrote in 1679:

Sir, There is one thing more, which would restore the ancient Prudence of this Nation, and add much Honour to you, and that is, to establish sumptuary laws amongst us, as to Apparel, and superfluous expenses, according to the several degrees and qualities of persons, which would in a short time recover this Nation: which is no other than a wise and laudable parsimony, which the Romans and other well-governed states have used. . . .

Then, Sir, all the Vanities, Toys, and Fripperies, which *Madame La Mode* shall bring us, will be laid aside.

For want of such a Law, our Servants here imitating their Masters and Mistresses, must go very gay, and to support that vanity, demand three times more Wages than formerly, though they perform ten times less service, which is a great infelicity amongst us, and will lay a foundation of our ruine, if not timely prevented.[35]

Half a century later George Blewitt was saying the same thing, with perhaps a little more force and precision:

The Dearness of Labour of all sorts, the Largeness of Wages and other Perquisites to Servants, their Idleness and Insolence are all the effects of Luxury; of which, as Sir William Temple observes, though the Example arise among idle Persons, yet the Imitation is run into all Degrees, even of those Men by whose Industry the Nation subsists. To this we owe the Scarcity of Servants where they are *really* wanted: and from hence arises that prodigious loss to the Publick, that Draught of lusty and able-bodied men from Husbandry or Country Business, to add to the magnificence of Equipages: *A sort of idle and rioting Vermin, by which,* (we are told)

[35] [B., J.], *An Account of the French Usurpation upon the Trade of England*, London, 1679, pp. 19-21, passim.

the Kingdom is almost devoured, and which are everywhere become a public nuisance.[36]

It was feared that the gentry might misdirect the energy of the whole nation by purchasing the wrong things; but they could do even worse; they might deprave the virtues of the laboring class by setting an evil example of idleness and extravagance.

Dives had a needle's eye to creep through in the Kingdom of England of the seventeenth and eighteenth centuries. Round him were raised all the inhibitions which his duty as an example to the general public demanded; if the grossness of his nature escaped these bounds, the least he could do was to expend his substance on the product of home industries.

But spend he must; for it was his duty, by judicious spending of a sufficient freedom, to set the poor upon employment. Bishop Berkeley counseled him to put labor to work upon houses and gardens. Thomas Mun had no complaint of "the Pomp of Buildings, Apparel, and the like, in the Nobility, Gentry, and other able persons." Such expenditure, he felt, was useful and "cannot impoverish the Kingdom; if it be done with curious and costly works upon our Materials, and by our own people it will maintain the poor with the purse of the rich, which is the best distribution of the Common-wealth." Barbon, though he was one of the heretics identified in the preceding chapter, thought that "Liberality in the Rich" was one of "the Chief Causes that promote Trade." He continued:

The Two Extreams to this Vertue, are Prodigality and Covetousness: Prodigality is a Vice that is prejudicial to Man, but not to Trade. . . . Covetousness is a Vice prejudicial both

---

[36] Blewitt, George, *An Enquiry whether a General Practice of Virtue tends to the Wealth or Poverty, Benefit, or Disadvantage of a People?*, London, 1725, p. 208.

to Man and Trade . . . Liberality ought.Chiefly to be Exercised in an equal Division of the Expence amongst those things that relate to Food, Cloaths, and Lodging; according to the Portion, or Station, that is allotted to every man.[37]

He agreed with Mun and Berkeley that the building of homes is an appropriate object of this "Liberality."

The rich, therefore, bore their responsibility in contributing to the strength of the realm. It was a less arduous task than that allotted to the poor; but it is apparent that it had its difficulties. The expenditure of the rich was to serve to set the poor to work, hence the necessity of government control through sumptuary legislation.[38] With scarcely a dissenting voice, the mercantilists demanded that the gentry should discipline their tastes—and, by example, the tastes of the community—to the end that both the laborer's work and the rich man's expenditure should contribute to the nation's economic strength.

The predominant interest in promoting the strength and power of the state was not sufficient, however, to produce a thoroughly consistent viewpoint among these writers on the delicate and difficult subject of luxury and its control by sumptuary legislation. Three different attitudes were expressed, and none was logically reconcilable with the others. A summary statement of each will show the inconsistencies: luxury and extravagance may be condoned if the objects of expenditure are of native origin; luxury and extravagance are necessary in order to furnish labor for the poor; luxury and extravagance are extremely dangerous to the nation, for the tastes of the poor may be corrupted by the rich. The first and second admonitions

[37] Berkeley, George, *The Querist,* London, 1734-1736, ed. J. H. Hollander, Baltimore, 1910, questions 120-133; Mun, Thomas, *England's Treasure by Forraign Trade,* London, 1664, ed. Sir William Ashley, New York, 1895, p. 81; Barbon, Nicholas, *A Discourse of Trade,* London, 1690, ed. J. H. Hollander, Baltimore, 1910, p. 32.

[38] For the arguments for sumptuary legislation, see p. 214.

13, 13, 14, 17 17
20 24 24 9 24 10

39 99 100 37 103

43 104 105

45 125 130 14

14   149 48

5'

Mercantilism

Carrying the point of view of capitalistic industry
into politics, the State is handled as if it consisted
exclusively of capitalistic entrepreneurs.

to the wealthy can be accommodated one to the other by not insisting too much on the moral implications of the sin of extravagance, but the third is clearly incompatible with the other two. The mercantilists placed the rich man in a hopeless dilemma; the very liberality that was to furnish work to the poor inevitably created a spectacle of high living that corrupted their industry and parsimony and damaged their usefulness to the community. The problem of the rich man was really insoluble; he was required to have his cake and eat it too, but it seemed best if he never had a cake at all.

Nevertheless the writers were nearly unanimous in their support of sumptuary legislation. They felt, somewhat vaguely and incoherently, that expenditure should be directed to useful purposes, and they all agreed that some control should be imposed upon it in order to safeguard the economic health of the nation. They were not at all clear as to the nature and the extent of the controls, but the need for national strength brought them all to the conclusion that the rich, as well as the poor, owed allegiance to the kingdom.

C. *The Merchants' and Manufacturers' Mandate*

The merchant and the manufacturer were the directors and managers of the active business of the nation. Upon their energy and ingenuity depended the employment of the people and the treasure of the kingdom. Their importance was repeatedly mentioned in the work of all these writers; their responsibilities were more often written between the lines, but frequently enough were given express and open statement.

The vital function of both merchant and manufacturer lay in their part in foreign trade. In the preceding chapter the value placed on treasure gained from the export of English goods and manufactures was shown to spring in large part from the conviction that the increase of the precious metals meant an increase in the circulating medium of the country, with all the ensuing stimulation of commercial and industrial activity. Gold as gold was important enough to the community; but gold as money was, as one of the authors put it in 1697, "not only the Sinews of War, but the Medium of Trade and Commerce: For Money in the Body Politick, is as Blood in the Body Natural, giving Life to every part . . ." [39] The means by which this indispensable ingredient of economic health could be brought into the realm were trade and manufacture:

That trade or Marchant that carrieth out our superfluities, or those commodities wee abound in, and bringeth those commodities that we want, for them; is a good trade, or Marchant, and deserveth to be nourished, countenanced, and maintained therein, and those that do the contrary, better ordered.[40]

These words were written in 1640; at the end of the seventeenth century John Cary, arguing for a bank, insisted upon the importance of the trader in more general terms:

Money passes through the Hands of the Nobility and Gentry, only as Water doth through conduit pipes into the Cistern, but centers in the Hands of Traders, where it circulates and may be said to be used . . . [41]

Everything that was said of the merchants or traders was said with equal emphasis for the manufacturers:

So that, if it be from our Manufacture that the Riches of this Nation comes, and if it be chiefly from thence that our shipping is employed, and our Mariners bred; if it be from

[39] S., T., *Reasons humbly offered for the passing a Bill hindering the Home Consumption of East-India Silks*, London 1697, pp. 8-9.
[40] Maddison or Maddestone, Ralph, *Englands Looking In and Out*, London, 1640, p. 18.
[41] Cary, John, *An Essay towards the Settlement of a National Credit*, London, 1696, p. 2.

our Trading alone, and from the Riches which our Trading brings in, that their Majesty's Customs are raised, and that our Fleets have been hitherto Built and Maintained, and the Dominion of the Seas preserved, then it is and must be from our Manufactures, that our Trade is increased, and by which the rents of the Nobility and Gentry have been advanced . . . Then in regard our Manufacture doth this, the Encouragement of it must necessarily be the Greatest Interest of the Nation, to preserve it . . .[42]

These sentiments persisted through the eighteenth century; Sir William Mildmay was saying much the same thing in 1765.

Despite the general agreement on the vital importance of the functions performed by merchants and manufacturers, a number of the mercantilists realized that private interest might not always coincide with the interest of the nation. Thomas Mun recognized this possibility in 1630:

A Merchant by his laudable endeavours may both carry out and bring in wares to his advantage by selling them and buying them to good profit, which is the end of his labours; when nevertheless the Commonwealth shall decline and grow poor by a disorder in the people, when through Pride and other excesses they do consume more forraign wares in value than the wealth of the Kingdome can satisfie. . . .[43]

Ralph Maddison, mindful of this risk, proposed state action to protect the welfare of the community, addressing his words to Parliament, and asking for control of the exchanges:

Wherefore our Merchants having no care nor regard of this I humbly conceive it behoveth our State (which you repre-

[42] [Carter, William], *The Usurpations of France upon the Woollen Manufacture of England*, London, 1696, p. 5; and Mildmay, Sir William, *The Laws and Policy of England Relating to Trade*, London, 1765, p. 101.
[43] Mun, Thomas, *England's Treasure by Forraign Trade*, London, 1664, ed. Sir William Ashley, New York, 1895, p. 37. (Written about 1630, published posthumously.) See also [Hales], *Discourse*, pp. 91-93.

sent at this time) to have a special care unto it, lest the want of money, when you stand in most need of it (now flying away from you) continue the fall of all home-commodities, and your rents and livelihood to fall with it, which will be the undoing of your Tenants, the improverishing of all men, turning up of your Farms and Grounds throughout the whole Nation in generall, which in truth is the Mother of commotion and rebellion, procured through a generall decay of all estates.[44]

The elaborate tariff controls proposed for the foreign trade, the demand for management of the exchanges, the regulations of manufacture were all instances of the dominant interest of the government in seeing that the merchants and manufacturers discharged their duties to the community.

One other clear recognition of the importance of this class was the repeated proposal for a council of trade, made up of merchants and sometimes having representation on it of other classes, which was either to advise the government in these weighty matters or to possess actual power to regulate commercial and industrial activity. This suggestion recurs again and again in the mercantilist literature, and may be regarded as a final token of the grave concern of the kingdom in "the noble profession of merchant."

D. *Rents and Rations: The Landlord's Task*

The duties of the landlord cannot be omitted from this catalogue of the subjects' obligations. It was his function to produce the subsistence of the laborers and the raw materials for manufacture. Thomas Mun, with many other writers, wanted spirited proprietors, who would bring the land of the kingdom into use:

[44] Maddison, Ralph, Kt., *Great Britain's Remembrancer, Looking In and Out*, London, 1655, p. 25.

For other expressions of the importance of the merchant and manufacturer, often calling for state regulation of their activities, see p. 215.

Although this Realm be already exceeding rich by nature, yet it might be much encreased by laying the waste grounds (which are infinite) into such employments as should no way hinder the present revenues of other manured lands, but hereby to supply ourselves and prevent the importations of Hemp, Flax, Cordage, Tobacco, and divers other things . . .[45]

In the preceding chapter the methods of achieving this result were discussed; the mercantilists placed a great reliance upon the enclosure of the common lands.

Far more important than the possibility of introducing new crops on the new lands, was the continuous need for supplying the laboring classes with a cheap subsistence. Postlethwayt foresaw dismal consequences if rents rose too high and corn became dear:

Where the rents are raised beyond the proportion of money existing to pay them, there everything will rise in its price and value; commerce grow worse and worse, relatively considered with that of other nations, its general balance turn more and more against the dearer nation; and at length, the country become stript of its money. And when the trade and the money are once fled to other countries, the people will follow.[46]

His method for avoiding this catastrophe was in part the same recommended by Mun, the improvement of waste lands. But he thought that more than this was needed; and he proposed the establishment of public granaries to maintain a steady price for corn, and approved bounties on export, in common with others of his time who were defending the corn laws.[47]

[45] Mun, Thomas, *op. cit.*, p. 16. There were occasional condemnations of enclosure at this time like Powell, Robert, *Depopulation Arraigned*, London, 1636.

[46] Postlethwayt, Malachy, *Great Britain's Commercial Interest Explained and Improved*, 2nd ed., London, 1759, Vol. I, p. 5.

[47] *Ibid.*, Dissertations II and III. See also Allen, William, *Ways and Means to Raise the Value of Land*, London, 1736; [Smith, Charles], *A Short Essay on the Corn Trade and the Corn Laws*, London, 1758; Steuart,

The nation's interest in the activity and spirit of the landed proprietors was succinctly and emphatically stated by Jacob Vanderlint in a pamphlet devoted chiefly to money and currency, published in 1734. Having begun with the premise that "all things come from the soil," he proceeded to the conclusion that the more land cultivated, the greater plenty of things, and the more people employed:

And as the Produce will hence be increased, so will the Consumption of all Things increase too; and the greater the Plenty becomes this Way, the cheaper will everything be. . . . The Plenty may be increased so much as to make Victuals and Drink half the Price they are at now; which will make the Price of the Labour of Working People much lower; for the Rates of Labour are always settled and constituted of the Price of Victuals and Drink. . . . We shall hence be enabled to make, and export our manufactures at much lower Prices, and this must needs cause us to export abundance more of them to those Nations that now take them of us; besides that it will enable us to carry out Produce, etc. further and cheaper, to induce other Nations to take them of us, who now perhaps do not take any of our Goods; whence the Cash of the Nation will certainly increase, by raising the value of our Exports above the value of our Imports.[48]

The importance of the landlord measured up well against that of the other classes of the community. The welfare and strength of the state required an active class of husbandmen and proprietors, who would supply a sufficient quantity of raw materials and foodstuffs, and still not demand too high a price nor exact exorbitant rents.

Sir James, *Principles of Political Economy*, London, 1767, Vol. I, Chs. III-V; XIV.

[48] Vanderlint, Jacob, *Money Answers All Things*, ed. J. H. Hollander, Baltimore, 1914, pp. 15-16. (First published London, 1734.)

See also Harte, Walter, *Essays on Husbandry*, London, 1764; and for other discussions of the importance of agriculture, and the interest of the state in it, Notes 76-85 of Ch. II, *supra*.

If necessary the power of the state could be invoked to put bounties on export or to erect public granaries to hold prices steady; for agriculture, with labor and commerce, provided the basic materials for the kingdom's economic power.

E. *The Harmony of Interests*

When the duties of the various classes were thus assigned, with the guiding hand of the state steadily granting aid or applying discipline, as the need might be, to assure that every man would be in his place and have a place to be in, the mercantilists had constructed a well-ordered national community. They were confronted with a final question, however: this was indeed order, but was it bliss? Many of the writers, it must be confessed, either thought that it was bliss enough or failed entirely to perceive that such a question might arise. To be an Englishman, whether laborer, merchant, gentleman, or landlord, should suffice, while the strength of the kingdom grew in Europe, and its economic activity increased at home.

Indeed, the declaration of the national interest served, in the minds of many of the mercantilists, to resolve any conflicts between the groups or classes within the nation. They placed implicit reliance on the assumption that if the prosperity and strength of the realm were assured, the participation of its subjects in those benefits could be taken for granted, whatever their station in the community. The touchstone of the kingdom's wealth and power might be trade, or shipping, or bullion; but whatever it was, the interests of all men and classes were involved in it. A few quotations from several writers over a long period of time, identifying various activities as fundamental to England's welfare, will show this:

As concerning ships, it is that which every one knoweth, and can say, they are our ornaments, they are our Strength, they are our pleasures, they are our defence, they are our profit; the subject by them is made rich, the kingdome through them strong, the Prince in them mighty; in a word by them in a manner we live, the kingdome is, the king reigneth. (1615)

Trade is the true and instrinsick Interest of England, without which it cannot subsist: From Trade there doth not only arise Riches to the Subjects, rendering a Nation considerable, but also increase of Revenue, and therein power and strength to the Soveraign . . . for every Nation is more or less considerable, according to the proportion that it hath of Trade, and it's more or less enriched by the ballance of its foreign Trade. (1679)

No commodity is truly an Increase of the National Stock, but that which is exported, and all other Trades receive their Vigour and Life from the Merchant. (1708)

. . . the Nation that hath that Balance in their Favour, must increase in Wealth; for this is the only Way to bring Money into any Nation, that has no natural Fund of it in Mines in its own Bowels; and the only Way to keep it in any Nation that has. Since therefore it is incontestable, that Money is introduced into a Nation by Trade only, and that Trade is chiefly supported by its Manufactures and Product, that these are increased by Labour, and Labour by People, it manifestly follows, that Numbers of People are the Cause of Wealth in a Nation. . . . (1735)

The Trade of the said Colonies, if directed in the right Channel, might be made of much greater Service to this Kingdom, in the Consumption of our Manufactures, than our Traffick to any other Part of the World, and the landed Interest in England would be more improved thereby, than by any other Branch of Trade whatsoever; as it is conceived that a great Distinction is to be made between that kind of Commerce, which is carried on by the Exchange of Foreign Commodities from one Country to another, and that which arises from the Manufactures of this Kingdom; for altho' one may enrich the Merchant and the Publick Stock, yet the other doth not only enrich the Merchant and the Publick, but at the same Time employs the Poor, and consequently much improves the landed Interest. (1755) [49]

These eloquent words, regardless of the time at which they were written, or the chief subject in each instance which evoked them, or even the identity of the earnest author who penned them, all point the same moral. There was a community of interest among the subjects of the realm, and all of them shared in its welfare, and suffered from its misfortunes. Of course, it may be that these were merely the rhetorical flourishes of special pleading, that each writer was merely making the best possible case for bullion, colonies, population increase, or whatever subject he might be advocating at the time. Even if this were true, the idiom he employed was significant. The actor who raises a roar of applause from the galleries does not do it by strange metaphors and unexpected sentiments; the familiar and hackneyed lines are the ones that bring down the house. It may be admitted that these are quotations from advocates; still there is in them a substance of sincere belief that the interests of the classes are bound up with the fortunes of the commonwealth.

Such harmonies were built upon one dominant note; but there were closer and more celestial harmonies in which all the voices sang together. All the mercantilists conceived of an ordered national community, with every person and each group or class performing its function and receiving its due reward in a share of the general welfare. One of the famous writers, Gerard de Malynes, pictured

---

[49] [R., I.], *The Trades Increase,* London, 1615, p. 2; [B., J.], *An Account of the French Usurpation upon the Trade of England,* London, 1679, p. 4; [Oldmixon, John], *The British Empire in America,* London, 1708, 2 vols. introduction to Vol. I, pp. xxi-xxii; [Hay, William], *Remarks on the Laws relating to the Poor,* London, 1735, pp. 22-23; [McCulloch, William T.], *A Miscellaneous Essay concerning the Courses pursued by Great Britain in the Affairs of Her Colonies,* London, 1755, pp. 99-100.

this happy state in a long preface to one of his earliest pamphlets, in a parable of a lovely island inhabited by an ideal community:

> . . . a certaine equalitie and concord is required in every well governed commonwealth, the prince or governor having the disposing both of the one and the other. Equalitie concerning the trafficke and negotiation betwixt his dominions and other countries in the trade of merchandize: and Concord amongst the members of a commonwealth, when every member thereof doth live contentedly and proportionably in his vocation.[50]

This was written in 1601; sixty years later an anonymous writer opened his pamphlet on the fishing trade with a similar exhortation:

> As most men differ in Feature of Face, in Diet, in Condition, and Education, so all good men agree in a unity in the service of God, their Prince, and Country, in their several degrees and stations; the Divine in his Prayers, the Souldier with his Armes, wise men with Counsel, and Rich Men with Treasure. This being done willingly, makes sweet Harmony between King and Commonwealth: For that Prince is happy that hath young men to take pains, and old men to counsel; the one doth sustain the other in convenient time . . . some teaching, and others obeying.
>
> The next consideration is, how to make the people to subsist in the service of God, Prince, and Country. For there must be a rational means to work by; neither can a Monarchie be upheld and supported without people employed and set on work in their several stations . . . [51]

Sometimes the injunction to the subjects to love one another, the king, and the kingdom was sharpened from exhortation to admonition:

---

[50] Malynes, Gerard de., *St. George for England*, London, 1601, p. 3, unnumbered, of the preface.

[51] Anon., ΙΧΘΥΟΘΡΑ, *or The Royal Trade of Fishing*, London, 1661, pp. 2-3.

The hewers of timber and drawers of water are more service-able in any Kingdom than the idle and lascivious person, spending his body, his time, and estate in nothing but pleasure, debauchery, unprofitable and unnecessary expences. But while I speak of expences of all people, thus generally, by which the mis-imployment as well as mischief, doth certainly follow; let me not be mis-understood, as though the expences of all men ought to be alike, but rather admit of the several orders and degrees of men, to which their expences ought to be responsible. What is requisite for the service of a Prince, is Pride and Lasciviousness in a Duke. . . . The same distinction holds good between the Mistress and her maid, though nowadays 'tis hard to know the one from the other. . . . And I should think it were better for a Bakers, Butchers, or Barbers Wife, a Butler, a Prentice, and the Chamber Maid to return the price of their Silks, their pieces of Ribbons, their fine Laces, and their Flap-shoes, into his Majesties Exchequer, rather than to spend their money upon what they so little want, and doth less become them . . . they neither consider their estates given them, as well to the maintaining all things necessary for themselves, according to every man's degrees and quality, as to contribute part thereof for the publick good of the Country wherein they dwell.[52]

These statements, made during the course of the seventeenth century, were matched by Robert Ferguson just before the eighteenth century opened, though he placed more emphasis upon "the Peasants and ordinary Sort and such as are reckon'd for the Mobb and Commonalty." In fact, he said, "provided their Labour and Industry" was "pertinently and usefully apply'd" they were of great service to the community and "as contributary to the making a Country Opulent and Wealthy, as those of any Rank and Quality whatsoever, if not considerably more."[53]

[52] Anon., *The Use and Abuses of Money*, London, 1671, pp. 6-8, passim.
[53] Ferguson, Robert, *A Just and Modest Vindication of the Scots Design*, Edinburgh, 1699, p. 26.
For other expressions of a harmony of interests, see p. 216.

Similar declarations of mutual interest continued in the writings of the eighteenth century, but lost some of their fine moral flavor and became more strictly economic in tone. Henry Elking saw the benefits of the whaling fishery, if it could be established, distributed throughout the kingdom. Daniel Defoe devoted the opening chapter of the first part of *A Plan of the English Commerce,* to showing how the nation and all its classes participated in the advantages of an active trade. Malachy Postlethwayt, whose works are a summary of all the mercantilist views, wrote in 1757 that the nations which maintained a favorable balance of trade had secured "the only thing capable of augmenting the positive and relative mass of their metals, of encreasing their populousness, and of giving circulation that activity which distributes ease, the useful principle of luxury, through every class of people." [54]

The mercantilists were convinced that in an orderly state the interests of the classes would be resolved into a harmony. The service of every subject would be rewarded by the state in a comfort and security suited to his station. The wage of the laborer was low, but his employment was certain; the spending of the rich furnished that employment, and guided the tastes of the commonwealth; the landlord's rents were allowed to reach a level which would provide subsistence for the working classes; the enterprise of the merchant and the manufacturer supplied the directing force for the activity of the nation, but was subjected to supervision and control. Adam Smith was later to put

[54] Elking, Henry, *A View of the Greenland Trade and Whale Fishery,* London, 1722 (in McCulloch, J. R., *A Select Collection of Scarce and Valuable Economic Tracts,* London, 1859, pp. 102-103); Defoe, Daniel, *A Plan of the English Commerce,* reprinted, Oxford, 1928, Ch. I of Part I (first published, London, 1728); Postlethwayt, Malachy, *Great-Britain's Commercial Interest Explained and Improved,* 2nd ed., London, 1759, Vol. II, pp. 525-526 (first published, London, 1757). The same sentiments appear again and again in Sir James Steuart's two volumes, *Principles of Political Economy,* London, 1767.

his trust in an invisible hand that beneficently guided individual initiative into the way of serving the community; his predecessors readily perceived a visible and omnipresent hand, that of the state, governing the work of the classes of the nation and distributing rewards for service loyally performed.

III. THE INTERNATIONAL ANARCHY AMONG THE MERCANTILIST STATES

There might be peace, and order, and happiness at home; but there could be nothing but war abroad. The very same conception of national strength which served to reconcile the various interests into a harmony within the state led to an irreconcilable rivalry between states. The twentieth century has now accustomed itself to the notion that economic penetration is frequently a prelude to territorial expansion; we speak of "wars" of concessions and tariffs and regard with apprehension the effect of economic imperialism upon world politics. Such discussions would strike the mercantilist as tentative and hesitant; his conception of the nature and the powers of the state gave him a harder and clearer view of such phenomena. To him economic competition *was* political rivalry; commercial transactions had always a political significance. What else could he expect from the international scene but bitter competition which frequently rose to the pitch of war? He saw a group of national states, organized domestically to develop their full economic strength and appealing to their subjects to contribute their utmost to that end, competing with each other for a limited amount of trade and treasure, hoping always to sell and never to buy, and continually willing to use force to achieve their greatness.

In 1436 the author of the *Libelle of Englyshe Polycye* surveyed the trade of England to determine how it contributed to English maritime power.[55]   Henry Robinson described the situation bluntly in 1641:

[Since] the enlarging of our trade would keep us still predominant over all other states and Princes, I will set downe some few indigested Notions towards the producing and continuing a flourishing State of commerce, which if wee do not seriously apply ourselves unto, other States will questionlesse bee too hard for us, and whatsoever trade they beate us out of and engrosse into their owne hands, will bleede us with a bit and blow, making us pay for it what they please, which will not only impoverish us, but ruine our Navigation, and subject us to become a prey at pleasure.[56]

In the same year a petition put forward by the East India Company declared:

The safety of the Kingdom consists not onely in it's own strength and wealth but also in the laudable and lawful performance of those things which will weaken and impoverish such powerful Princes, as either are, or may become our Enemies. . . .[57]

It is easy to match the bluntness of the seventeenth century with the callousness of the eighteenth; Robert Ferguson wrote at the turn of the century:

Nor will it I suppose be denyed, but that according to the Share which England and Scotland shall acquire and obtain of the Trade of the World, the Less will fall to the Portion of the French, and the Less vent they will have, as well everywhere for their own Natural and Artificial productions, as for what they do Import from Foreign and Remote places.[58]

55 *The Libelle of Englyshe Polycye*, 1436, ed. Sir George Warner, Oxford, 1926, especially "chapitles" i, iij, xi.

56 Robinson, Henry, *England's Safety in Trades Encrease*, London, 1641, p. 3.

57 East India Company, The, (English) *The Petition and Remonstrance of the Governour and Company of Merchants of London trading to the East-Indies*, London, 1641, p. 16.

58 Ferguson, Robert, *A Just and Modest Vindication of the Scots Design*, Edinburgh, 1699, p. 16.

A pamphlet attributed to Defoe, discussing alleged breaches of a trade treaty, laid down this axiom in 1727:

> Invading our Commerce is invading our Property; especially where the exclusive right to that Commerce is expressly stipulated; and invading a Nation's property is a War begun.[59]

This condition of international rivalry was embittered further by the assumption expressed by Ferguson in the quotation given above, and shared by many others, that the amount of trade in the world was limited. One nation could gain only at the expense of the others.[60]

The full strength of the chorus of voices clamoring for war is shown by the rarity of the pleas for peace. Sometimes the plea was quaintly put, as it was by Thomas Houghton in 1695. He deplored the wars of the French king in Europe, and proposed that the great states of Europe should unite together and make war upon the Turks, driving them out of Europe, and then make joint conquests in Africa. By this warfare upon the infidels, in the course of which the gold of the Guinea coast could be secured, the peace and prosperity of Europe could be achieved. There were more careful and closely reasoned condemnations of war during the course of the eighteenth century. Thomas Merchant, discussing *Peace and Trade, War and Taxes* in 1729, exclaimed, "War is Indolence, Trade is Industry; War is a Destroyer, Trade a Nurse (of and) to the Wealth and Prosperity of a Country; War is the Medium of Destruction, Poverty and Waste, Trade is

[59] [Defoe, Daniel], *The Evident Approach of a War*, London, 1727, p. 29. See also *The Evident Advantages to Great Britain and its Allies from the Approaching War*, London, 1727, and *Reasons for a War, in Order to Establish the Tranquility and Commerce of Europe*, London, 1729, both attributed to Defoe.

For other expressions of the rivalry of states, and the likelihood of war, see p. 216.

[60] See Ch. II, *supra*, pp. 28-29 and notes to same, numbers 21-24.

the Medium of Wealth, honest Labour, and Plenty" and went on to catalogue the injuries done to the merchant, the manufacturer, and the fisherman. A score of years later another pamphlet expressed a more positive view: "a trading Nation should enter, reluctantly, upon even a just War . . . because it can never be the Interest of a People subsisting by Trade and Industry, to be at Variance with any that take off their products and manufactures." The author of *The Universal Merchant* supported this argument, and even recognized the interests of the other nation:

> War devours, and Peace restores; the Sovereign or State that proposes to enrich their Country, must avoid War with their Neighbours, encourage Virtue and Industry, and preserve Peace and good Order at Home. . . .
> War has the same Effect on Nations, as Contentions on private Families; they at last both set down Losers.

These men, and a few others, raised their voices to argue for peace in Europe, but they were but a whisper against the swelling chorus that demanded war to protect the national interest.[61]

The tactics of this international rivalry were familiar to all the mercantilists. The greatest resource to be depended on was the nation's economic strength. The second Duke of Buckingham has been credited with these trenchant phrases published under the title of *A Letter to Sir Thomas Osborn* in 1672:

[61] Houghton, Thomas, *Europe's Glory, or Peace and Plenty to the People Thereof,* London, 1695; Merchant, Thomas, *Peace and Trade, War and Taxes,* London, 1729; p. 8; Anon., *National Prejudice opposed to the National Interest,* London, 1748, p. 10; [Horsley, William], *The Universal Merchant,* London, 1753, p. 9, 23.

The few other advocates of peaceful international relations, which an extensive search of the writings revealed, follow: Anon., *An Enquiry into the Danger and Consequences of a War with the Dutch,* London, 1712; Anon., *Britons Awake, and Look About You,* London, 1743; Anon., *An Enquiry into the Present System,* London, 1756.

The undoubted Interest of England is *Trade,* since it is that only which can make us *Rich* or *Safe;* for without a *powerful Navy* we should be a *Prey* to our *Neighbours,* and without *Trade,* we could neither have *Sea-men* nor *Ships.* From hence it does follow, that we ought not to suffer any other Nation to be our *Equals* at *Sea,* because when they are once our *Equals,* it is but an even *Lay,* whether they or we shall be the *Superiors.*[62]

At the end of the same century two of the writers conducted a duet on the same theme. Simon Clement pointed out that "according to the present Constitution of these Parts of the World, he that hath the longest Purse, will certainly have the longest Sword"; whereupon an anonymous author echoed the sentiment, and went on to demand that the government take action:

. . . so as whoever will give himself the pains to enquire into the conquests other Nations have made upon our Trade, and then add the dismal Effects of this War, will find no solid Grounds to expect that England should recover her former Glory, Wealth, and Dominion at Sea, without some new Advantages to Trafficke from the Government; which if it had in any proportion to what other countries give . . . we should no doubt out-strip our Emulous Neighbours . . .[63]

The battery of weapons described in the preceding chapter was rolled into action: customs duties and prohibitions to manipulate the foreign trade, the navigation laws to stimulate shipping, the management of the colonial economy to build the strength of the empire. Defoe perceived, before half the eighteenth century had elapsed, that the persistent use of such tactics was a permanent feature of the international scene:

[62] [Buckingham, George Villiers, 2nd Duke of], *A Letter to Sir Thomas Osborn,* London, 1672, p. 13.
[63] Clement, Simon, *A Discourse of the General Notions of Money, Trade, and Exchanges,* London, 1695, p. 32; Anon., *Considerations requiring greater Care for Trade,* London, 1695, p. 11.

Hence we cannot blame the French or Germans for endeavouring to get over the British Wool into their Hands, by the hope of which they may bring their People to imitate our Manufactures, which are so esteem'd in the World, as well as gainfull at Home. Nor can we blame any foreign Nation for prohibiting the Use and Wearing of our Manufacture; if they can either make them at Home, or make any which they shift with in their stead. The reason is plain; 'tis the Interest of every Nation to encourage their own Trade; to encourage those Manufactures that will employe their own Subjects, consume their own Growth of Provisions, as well as Materials of Commerce, and such as will keep their Money or Species at Home. . . .

Trade is the Wealth of the World; Trade makes the difference between Rich or Poor, between one Nation and another. . . .[64]

Having set all the nations of the world at each other's throats, the mercantilists were ready and anxious to point out England's most dangerous adversaries. Of these the head and chief was France; upon her they were eager to let loose the dogs of trade. The anonymous author of *The Proverb Crossed* demanded in 1677 that the laws permitting the transportation of wool be repealed, because the "French King hath laid all this method in readiness, to rob us of our Clothing trade . . . we must be very short sighted if we understand not that after he hath supplyed his own Countrey he will not only endeavour, but will soon be able to supply Flanders, Portugal, Spain, and the Streights, to gain and advantage his own subjects." [65] Nearly a century later the French were still being identified as the arch-enemies of the English: "It is to be apprehended that they will in time monopolize our trade. We should seize the present opportunity of checking their

---

[64] Defoe, Daniel, *A Plan of the English Commerce*, London, 1728, reprinted Oxford, 1928, pp. 41, 51. See also Steuart, Sir James, *Principles of Political Economy*, London, 1767, Vol. I, Book II, Ch. XII.

[65] Anon., *The Proverb Crossed*, London, 1677, pp. 2-3.

progress, and restraining them within such bounds as may leave us nothing to fear from their competition." [66] During the interval many other writers had been repeating the same warning.

Holland could often be used as a barrier against the French, so at times policy seemed to dictate friendship with the Dutch. Still they were dangerous. Even Roger Coke, who had tried to make economics into a passionless science like mathematics, regarded them with fear and distrust:

So as now the Dutch are swelled to such a prodigious greatness by Sea, that it is a Question whether it can be controuled by any Power in the World; and what the Consequences hereof will be, God only knows: I do not believe the Dutch intend us any good by it. [67]

During the eighteenth century this alarm subsided; the attacks upon the Netherlands were the product in large part of Cromwell's policies.

Spain appeared in the role of England's adversary occasionally. Early in the seventeenth century she was often paired with France; the two being regarded separately as worthy of constant watchfulness, and the chance of their association constituting a frightful menace. In the eighteenth century the Spanish colonial empire seemed a danger to the English colonial trade, and so the Spaniard once more was named as a foe. [68]

Colonial policy was one of the weapons of international rivalry. In the preceding chapter its usefulness in this field was sufficiently explained. The plantations served to supply essential raw materials; their trade was reserved

[66] [Young, Arthur], *Reflections on the Present State of Affairs,* London, 1759, p. 21.
For other demands for action against France, see p. 216.
[67] Coke, Roger, *Treatise,* London, 1671, p. 129.
For other attacks on the Dutch, see p. 218.
[68] For the writings identifying Spain as an enemy, see p. 218.

to the mother country and thus constituted a backlog upon which the merchants, shippers, and manufacturers could depend; their existence was a strategic advantage against the development of other countries. In Britain's armory of economic weapons against the French, the Spanish, and the Dutch, they were both a shield and a sword.

For the advocates of the mercantile system, then, the counterpart of peace at home was war abroad. War in peacetime, relentlessly waged with tariffs, shipping, and colonial policy; armed force in wartime, deriving its strength from commercial and industrial activity, fostered by the guiding hand of the state. The very measures of domestic prosperity and welfare were the marks of international superiority: the favorable balance of trade, the gain in treasure, the employment of the people, the acquisition of territory overseas. The only prospect of international peace lay in the maintenance of a precarious balance of power; and constant watchfulness was needed to protect the ordered welfare of Britain and her empire.

IV. SUMMARY

The term, economic planning, has been much abused; but mercantilism might be called a planned economy for the nation. Naturally enough it was put in terms of the conditions in which the mercantilists lived and wrote. Judged by the circumstances and measured by the economic and political knowledge of their time, it showed itself to be comprehensive in scope and ingenious in detail. The fundamental assumption, implicit in the work of every author and made explicit by many, was that the state was justified in exercising its powers in any department of the national economy in order to secure the power and welfare of the nation.

This general assertion of the sovereignty of the state in the affairs of business was made more precise by stating the duties of the subjects. The laborer was to work; and most of the writers would have him work for a bare subsistence. The rich were to spend, upon objects which the state could sanction; these should be the product of home industries and, if the natural man could be curbed, not of a nature to corrupt the public taste. The merchant and the manufacturer carried grave responsibilities; their functions of organizing and managing trade and industry made them at once the subjects of eulogy and the objects of some suspicion. The landlord and cultivator supplied the indispensable raw materials and a sufficiently plentiful supply of foodstuffs to guarantee cheap living and low wages. The reward for faithful performance of these duties lay in the station allotted to each class. The laborer was assured employment; the rich had the perquisites as well as the responsibilities of regulated conspicuous spending; the merchant had his profits and the attentive regard of the governing authorities; the landlord's rents, though low, were to be sustained by the corn laws and the public granaries.

The interdependence of politics and economics is a commonplace of such a system. Economic questions were always considered in the light of their political aspects; political proposals were implemented with economic devices. The wide scope of state powers and the assertion of political sovereignty in the field of economic affairs might be briefly summarized by saying that their politics controlled their economics. At the same time it is possible to say that their economics controlled their politics. Since the obligations of the subjects and the classes required definition if a balanced and ordered national economy was to be established, the demand for the exercise of government authority continually arose out of the harmonious relations of the classes to each other and each individual's part in the economic activities of the community. The mercantilists' analysis of any problem, therefore, was always influenced by both political and economic considerations; in fact, it presented itself to them as simply a *national* problem.   If their work is viewed from such a standpoint, some of the errors in economic thought they have been charged with, appear less mistaken; even their cardinal sin of over-valuing treasure and the favorable balance of trade rose from quite a clear view of the political considerations involved.

They faced with equanimity, and even enthusiasm, the hard consequence that domestic order must be won at the price of international anarchy.   Europe was inhabited by a group of self-contained and self-seeking national communities, the most dangerous being the French, the Dutch, and the Spanish.   If Britain was to remain secure in the possession of wealth, ships, trade, or employment for her people, she must be always watchful of her competitors and constantly ready to employ the tricks of peace time and the arts of war for her protection.

These were the political implications of the mercantilist economics.   Underlying all of them was the great authority of the state.   Of what was their Caesar made, that he should wax so great?   The structure of the mercantilist state must now be examined; the governing machinery in which such power was lodged should next be described.

CHAPTER IV

The Structure of the Mercantilist State

THE mercantilists might possibly have defended the powers of the state—had they thought a defense was required—by reference to its structure. Fortunately for most of them, they saw little need for any carefully reasoned justification of government authority; for had they attempted it, the state they envisaged would scarcely have borne the weight of such a philosophical necessity. Their tendency was to take the machinery of government for granted in much the same way that they had assumed the extent of its powers was not subject to question. They displayed, once more, the businessman's preoccupation with immediate problems, and disregarded the theoretical implications of their plans. There was a state in action, run with great success by the Tudors and, barring some periods of revolution, with sufficient effectiveness by the Stuarts. The mercantilists simply fitted their suggestions, whenever possible, to the existing patterns of government organization.

It is not surprising, then, that the mercantilist state confided great powers to the king. Royal authority, the executive agency of government, was the means of getting things done. But though the will of the king could be depended upon, his wit might at times need assistance; so the mercantilist proposed a rudimentary bureaucracy, most often a council of trade, to help administer the economic affairs of the realm. Still, despite the great trust they reposed in princes, they also valued the liberties of the subject and the representative character of the Parliament; for they were convinced that both contributed to activity of trade. It is fair to say, however, that the people and Parliament were expected to consent to the policies, and support the action, of the executive.

These views of king and Parliament were quite generally agreed to by most of these writers; but on one subject, the place of the monopolistic companies, there was a continuous and irreconcilable dispute among them. The companies had their opponents and their defenders, and both sides recognized that political as well as economic issues were at stake.

One last feature of the mercantilists' political doctrines is worthy of notice; their design for the structure of the state owed little to the political philosophy of their time. Some ideas they might have borrowed, but in the main they confined themselves to the task of constructing a practical, working mechanism, very like the government in power as they saw it in the seventeenth and eighteenth centuries.

I. THE COMPETENCE AND INTEGRITY OF EXECUTIVE AUTHORITY

Confidence in monarchy as an effective instrument for accomplishing the purposes of economic policy could scarcely sustain itself unchanged through the Puritan Commonwealth and the Glorious Revolution. Nevertheless, though Charles I was thrust out of this world and James II was forced to flee from England, the mercantilists clung to their opinion that the administrative authority of a monarch and his ministers afforded the quickest and most serviceable means of regulating trade and industry. Fundamentally, what was expressed throughout both the sixteenth and seventeenth centuries was a reliance on the executive department of the government, for obvious practical reasons; a change in viewpoint did appear with respect to the personal power of the king. The experience of the Rebellion shook their faith only a little; after 1689 they still expected the king to rule as well as reign, but his powers were those that properly attached to one of the important estates of the realm.

The most attractive feature of monarchy for the writers of the seventeenth century was its promise of stable and orderly government. A glance at the quotations given in the preceding chapter shows how often the power of the state was put in terms of royal authority.[1] "The Prince" or "the King" was addressed by these men when they wanted regulation of the commercial and industrial affairs of the realm; and this was not a mere form of words, for they expected decisive and consistent action from the executive power. A considerable number took the trouble to argue the case briefly. Thomas Mun in 1630 asked in a tone of general exhortation, "shall not the wealthy and loyal subjects of such a great and just Prince maintain his Honour and their own liberties with life and goods, always supplying the Treasure of their Soveraign, untill by a well ordered War he may inforce a happy Peace?" [2]

Gerard de Malynes, describing his ideal commonwealth in 1601, attributed its harmonious peace to its ruler:

> . . . and from the Prince as from a lively fountaine all vertues did descend into the bosome of that commonwealth, his worthy counsellors were with the magistrates as ornaments of the Law . . . every man was contented to live in his vocation with obedience. . . .[3]

[1] Ch. III, *supra*, pp. 75, 79-80, 83, 107-108, 110, 114.

[2] Mun, Thomas, *England's Treasure by Forraign Trade*, London, 1664, ed. Sir William Ashley, New York, 1895, p. 87. (Written about 1630, published posthumously.)

[3] Malynes, Gerard de, *St. George for England*, London, 1601, p. 14.

Two years later, having doubtless meditated further upon the matter, he gave a much more carefully reasoned statement:

> . . . Princes, that are the fathers of the great families of Commonweales: . . . are to provide carefully for the two seasons, namely, the time of warre when armes are necessarie, and the time of peace more fitting wholesome lawes . . . it cannot properly be said, that the office of a Prince is wholy employed about the government of the persons of men . . . but rather in the observation of Religion towards God, and administration of justice towards man. . . . Justice is as a measure ordained by God amongst men to defend the feeble from the mightie. Hence proceedeth that the causes of seditions and civill warres, is the deniall of justice. . . . Now, as Princes raigne by God, so must they be directed by him. . . . Serve him they cannot but according to his will, and his will is not known, but by his word and lawe . . . as justice is administered and prescribed by lawes and customs: so reason requireth, that this gradation shoud be observed concerning all lawes: that even as the wills, contracts or testaments of particular men cannot derogate the ordinances of the Magistrates, and the order of the Magistrates cannot abolish customs, nor the customs can abridge the generall lawes of an absolute Prince: nor more can the lawes of Princes alter or chaunge the lawe of God and Nature. By Justice (properly called distributive) is the harmonie of the members of a Common-weale maintained in good concord. . . .[4]

In one of his last, and most important works, published in 1636, his defense of monarchy became even more dogmatic:

> . . . so it is between the King and his subjects, who is therefore called Parens patriae, who like a father of the great family of the common-wealth, doth studie for the welfare thereof . . . Aristocracie is the government of the lesse number of people of a common-wealth in soveraigntie, and Democracie (being

[4] Malynes, Gerard de, *England's View, in the Unmasking of two Paradoxes*, London, 1603, pp. 1-9, passim.

contrary unto it) is the greater number of people governing. Whereas a monarchie is a common-wealth where one sole Prince hath the absolute government, here the peace, unitie, concord, and tranquilitie of subjects consisteth by meanes of one head, by whose power common-weales are fortified, vertue thereby being united and more corroborated, than if it were dispersed into many parts which give occasion of strifes, turmoiles, and controversies by the divided powers and emulation of greatnesse: whenas one person (imitating nature) doth governe (as the head) all the parts and members of the body, for the generall safeguard and weale publike.[5]

This interest in order and stability was the spring of support for the kingship with other writers. Sir William Temple pointed out that "Trade cannot live without mutual trust among private men" nor could it increase without "a confidence both of public and private safety, and consequently a great trust in government." [6] In another work he described the ideal form of the state, making use of the metaphor of a pyramid. The base of the pyramid was the consent of the people, and he concluded:

Now that government which . . . takes in the consent of the greatest number of the people, and consequently their desires and resolutions to support it, may justly be said to have the broadest bottom, and to stand upon the largest compass of ground; and, if it terminate in the authority of one single person, it may likewise be said to have the narrowest top, and so to make the figure of the firmest sort of pyramid.

By these measures, it will appear, that a monarchy where the prince governs by the affections, and according to the opinions of his people, or the bulk of them (that is, by many degrees the greatest or the strongest part of them); makes of all others the safest and firmest government: and on the contrary, a popular state which is not founded in the general hu-

[5] Malynes, Gerard de, *Consuetudo, vel, Lex Mercatoria,* London, 1636, p. 47.
[6] Temple, Sir William, *Observations upon the United Provinces of the Netherlands,* London, 1673 (in *Works,* London, 1814, Vol. I, p. 166).

mours and interest of the people, but only of the persons who share in the government, or depend upon it, is of all others the most uncertain, unstable, and subject to the most frequent and easy changes.[7]

Similar opinions were expressed by a number of others. At about the same time, the author of *The Use and Abuses of Money* remarked that the Prince had the duty of governing, "every kingdom being a body politick, ex institutione Dei, by whose omnipotence Kings reign; by him the People are brought to their obedience," and then went on to discuss the duties of the subjects, as they should be carried out under this direction.[8]   Davenant, more cautious than some of his contemporaries in the last decade of the seventeenth century, made some mention of Parliament when he discussed the royal authority.   He was sure that "the Care of Trade does indeed belong to the executive power now in being, and is properly the business of the established ministry," but if they needed laws, then the legislative body might have occasion to act.[9]   He likewise had a high regard for the monarchy as a guarantee of stable government, and fifteen years after the Glorious Revolution was writing:

The harmony that is to make England subsist and flourish, must have its rise from a due respect and obedience to be paid by the whole people, to that authority with which the laws have vested the different parts that compose this government: As first the Prince who is head of the republick; then the two pillars supporting the royal dignity, which are the House of Lords, and the House of Commons.   When by the arts of wicked men the multitude are brought to slight the regal

[7] Temple, Sir William, *An Essay upon the Original and Nature of Government*, London, 1672 (in *Works*, London, 1814, Vol. I, pp. 23-24).

[8] Anon., *The Use and Abuse of Money*, London, 1671, pp. 6-8, passim.

[9] Davenant, Charles, *Discourses of the Public Revenues and on Trade*, London, 1698 (in *Works*, ed. Sir Charles Whitworth, London, 1771, Vol. I, pp. 422-423).

power, in a little time sedition begins, and civil war follows; and our histories are full of such commotions. . . . The art of governing is to rule the many by a few; but when the many are suffered to sway, direct and lead the few, which way they please, it is quite returning into the wild state of nature, and giving to force that empire and dominion, which reason and wisdom ought to have.[10]

To the value of stability there was added another merit of monarchy; the interest of the king must of necessity be at the same time the welfare of the people. Malynes stated this argument with a terseness unusual in his style:

> . . . Sacred wisdome hath approved this Axiom: That a King is miserable (how rich soever he be) if he Raignes over a poore people; and that, that Kingdome is not able to subsist (how Rich and Potent soever the people be:) if the King bee not able to maintaine his estate. Both which (being Relatives) are depending upon Traffique and Trade. . . .[11]

Naturally the persistent preoccupation with the importance of trade led Malynes to hasten to add it to his axiom, and many writers were willing to put the mutual interest of king and people specifically in those terms:

> And now, as from the growth of Trade, there doth naturally arise, not alone riches to the Subject, rendering a Nation considerable, but also increase of Revenue, and therein power and strength to the Soveraign; so it is the undoubted Interest of his Majesty, to advance and promote Trade, by removing all obstructions, and giving it all manner of incouragement.[12]

The quick and easy way of making evident the trustworthiness of royal power in all matters where the economic wel-

[10] Davenant, Charles, *Essays upon Peace at Home and War Abroad,* London, 1704 (in *Works,* Vol. IV, pp. 289-291).

[11] Malynes, Gerard de, *The Maintenance of Free Trade,* London, 1622, p. 2, unnumbered, of dedicatory epistle.

[12] [Bethel, Slingsby], *The Present Interest of England Stated,* London, 1671, p. 8.

fare of the realm was at stake was to resort to the favorite metaphor of the national family, with the king in the role of the father. Davenant made use of this analogy in 1700:

> Kings are the fathers of their country. . . . The Prince is our common father, and therefore all that tends to his safety, ease and state is due him; however, the less he is necessitated to depend upon his children the more he is respcted.[18]

Davenant's last clause in this instance was evidently designed to keep the children in their place, but the fact of paternity was stressed by many writers, and echoes through all their works. Sometimes the metaphor was quaintly varied. Thomas Mun, writing in the first part of the seventeenth century, made a catalogue of all the uses to which the king should put his revenue in order to give activity to commerce and industry in the country and concluded by saying, "for a Prince (in this case) is like the stomach in the body, which if it cease to digest and distribute to the other members, it doth no sooner corrupt them, but it destroys itself." [14]   Joshua Gee and Lewis Roberts might be added to a list of the defenders of monarchy as an instrument for the accomplishment of plans for building economic strength.[15]

There were a few doubters, like Henry Robinson and the author of *The Grand Concernments of England Ensured,* who did not join in the prevailing praise of mon-

[18] Davenant, Charles, *Discourse upon Grants and Resumptions,* London, 1700 (in *Works,* Vol. III, p. 7).

[14] Mun, Thomas, *op. cit.,* pp. 94-95.

[15] Gee, Joshua, *The Trade and Navigation of Great Britain Considered,* 3rd ed., London, 1731, preface (first published in 1729); Roberts, Lewis, *The Treasure of Trafficke,* London, 1641 (in McCulloch, J. R., *Early English Tracts on Commerce,* London, 1856, pp. 72-73).

In this connection there should be cited Raleigh, Sir Walter, *The Prerogative of Parliaments,* London, 1628, and *The Arts of Empire, and the Mysteries of State Discabineted,* London, 1692, published by John Milton; Anon., *The Vindication and Advancement of Our National Constitution and Credit,* London, 1710, pp. 1-21.

archy and monarchs in the seventeenth century.[16]   The faint echoes of their skepticism were reinforced by the political disturbances of a century in which royal prerogative suffered at the hands of Parliament.   The orthodox attitude adopted by the mercantilists in the succeeding hundred years was to praise the balance of crown and representative legislature, the "mixt English constitution" in which the authority of the king furnished active leadership and administrative power while the Parliament gave advice and mobilized popular support.   Malachy Postlethwayt was pursuing this line of thought when he pointed out the danger of the people falling under the influence of demagogues and proceeded to declare the best safeguard against this misfortune: "If public affairs should ever happen to light into such hands and reduce the state into great disorder and confusion, we must put our chief hopes in the king, at the head of a parliament." [17]   A long series of "Remarks on the English Constitution" published in *The Craftsman* from 1730 to 1735 set forth the balanced character of the constitution, and deplored the growth of factions as destructive of this traditional merit of English government structure.[18]   Josiah Tucker, Dean of Gloucester, though only half a mercantilist, repeated these ideas at the end of the eighteenth century.[19]

Despite this eighteenth century dilution of the regard for kingship with the doctrines of popular consent, it was still possible in 1755 for a writer on colonial affairs to

16 Robinson, Henry, *Certain Proposals in order to the Peoples Freedome*, London, 1652, pp. 3-4; Anon., *The Grand Concernments of England Ensured*, London, 1659, pp. 15-17.

17 Postlethwayt, Malachy, *Dictionary of Trade and Commerce*, 4th ed., London, 1774, under title, "Parliament" (first published in London, 1760).

18 *The Craftsman*, London, issues from September 12, 1730, to September 6, 1735. In the collected edition, with authorship attributed to Caleb D'Anvers of Grays-Inn, the most important references are: Vol. VII, pp. 23 et seq., 86-90, 293-300, 394-395; Vol. XII, pp. 1-111, passim.

19 Tucker, Josiah, Dean of Gloucester, *A Treatise concerning Civil Government*, London, 1781, Part II, especially pp. 136 et. seq.

praise the efficiency and public spirit of the French monarchy as a model for the administration of economic affairs.
The French Council of State served to accomplish this
result:

> . . . in which Light the King is to be considered as the
> Center to which all Persons, employed in the Administration
> of Public Affairs, and all Matter relative to the Offices, ulti-
> mately resort; and from this there results a Spirit of Liberty in
> the Administration of Public Affairs. . . .
>
> It may be proper to observe further, that by the system of
> the French Government, the said Council of State is the high
> Watch-Tower, from which the King may survey all his Domin-
> ions, and sometimes all the Dominions of the World, in order
> to consult the Honour, Defence, Profit, and Peace of his Sub-
> jects. . . .[20]

It can be freely admitted that in all these expressions
of regard for the monarchy there was a large proportion
of conventional hyperbole. These expressions were not,
however, mere forms of words. Practical merchants and
administrators wanted active and consistent management
of the economic activities of the kingdom; and they steadily had recourse to the executive authority to obtain
speedy performance of their proposals. They certainly
did not concern themselves much about the political problems of the location of sovereignty in the state; what they
wanted was action from the government of the time. In
the third section of this chapter their ideas on the liberties
of the subject and the function of Parliament will be examined, to show what reconciliation they were able to
make between royal power and popular consent. Still,
however much they might have valued representative institutions, and conceding any change of heart they might

20 [McCulloch, William T.], *The Wisdom and Policy of the French,
in the Construction of their Great Offices*, London, 1755, pp. 17-19, and
32-33, passim.

have undergone in the course of the seventeenth and eighteenth centuries, it can be said that they had a high regard for executive authority embodied in the person of the monarch. Stability of government and devotion to a public interest mutually shared by king and people seemed to them powerful arguments for the extended use of this organ of the English constitution. Without much exaggeration of their real sentiments they might have paraphrased a famous dictum and declared, "No king, no trade; no trade, no king."

They could scarcely expect that the English monarch and his ministers, burdened with all the conventional tasks of government, would be able to undertake an extensive program of control of commerce and industry without some elaboration of the administrative agencies of the executive department of the government. Most of the proposals for creating this bureaucracy were a further mark of their confidence in executive power, for they were usually attached to the king. The Privy Council doubtless served as a model for these bodies. These suggestions have a further interest; they reveal, in their simplicity and uniformity, the unbounded confidence of the mercantilists that it would be a relatively easy task to set up the agencies of economic planning.

II. THE RUDIMENTARY BUREAUCRACY OF ECONOMIC CONTROL

The good will of the king was unimpeachable but his wisdom, particularly in matters of trade, might leave a little to be desired. More than this, if the state was to undertake an extensive program of regulation and supervision of both foreign trade and domestic industry, it was surely necessary to equip it with some specialized administrative mechanism. The surprising thing is that the mercantilists, so fertile in discovering tasks for the government to perform, should have been satisfied with so little in the way of a bureaucracy to execute these ambitious plans. A persistent plea for the establishment of a council of trade, and occasional suggestions for banks, workhouses, and similar semi-public bodies, exhausted their ingenuity.

A. *The Council of Trade*

Their stock proposal was a council of trade; many of the writers advanced it and it was never opposed by any. One of the best marks of the general acceptance of the idea lies in the fact that a considerable number added it to their programs for the regulation of economic affairs as a matter of course, without taking trouble to set up the details of its structure or powers.

It was scarcely necessary to argue the necessity for such a body; it rose naturally out of the mercantilists' general attitude toward the relationship of the state to commerce and industry. Roger Coke, though he argued for greater freedom of enterprise and attacked the tariffs and the navigation laws, deplored the fact that England possessed no agency of this kind:

And though the forrein Trade of our Manufactures, and the Fish caught upon the Coasts of England and Scotland, and the Navigation depending thereon, be the Soul of the well-being and safety of the Nation; yet in it is not so much as a Council of Trade, or any established Power, to Govern or Regulate it.[21]

William Paterson, who had much to do with the establishment of the bank of England, said much the same thing in 1701: "Princes and states are not now, as formerly, only obliged to promote trade and industry for their advantage, but even in their defence—not only for their benefit, but

21 Coke, Roger, *England's Improvements*, London, 1675, p. 115.

also of necessity." [22]   This was the preface to his scheme
for a council of trade.

The structure of the council was usually simple: a board
of merchants appointed by the king. Lacking the profes-
sional economist, the commercial community naturally
was expected to furnish expert knowledge and the wisdom
of experience. The author of *Trade Revived* described
and nominated these worthies in 1659:

> . . . to encourage and ease the trade and commerce of this
> Nation and its Dominions, . . . there might be a Committee
> of Merchants settled, consisting of a meet number, either fif-
> teen or seventeen, or more or less, as shall be thought fit, five
> or seven of which to be the Corum to settle any business; the
> which Merchants to be of the ablest, understandingest, and
> experiencedst men trading into foreign parts, who shouldst
> meet (a place being appropriated to the commerce for that
> purpose) once in fourteen days or oftener, as affairs required.[23]

To some it seemed advisable to include the manufacturing
interest as well; in *The Ancient Trades Decayed, Repaired
Again* the members suggested were "some eminent tradesmen of the City of London, mixt with some of the Country, and some eminent Clothiers, who might consider what
might be necessary for the promotion of trade, and for the
right settling thereof. . . ." [24]   John Cary wanted men
"well verst" in matters of trade, warning that "great Care
must be taken, that these Places be not fill'd up with such
who know nothing of the Business, and thereby this Excellent Constitution become only a Matter of Form and
Expence." [25]

[22] Paterson, William, *Proposals for a Council of Trade*, London, 1701
(in *Works*, ed. Saxe Bannister, London, 1859, Vol. I, editor's introduction,
p. cxxv).

[23] [Bland, John], *Trade Revived*, London, 1659, pp. 45-46.

[24] Anon., *The Ancient Trades Decayed, Repaired Again*, London, 1678,
p. 50.

[25] Cary, John, *An Essay, towards Regulating the Trade*, London, 1717,
pp. 85-86.

Sir Josiah Child was a little skeptical of the devotion of the merchants to the interest of the nation, and wanted a more representative body:

That Trading Merchants while they are in the busie and eager prosecution of their particular Trade, although they be very wise and good men, are not always the best Judges of Trade, as it relates to the Profit or Power of a Kingdom. The reason may be because their Eyes are so continually fixt, and their Minds intent upon what makes for their peculiar Gain or Loss, that they have not leasure to expatiate or turn their thoughts to what is most Advantagious to the Kingdom in General. This I am told was the Opinion anciently of M. T. Cicero, and also Boden, that learned French Author, and lately of the Lord Chief Justice St. John. . . . But whether it was their opinion or not, I am sure it's true by manifold experience. . . . The like may be said of all Shopkeepers, Artificers, Clothiers, and other Manufacturers, until they leave off their Trades and being Rich, by the purchase of Lands, become of the same common interest with most of their Countreymen.

And upon the same reason I am of Opinion, and have found by Experience, that a mixt Assembly of Noblemen, Gentlemen, and Merchants, are the best Constitution that can be established for the making Rules, Orders, and By-Laws, for the carrying on any Trade for the publick Utility of the Kingdom.[26]

Consciousness of such considerations led William Paterson to suggest a membership of twelve: three chosen by the nobility, three by the estate of the barons, three by the boroughs, and three by the Indian and African companies. The president was to be appointed by the king, and the whole membership was to be renewed one-third annually, each member having a three-year term.[27]   Both Child's doubts of the traders, and Paterson's careful machinery of

---

[26] Child, Sir Josiah, *A Treatise wherein is Demonstrated, that the East India Trade is the most National of all Foreign Trades*, London, 1681, pp. 1-2.

[27] Paterson, William, *op. cit.* (in *Works*, Vol. I, pp. 1-15).

representation of various interests, are not characteristic mercantilism; most of their contemporaries relied upon the merchants and manufacturers.

The powers vested in these bodies were nearly as wide and as various as the general program of state control advocated by their supporters. The least they could do was to advise the king and Parliament. Here is a catalogue of advisory tasks enumerated in *Trade Revived* in 1659:

1. To consult of such forein trade as may be promoted and carried on, for the advantage of this Nations commerce and people. 2. To consider of all such inconveniences as arise in forein trades and traders, and how to regulate and redress them. 3. To compose what hath been consulted of, and to draw up the same to a head, if found advantagious for the commerce, and so presented to the Power that they may approve thereof, and order its execution and practice, whereby, as occasion shall offer, all Traders may by this Committee find relief at an easie attendance when any interruption shall be imposed on them at home or abroad to discourage or destroy trade. 4. To find out by their experienced knowledge, and examination of all things in reference to our trade at home and abroad, a means to settle the same upon such a continued succession of advantages, that it may be an incouragement to all persons that desire to employ themselves in a forein trade.[28]

There was one difficulty, which was felt by those of a delicacy as nice as that of Roger Coke. He apologized for suggesting that His Majesty and his Privy Council should need aid in looking out for the welfare of the kingdom, but still clung to the need for such specialized advice.[29] John Cary, referring to the Parliament, did not spare the sensibilities of the honorable members:

. . . it hath sometimes been thought, that when that Great and Glorious Assembly hath medled with Trade, they have

[28] [Bland, John], *op. cit.*, pp. 45-46.
[29] Coke, Roger, *Treatise*, London, 1671, pp. 135 *et. seq.*

left it worse than they found it; and the Reason is, because the Laws relating to Trade, require more time to look into their distant Consequences, than a Session will admit, whereof we have had many instances.[30]

A considerable number of the mercantilists would have had the council go on from advice to actual administration.   Roger Coke, despite the tincture of laisser-faire in his views, wanted his council to "inspect and regulate our Native and Forein Trade, but also be advising and assisting to his Majesty in such Treaties with other Princes and States, wherein Trade is concerned." [31]   Twenty years later the words "inspect and regulate" are given a little more specific meaning by another writer:

The proper work of this proposed Council might be during War, to offer Directions to the Admiralty for the assignment of Convoys, and prescribe time of Sailing to our most distant Voyages.   In Peace, to enquire narrowly into the Balance of Trade with every Nation, to examine the making of manufactures, to draw up Results and Methods for Improvement of Navigation and Commerce, and intend studiously the welfare of them in every regard; in some cases to determine of themselves, in others to have recourse to the Privy-Council or the Admiralty, in others to digest Matters for information or Sanction of Parliaments.   All which may be easily contrived to the vast emolument of the Kingdom, without interfering, I conceive with any part of our Constitution.[32]

Paterson's council was to have the management of funds raised by a tax of one-fortieth on the sale of property or succession to title, one-fortieth on manufactures, one-twentieth on the value of lawsuits, and one-tenth on the wheat, rye, pease, barley, beer, malt, and oats collected at the kilns and mills.   These were to be granted for a period of

[30] Cary, John, *op. cit.*, pp. 87-88.
[31] Coke, Roger, *Treatise*, London, 1671, pp. 136-137.
[32] Anon., *Considerations requiring greater Care for Trade*, London, 1695, pp. 15-16.

twenty years, and in addition there was power to borrow a million pounds.

Thus armed, he could well expect the agency to carry out the following projects:

1st. The employing and relieving the poor, and the repressing of idleness and sloth; 2ndly. Erecting of national granaries and stores of corn, so as that the industry of this kingdom may not, as hitherto, be at any time clogged by extreme cheapness, nor crushed by extreme dearth of grain; 3rdly. The improvement of the mines, minerals, and other ordinary and extraordinary products of this kingdom; 4thly. The improving and advancement of our manufactures, both in quantity and quality; 5thly. The setting on foot, promoting, and carrying on that great work of making salt upon salt, or refined salt, and therewith the fisheries of this kingdom; 6thly. The reducing of the interest of money to three per cent. per annum or less, not by force or restraint, but by easy and effectual means, and which can never be done but by such a constitution as a council of trade ought to be; 7thly. The effectually carrying on, countenancing, protecting, and supporting the foreign trade.[33]

This is a most impressive list of functions, but in all probability Sir William Mildmay had an equally wide range of powers and duties in his mind in 1765 when he declared:

These difficulties in guiding the separate interest of each Trade to the general interest of the Whole, make it necessary for a government to appoint a particular department in its administration, to superintend the affairs of commerce, and examine all proposals for its advancement, or complaints of its decay.[34]

The council of trade envisaged by the mercantilist writers was always to advise, but frequently it was to administer as well. Whether it acted in the first capacity only, or in

[33] Paterson, William, *op. cit.* (in *Works*, Vol. I, p. 28).
[34] Mildmay, Sir William, *The Laws and Policy of England, Relating to Trade,* London, 1765, p. 101.

both, it was regarded by a great number of the mercantilists as a necessary addition to the administrative structure of the government.[35]

These repeated proposals reveal two important characteristics of mercantilist political doctrines. Though the point should not be pressed too far, these bodies may be fairly taken as evidence of the reliance upon executive authority, and often they were definitely attached to the king as embodying that authority. In the second place, they reflect the insistence upon a wide range of government power in economic affairs.

This readiness to entrust matters of such moment to the king, his ministers, and the council of trade also rose from the general nature of the economic doctrines. A group of merchants, sometimes associated with a few of the gentry, could be expected to perform successfully a set of tasks which would now terrify a calloused corps of economists in a well-established civil service, because the formulas to be applied were simple. The fundamental rules bore a strong resemblance to the orthodox principles of family housekeeping. So long as the export trade overbalanced imports, so long as wages and living costs were held down, so long as familiar standards of quality were maintained and natural resources actively developed and also carefully husbanded, the realm would prosper. Any monarch anxious to maintain the prestige of his crown and his people could, with the assistance of a group of loyal merchants who had a trader's watchfulness for profit, direct the economy of the commonwealth in such a way as to secure the safety and the welfare of the whole community.

B. *The Miscellaneous Semi-Public Bodies*

There were a few problems which seemed to call for special agencies. Most of the mercantilists would have

[35] For other proposals for a council of trade, see p. 218.

been satisfied with the establishment of a council of trade possessing the powers that Paterson had enumerated, but those who had their attention fixed upon one aspect of the national economy might still have demanded a national bank, or parish workhouses organized throughout the land, or courts merchant in the principal cities. Since these projects have already had some notice in the two preceding chapters, it is unnecessary to do more than summarize them briefly here.

There were many advocates for a national bank; for a sufficient supply of money to keep trade active, and available credit to set enterprise in motion, seemed essential to all the mercantilists. John Cary wanted what would now be regarded as a sound bank, doing a regular commercial business, though it was to be established by government initiative. As such, it would be of great value: "Banks, as I humbly conceive, ought chiefly to be calculated for the use of Trade, and modeled so as may best content the Traders. What gives them satisfaction will answer all other Occasions of the Kingdom." [36] Some of the banks, like John Asgill's and John Briscoe's, were designed to issue notes against the value of land; others, like William Killigrew's, were to be based upon the government's credit.[37] All, however, were designed to achieve the same end, to stimulate the nation's commerce by furnishing a circulating medium and a supply of credit, and all were to be created, and to a considerable degree, managed by the government.

[36] Cary, John, *An Essay towards the Settlement of a National Credit,* London, 1696.

[37] Asgill, John, *Several Assertions Proved,* London, 1696; Briscoe, John, *An Explanatory Dialogue of a late Treatise,* London, 1694, and *Proposals for Raising Money for a National Land-Bank,* London, 1695; Killigrew, William, *A Proposal shewing how this Nation may be vast Gainers by all the sums of Money, given to the Crown, without lessening the Prerogative,* London [1663].

For other discussions of the need of a national bank, see p. 219.

Besides the banks, the other frequently offered project was the parish workhouse, sometimes dignified by the title John Bellers gave it, "Colledge of Industry." [38]   The importance of an agency designed to keep the laboring poor at work has been sufficiently explained in the preceding chapter.   It is worth noticing that the managers of these charitable enterprises were the local magistrates, both merchants and landlords, so that the discipline of the nation's labor force was sure to be kept in safe hands.

Courts merchant in the principal cities, and the great monopolistic trading companies which will be dealt with later, completed the suggestions for the bureaucracy which was to serve the state in directing the national economy. The marvel was that so few agencies could do so much. Clearly the bulk of the work would have to be done by existing administrative officers: the customs officials, the justices of the peace, the Privy Council, and the directors of the chartered companies.   Nevertheless, it remains surprising that such an extensive program of planning and regulation of the national economy should not carry with it more in the way of a skilled staff for its accomplishment.

The fact is that the mercantilists took the capabilities of the existing state for granted much as they had assumed that its powers were extensive.   In addition, the specific character of the proposals they made assisted them in ignoring the difficulties of administration.   Any industrious customs official could compute the balance of trade according to the rules laid down for him by Mun or Child; any director of the mint should be able to detect the decline of the supply of bullion or coin.   The principles governing trading policies presented to these optimistic analysts none of the mystifications which the Tariff Commission of the United States has had such difficulties in

[38] Bellers, John, *Proposals for raising a Colledge of Industry*, London, 1696.   For other proposals of workhouse schemes, see Ch. III, *supra*, p. 95, and note on p. 213.

unraveling. There might well be some dispute on details, but the economic science offered in this period gave reasonably definite solutions to the problems of management of the foreign trade.

The measurement and control of phenomena in the domestic economy was likewise no impossible task. The local justices were competent to compute wages in terms of subsistence; the traditional practices of the crafts furnished the standards of quality for goods; the luxuries which should be controlled by sumptuary laws were identifiable by reference to the rules of common morality and traditional habits of living.

The analogy of the national household made the whole range of economic phenomena intelligible and controllable. If the ruler could be convinced of the value of specific policies, and the citizens induced to obey his decrees, the actual administration of affairs became a relatively simple matter. It might be advisable to elaborate the executive machinery somewhat, particularly by creating a council of trade; but actually the achievement of national prosperity was as easily practicable as it was vitally necessary.

The mercantilists recognized the value of individual activity, and the importance of public consent to national policy, if these projects for strengthening the economic power of the kingdom were to be steadily carried out. In these connections the rights of the citizens and the function of the Parliament acquired significance.

III. THE PROVINCE OF POPULAR ASSENT

Resorting once more to the metaphor of the national household, a metaphor of which the mercantilists never tired, it seemed obvious to them that a well-knit family should depend upon ties of affection and loyalty rather than the stern exercise of parental authority to give it

unity in spirit and vigor of action. The rights of the
members should be respected and even encouraged whenever possible; and the use of consultation among them was
in the highest degree desirable. This all meant that the
rights and liberties of the subject were valuable in stimulating the economic activity of the community, and that
the deliberations of the Parliament should serve the executive power by offering advice and by expressing popular support for policies. These liberal notions did not
contradict the confidence the authors expressed in the
king; in fact, the happy resolution of popular support and
executive leadership seemed to them a most valuable asset
to the welfare of the kingdom; and it could be achieved
without any serious difficulties.

A. *The Liberties of the Subject*

Individual freedom has been often defended as an in-
alienable right of man and a necessary condition of the ful-
fillment of the high destiny of mankind. The mercantilists found no occasion to make use of the resounding eloquence of philosophical justification; they placed their reliance upon much more prosaic grounds. Liberty might
well be one of the glories of the race, and none of these
men would have denied its importance; the fact that im-
pressed them was that liberty contributed directly to economic activity and they defended it because it was a commercial asset of undoubted value.

The author of *Britannia Languens* put this argument
forward in 1680:

The English Freedoms are at this day so great an advantage
to his most Sacred Majesty of England, that they are a Weapon
left in his hands, with which, and a Concurrent Regulation of
our Trade, he may with ease and assurance attain a Superiority
over all the Monarchs and Powers of Europe put together; he
will cut the Grass under their Feet, and *draw* away all their

Treasures and People, notwithstanding all the Policies which can be used. . . .[39]

Davenant made the argument more precise and specific about twenty years later:

Nothing therefore can more contribute to the rendering England Populous and Strong, than to have Liberty upon a right Foot, and our legal Constitution firmly preserved. . . . For Liberty encourages procreation, and not only keeps our own inhabitants among us, but invites Strangers to come and live under the shelter of our laws. . . .

And if it should be asked, why the Care of Liberty and preserving our Civil Rights should be so much recommended in a Paper relating to Trade We answer, that herein we follow Machiavel, who says, "that when a Free State degenerates into a Tyranny, the least mischief that it can expect, is to make no farther Advancement in its Empire; and no farther increase either in Riches or Power. . . ." If the Wealth and power of a Country depend upon Good Government and Stability of its Affairs, it must certainly import that all the different ranks of Men contribute their utmost that Things may be well administer'd.[40]

More could be expected of this freedom than merely the general advantage of stimulating the activity of the citizens in commercial and industrial affairs. It could be harnessed occasionally to the successful continuance of some particular institution which would benefit the community. John Cary saw it as a valuable support to the establishment and maintenance of a national bank:

It hath the Legislative Power of the Kingdom of England for its foundation. . . . So long as the Peoples Liberties last . . . so long as the People of England have a hand in making their own Laws, whose Common Interest will be so united and

---

[39] [Petyt, William], *Britannia Languens*, p. 292.

[40] Davenant, Charles, *An Essay upon the Probable Methods of making a People Gainers in the Balance of Trade*, 2nd ed., London, 1700, pp. 17-18, 261-263 (1st ed., London, 1699).

made up with the Security of this Bank, that they will in a short time become one thing. . . .[41]

As a clinching argument he pointed out that such a bank could not be set up in France, England's most dangerous commercial rival, because the absolute monarchy in France made impossible this practical use of civil liberty.

Cary's view that absolute monarchy was incompatible with financial activity and stability was used by others in a more general form as a demonstration of the value of individual freedom. The anonymous author of *The Grand Concernments of England Ensured* condemned absolute power in the monarch as a real danger to trade; it discouraged the trader and exalted the court.[42] A pamphlet published in 1697, devoted principally to showing that a standing army was dangerous to English institutions, began by arguing with some care the connection between the enjoyment of freedom and the stimulation of trade, and pointed to the economic risks of autocratic rule.[43]

In the eighteenth century the same sort of reasoning made an appearance. One of the many productions attributed to Daniel Defoe pointed the moral in terms of France:

Thus the Arbitrary Government of the King of France, the Property of every Man being entirely at his Dispose, destroy'd the very Reason and Nature of Publick Credit; and the Limited Power of Great-Britain's Crown, the Strings of the Purse being in the hands of the Parliament, whose Appropriations, if I may be allow'd to speak so plain, even our Kings themselves durst not break in upon, has been the Reason and Foun-

---

[41] Cary, John, *An Essay towards the Settlement of a National Credit*, London, 1696, p. 7.

[42] Anon., *The Grand Concernments of England Ensured*, London, 1659, pp. 15-17.

[43] [Moyle, Walter], *An argument showing that a Standing Army is inconsistent with a Free Government*, London, 1697.

dation of such an immense, boundless Credit, that nothing can hurt or destroy, unless the Parliament should invert their way of acting. . . .[44]

As late as 1758 the argument was being repeated by other writers, with continued insistence upon the relationship of liberty and freedom to an active trade.[45] It might be added that many of those who attacked France as one of England's most dangerous enemies counted upon this weakness of absolute rule to give their own country an economic advantage in whatever struggle might be ultimately necessary to remove this menacing opponent.

It can be said, then, that there was quite general agreement among the mercantilists as to the value of individual liberty. They made little effort to define with any precision what that freedom comprised. Their arguments for its value were based on strictly practical considerations; they saw a general connection between civil rights and commercial and industrial activity. This relationship could also yield specific and particular results; such institutions as a national bank would derive efficiency and stability from the nature of the English political system. They clinched the argument by displaying the dangers of absolute monarchy and insisted that it had a stifling effect upon trading initiative.

Since they were never troubled by logical inconsistencies, none of them perceived any contradiction between their reliance upon the good faith of the monarch and the effectiveness of executive authority, and a simultaneous defense of the value of individual rights and the limitation of royal power. Nor were they any more disturbed by the possibility of a theoretical conflict between the broad powers of the state and the sphere of private initia-

[44] [Defoe, Daniel], *The Chimera: or the French Way of Paying National Debts,* London, 1720, p. 5.

[45] [Williamson, Peter], *Occasional Reflections on the Importance of the War in America,* London, 1758, pp. 8-9.

tive. The ease with which they avoided these philosophical difficulties is demonstrated in the views they held of the place of the Parliament, for in assigning its place in the constitutional system they made use of a conception of popular agreement between king and people expressed through the medium of a representative assembly.

B. *The Function of Parliament*

There were, undoubtedly, the seeds of dispute in the insistence upon the subject's rights at the same time that approval was given to the royal prerogative. This was recognized in the middle of the seventeenth century by a staunch mercantilist, Henry Robinson. In the opening pages of his *Certain Proposals in order to the People's Freedom* he expressed doubts as to whether princes managed the affairs of the commonwealth as well as might be desired, and made a plea for greater rights of petition to the Commons.[46] When he emphasized the importance of Parliament he laid hold of the means of reconciling difficulties between king and people which seemed most attractive to all the mercantilists. The representative assembly of the realm was regarded as a sort of family council, in which a real unanimity might be established among all the members of the family. Indeed, William Hodges domesticated this constitutional relationship in 1696: "And in short, I look upon England as a Family, and the King and Parliament as Husband and Wife. . . ." [47]

Whether this pretty picture invariably meant domestic agreement is, of course, open to question; but certainly a family conclave is most satisfactory to all concerned when the views of the head of the house are accepted by the rest of the members of the household. Thomas Mun delicately assigned such a function to Parliament:

[46] Robinson, Henry, *Certain Proposals in order to the Peoples Freedom*, etc., London, 1652, pp. 3-4.

[47] Hodges, William, *The Groans of the Poor*, London, 1696, p. 4.

I will add this as a necessary rule to be observed, that when more treasure must be raised than can be received by the ordinary taxes, it ought ever to be done with equality to avoid the hate of the people, who are never pleased except their contributions be granted by general consent: For which purpose the invention of Parliaments is an excellent policie of Government, to keep a sweet concord between a King and his Subjects, by restraining the Insolency of the Nobility, and redressing the Injuries of the Commons, without engaging a Prince to adhere to either party, but indifferently to favour both. There could be nothing devised with more judgment for the common quiet of a Kingdom, or with greater care for the safety of a King, who hereby hath also good means to dispatch those things by others, which will move envy, and to execute that himself which will merit thanks.[48]

This bluntness very nearly amounted to cynicism; the author of *Britannia Languens* attempted to define these relationships much more carefully in 1680:

A great part of the transcendent Policy of this our form of government consists in the high *Obligations* and *means* of a *Union:* The Prince being invested with the mighty *prerogatives* of making War and Peace, Calling, Proroguing, and Dissolving Parliaments, and as many others as fill Volumes, hath such controll on the Parliament, that it is generally to be presumed they will ever gratifie him in whatsoever is any way consistent with that *Trust* they are under; on the other side, the Parliament, being the great and High Council, and their Consent requesite to all new Taxes, whensoever the Prince on any Emergency desires their Advice, or a supply of Money, the People must necessarily have time to represent their true grievances to Him whose Princely favour and occasions, will then equally call upon him to redress what is really amiss; *in which Commutation* he must have a far greater advantage than any *bare Tax* he receives; since as it appears the true strength of all Monarchies and Governments depend upon well-being Abilities, and Increase of the *Populacy*, which no other Prince

48 Mun, Thomas, *op. cit.*, p. 91.

hath Comparably so certain a means to understand and Improve, as he that hath a Parliament: To all which may be added, that *mutual Affection* which must naturally follow these endearments, and which must render the Prince and the Nation much the stronger, never to be hoped for in any other kind of Monarchy; there are yet farther obligations to this *Union* between the Prince and the People from a just sense of these fatalities which must follow a *disunion;* we need not resort farther than to the Fable where we have an Accompt of a quarrel among the several Limbs of the Body Natural, whereof the consequence was, that every part grew presently Languid and Impotent, and ready to yield itself a Feast to the Ravens.[49]

This idea of a natural "Union" between the king and Parliament, with some mysterious formulation of a national will taking place as the two worked harmoniously together, was a favorite. notion of the mercantilists. Roger Coke, though he did not fully subscribe to all the doctrines of his contemporaries, was ready to give this interpretation of the British constitution his support. In the preface to his *Detection of the Court and State of England,* really his last extensive work, he made a careful statement of this viewpoint. He argued that "in our English government, the Constitution and Laws of it, are as well the Rules of the King's Dominion, as of the Subject's Allegiance to the King." So long, then, as the king acted within this constitutional framework, "for Subjects to resist him is High Treason in this World, and Damnation in that to come . . . no People in the World are more Honourers of their Kings, yet more jealous of preserving their Constitution and Laws than the English." From this it also followed that if the king did not act in accord with these customs and rules, he forfeited the claim to this devotion on the part of his subjects. The normal practice, however, was for both to conform to the dictates of this harmonious relationship:

[49] [Petyt, William], *Britannia Languens,* London, 1680, pp. 250-251.

In this regular Monarchy, the Kings of England do not abrogate old Laws, nor impose new, nor raise Monies from the Subject above the Revenues of the Crown, without Consent in Parliament, and hereby the Kings of England reign in the Love and Obedience of their Subjects, and are freed from the imputation of Tyranny in Sanguinary Laws, and from Oppression in the Taxes granted in Parliament, which no Absolute Monarch is, and are more absolutely obeyed in both, than any absolute Monarch, who makes his Will the Law of his Subjects.[50]

Farther on in the first volume he gives a more precise definition of the function of Parliament. Having made clear that the "King is the Head, Principle, and End of the Parliament," he argues that its function is to give advice and information:

So does a Parliament discharge the great Objection against Hereditary Monarchies, that tho' Princes see only with their own Eyes, and hear with their own Ears, as other Men do; yet so as it is impossible without a true Representation of the State of their Subjects, they can see or hear of the true State of them; whereby Minions and Flatterers, whose interest is different from that of the Kingdom, which is the Throne of the Prince, is not conceal'd from the Prince, but false representations made by them of it; whereas the Parliament is the Eye of the Nation, which sees the Abuses, which Flatterers by abusing the King's Name, and making it subservient to their Interest, impose upon it. The great Ends of the Meetings of Parliament are, First, to redress the Grievances of the Nation, if any be, by representing them to the King. Secondly, to punish Men, which are out of reach of the ordinary Rules of Justice, which either abuse the King's name to attain their Ends, or may prove dangerous to the Government. Thirdly, to make Laws against growing Evils, and to repeal Laws which have been found inconvenient to the Nation; and Fourthly, to supply the King upon extraordinary Occasions for support of the Nation, as Times and Accidents may happen.[51]

[50] Coke, Roger, *A Detection*, London, 1694, Vol. I, pp. 2-4, of the "Apology to the Reader," unnumbered.
[51] *Ibid.*, Vol. I, pp. 30-32.

These quotations from writings of the seventeenth century have been set forth at some length in order to show
the faith of their authors that the interests of king, Parliament, and people could be expressed through the time-
honored institutions of the British kingdom.   Similar
statements can be found, for example, in the works of Sir
William Temple and Charles Davenant.[52]

In the eighteenth century the mercantilists seized upon
what they called the "mixt English constitution"; but they
were still relying upon the recognition by both king and
Parliament of the evident interest of the whole nation to
produce a harmonious accord between the governor and
the governed.   Charles Davenant's *Essays upon Peace' at
Home and War Abroad,* published in 1704, are quite
fairly representative of this approval of the balance of
power in the government authorities:

> When the commonalty have once made their choice, [of a
> Parliament] their whole power is devolved and delegated; and
> whether their representatives do well or ill, their Princes are
> to judge; who by their prerogative they have to call them to-
> gether and dissolve them, as they and their council shall think
> expedient, can rectify any material error in their proceed-
> ings. . . .[53]

Having established the importance of regularly constituted authority, he then devotes the bulk of the essay to
an analysis of the evils of parties and factions, and con-
cludes with a sketch of administrative organization:

> Our constitution lodges the executive power originally in
> princes, who devolve such functions of it as they cannot per-

[52] Temple, Sir William, *Of Popular Discontents* (in *Works,* London,
1814, Vol. III, pp. 44-45); Davenant, Charles, *An Essay upon the Probable Methods of making a People Gainers in the Ballance of Trade,* 2nd
ed., London, 1700, pp. 17-18.   (First published, London, 1699.)

[53] Davenant, Charles, *Essays upon Peace at Home and War Abroad,*
London, 1704 (in *Works,* ed. Sir Charles Whitworth, London, 1771, Vol.
IV, p. 294).

form in their own persons, upon the different members that compose a well-ordered commonwealth, of which the chief are called ministers of state. . . . In a government of the laws, and not of men, princes are a part, but at the head of the legislature, and either in person, or by their ministers, execute what the constitution requires, what the legislature has already ordained, and what it enacts from time to time upon new emergencies; and where this is fully done, the administration is compleat.[54]

Throughout the eighteenth century this reliance upon the cooperative action of king and Parliament, coupled with condemnation of parties and factions whose action was sure to obscure the clear view of the national interest, was characteristic of the mercantilist view of the state. Conflicts of power could be resolved by the solvent of patriotic devotion to the paramount goal of the strength and welfare of the kingdom.

This happy union of the force of popular assent and the stability of royal power and dignity, described somewhat vaguely in terms like those of the ending of a pretty fairy tale, offered the best form of government if the objects of commercial prosperity and national strength were to be maintained. A machinery of popular assent, rather than popular control, was an indispensable part of the structure of the state. The activity and enthusiasm of the citizens could be encouraged by seeing that their civil liberties, at least from class to class, were respected. Political participation of the subjects in the government was provided, but these privileges were to be exercised by supporting the policies proposed by the monarch and his ministers. Parliaments were in large part simply means for registering the loyalty of the citizen, for mobilizing the support needed to build a strong state; though there

[54] *Ibid.*, Vol. V, pp. 1-2. For other works in the eighteenth century, placing a similar emphasis on the "mixt elements" of the British Constitution, see p. 220.

was some value in the advice they could occasionally offer to the ruler.

The fundamental problem of defining the relationship of the governed to the governor was really avoided, though most of the writers seemed to think that it was solved. The apparent solution was, nevertheless, quite consistent with the economic and political doctrines to which they subscribed. Granted that great powers had to be assigned to the state because the relations among states took the form of an irreconcilable rivalry, the structure designed for England required confidence in the executive expressed through a national assembly which performed the function of organizing general consent. After all, state making was the chief concern of the mercantilists, and interpreted in the light of this guiding principle, the pattern of their political system conformed to the demands of their economic views.

IV. THE PROBLEM OF MONOPOLISTIC PRIVILEGE

The pattern of the sovereign state itself evoked an agreement that approached unanimity; but the problem of the little states within the state was a bone of contention throughout the sixteenth and seventeenth centuries. It remained unsettled till the triumph of laissez-faire doctrines condemned both monopoly and mercantilism as enemies of economic freedom. This unresolved conflict is all the more striking because it makes its appearance in the earliest literature; it is, in fact, only a slight exaggeration to say that mercantilism originated from disputes over the status of the privileged trading companies—particularly the Merchant Adventurers and the East India Company—and their relation to the welfare of the kingdom. The controversy among the writers ranged over various aspects of monopoly but it is possible to reduce the issues to only two subjects of general importance: first, the economic features of exclusive trading and manufacturing companies, as related to the economy of the realm; second, the political dangers which arose from the power of these organized groups. On each subject there were both opponents and defenders of the companies among the most orthodox of these merchant-philosophers.

A. *The Dispute over Monopoly Economics*

Attack upon monopoly rested in essence upon two grounds, both important when regarded from the standpoint of a care for the national interest. The first and simplest accusation was that monopoly prices were too high, and increased the costs of living and of raw materials. The inevitable result would be to reduce the sale of English manufactures, in all industries which were affected by such high prices, and thus to injure England's foreign trade. This charge against the trading companies was brought forward early in the seventeenth century by an author who signed himself I. R. in a pamphlet entitled *The Trades Increase;* but John Wheeler's *A Treatise of Commerce* which appeared in 1601 reveals, as he defends the Merchant Adventurers from the same complaints, that the grievance was one of long standing.[55] More sophisticated and careful statements of this argument appeared in the eighteenth century; the anonymous editor of *A Collection of Papers relating to the East India Trade,* published in 1730, put it forcibly:

The Success and Improvements of Trade, depend wholly upon supplying the Commodities cheap at Market, and whoever can afford those of equal Goodness at but half per Cent. cheaper than his Neighbours, will command the Sale. Now 'tis impossible any Company can do this upon equal terms

[55] [R., I.], *The Trades Increase,* London, 1615; Wheeler, John, *A Treatise of Commerce,* London, 1601.

with a private Merchant, nor would they if they could: Private Men will think of every Way to come at their Goods cheap . . . but nothing of this is ever done by Companies. . . .

Besides, it is the Interest of the Nation to sell their Commodities at as good a Price as the Markets abroad can afford to buy them, and to bring in foreign Commodities as cheap as they can afford to sell them; especially such as do not interfere with our own . . . and the Interest of Companies is directly contrary to all this; for other People being prohibited to deal in the same Commodities, they can put what Price they please upon both, and ever will put what is most for their own advantage . . . often to the discouragement of our own Manufactures, which depend upon their Cheapness, their business being always to encrease the Price of Stock, without encreasing Trade.[56]

Nearly all the writers who criticized monopoly and exclusive companies resorted to this type of argument among others.

The second, and from the mercantilist standpoint, the graver fault of privileged companies both in trade and in manufacture, lay in the restrictions their special rights imposed upon activity and enterprise. An anonymous critic of the Merchant Adventurers wrote in 1645:

The strength of a kingdome consists in the riches of many subjects, not of a few, in so much that were this trade enlarged, it would tend to the multiplying of able and wealthy Merchants, it would disperse it to a greater latitude, and further ennobling the Trade, and prevent the encrease of poore men and beggars up and downe the Land: for it is one of the maine reasons why there are fewer beggars seen in Commonwealths than in Kingdoms, because of community and freedome of trading, by which means the wealth of the Land is more equally distributed amongst the natives. . . .

Trade (though the comparison be homely) is like Dung,

---

[56] Anon., ed. *A Collection of Papers relating to the East India Trade*, London, 1730, preface, pp. viii-ix.

which being close kept in a heap or two stinks, but being spread abroad, it doth fertilize the earth and make it fructifie.[57]

Roger Coke, who was something of a heretic in his economic views but who agreed with a considerable part of the opinions of his contemporaries, was willing to generalize this argument further, and put it in terms of labor, condemning the corporations and even the Statute of Apprentices, lamenting the fact that "more poor children are born than can be employed in Rural or Country Affairs, and their poor parents have not the means to bind them Apprentice in Market-Towns and corporations." These restrictions, applied by the corporations and sanctioned by the statute, forced these unfortunate youths "either to fly their Country, or to be Tapsters, Ostlers, and Drawers. . . ." This resulted in a grave injury to the nation, for its strength depended upon the industry of its people, "and therefore to neglect to instruct Youth how to Imploy themselves, or to debar any man from the benefit of his honest Imployment, is not only unjust, but Impolitick." [58]

If the companies and the corporations were to stand convicted both of undue enhancement of prices and restriction of enterprise they were grievous offenders indeed, guilty of crimes against the life of the state itself. Defenders rushed forward to clear them of both indictments. The reply to the argument on prices was a simple head-on collision; the supporters of the companies flatly denied that the prices were high, or at the very least asserted that they were not much too high. Dudley Digges refuted the allegations of I. R. by citing figures on the reexport of Indian commodities, and claimed that such

[57] Anon., *A Discourse consisting of Motives for the Enlargement and Freedome of Trade,* London, 1645, pp. 22-23; 25.

[58] Coke, Roger, *A Detection,* London, 1696, Vol. I, pp. 43-44 of the Introduction, unnumbered.

goods had been cheapened in England by virtue of the work of the East India Company.[59]   Even Malynes, usually hostile to monopoly, in one of his pamphlets absolved the Merchant Adventurers of blame for raising domestic prices for cloth by comparing home and foreign prices, and showing the former to be lower.[60]

According to the tenets of mercantilist doctrine, the second charge that monopoly restricted enterprise by excluding deserving citizens from trade, manufacture, or employment was even more important than any quarrel over price levels.   The friends of the companies and corporations evaded this accusation by emphasizing the promotional activities of the great companies, particularly those engaged in trade.   Such were John Wheeler's arguments in 1601, and two years later Malynes admitted that "the dissolution of that societie [the Merchant Adventurers] would be the undoing of all the trade, and bring a great confusion to the Realme." [61]   Toward the end of the seventeenth century John Collins, in a little pamphlet entitled *Salt and Fishery,* demonstrated the need of societies with monopoly rights in order to initiate the manufacture of salt and thus stimulate activity and employment.   Struck by the merits of his formula for a salt industry, he then proposed its application to tin, linen, and various other enterprises.[62]

In the eighteenth century there were a host of defenders for the companies, particularly in the African and Indian trades, who glossed over the question of price while they pointed out that joint stock was necessary to drive these ventures, for it was imperative to maintain forts and troops to protect the traders.   It was often proposed, indeed,

[59] Digges, Dudley, *The Defence of Trade,* London, 1615, especially pp. 42-45.   See also the quotation from Fortrey given in Ch. II, *supra,* p. 36.
[60] Malynes, Gerard de, *England's View, in the Unmasking of two Paradoxes,* London, 1603, pp. 84-85.
[61] Wheeler, John, *op. cit.*; Malynes, Gerard de., *op. cit.,* p. 85.
[62] Collins, John, *Salt and Fishery,* London, 1682.

that the nation should reimburse these societies for their expenditures in defending and improving these essential commercial activities. The frankness of these advocates is often refreshing; many admitted that they were stockholders, but expressed their entire willingness to accept personal profits in order to improve and maintain the public welfare.[63]

The argument that this type of organization was indispensable for the stimulation of new enterprises and the support of established trades raised another aspect of the whole question. A political controversy arose between those who believed the companies to be an important tool of state supervision and control of trade, and the critics who asserted that they were, on the contrary, little kingdoms within the kingdom imperiling the liberties of the subject and the authority of the commonwealth.

B. *The Political Aspects of Monopoly*

While the defenders of the companies expended a very considerable amount of ink and energy in refuting the economic accusations of their opponents, they frequently avoided direct combat over questions of price and enterprise, and shifted the debate into a field where they felt much more secure, the question of the means of state control over economic activity in general. Here was a battleground much more to their liking, where they occupied the heights of national prestige and had ranged behind them the big battalions of the sovereign power of the state. Regarded as instruments of regulation and direction of the trade and manufacture of the kingdom, the companies and corporations were elevated above all sordid questions of price or profit and became the props and stays of the nation's strength.

[63] For lists of writers who attacked monopoly, chiefly on economic grounds, and for the defenders of the companies against these charges, see p. 220.

Almost every advocate of these charters and privileges came quickly to this argument. "All Trades," wrote one of them in the mid-seventeenth century, "should center in Companies and Corporations, the only Foundation and Pillar upon which a lasting Monument of Trade and Manufactories is to be built and preserv'd . . ."; and then went on to sketch an economic community in which such organizations mobilized the capital and skill of many in order to further the well-being of the realm.[64]   The author of *The Ancient Trades Decayed, Repaired Again* deplored the decline of the London companies:

If all those of a Trade were of one and the same Company, and had power to make some by-laws for the good of their Trade, it would extremely conduce not only to the promotion of the same, but to the keeping of it in a right and good order, preserving (at least) a *temperamentum ad justitiam,* if not *ad pondus* in our trades and negotiations.

And doubtless *ab origine* it was so in London . . . the defect whereof, I judge, is the reason that the trade of that City is declining. . . . For if none were of a Company but those only that were of the same trade, they would be frequently whetting one another to do something that might be for the advancement thereof; and everyone would refrain the doing of anything that might give a wound to the fame, for fear of being reprehended by the Company.[65]

Comparable to these defenses of the companies as a means of securing a well-ordered trade and manufacture which were voiced in the seventeenth century, are the repeated assertions made in the eighteenth century that the great trading companies, particularly those to India and Africa, were the only means of driving those hazardous ventures where forts and garrisons must be maintained to protect the invested capital from both the barbarous natives and

[64] [Bland, John], *Trade Revived*, London, 1659, p. 3.
[65] Anon., *The Ancient Trades Decayed, Repaired Again*, London, 1678, pp. 50-54.

the civilized rival nations like the French and the Dutch.

Here, indeed, was a crushing retort to the foes of monopoly; for it not only reduced their case to insignificant dimensions compared to the importance of the nation's welfare, but impugned their patriotism as well. Like many resounding periods, however, it brought forth replies proclaimed with equal eloquence and put also in political terms. The critics of the companies first asserted the rights and liberties of the citizen as a counterblast to their opponent's claim that upon their side stood the authority and interest of the state in a well-regulated economy. In 1615 the orthodox mercantilist author of *The Trades Increase* attacked the Muscovy and East India companies thus:

> . . . merchandize sorting and setled in companies, confineth merchants into those limits that private orders tie them in, so that they may not helpe themselves through any discouragement in one trade, but by sute and submission of themselves to the other; though, I say, their trades faile them, and others have too much, nor may any else of the kingdome come amongst them, though never so able and well disposed, unlesse they come in on such conditions as the victor pleaseth to propound. A thing in ordinary sense somewhat harsh to follow, Subjects and equall Citizens in this great Monarkie, to be so serviceablie tied and subdued one unto the other, and the rather for that those priviledges by the indulgencie of the Prince being granted as a reward to some for their industries, and exemplary to other encouragements are strictly used to the eternall benefite of a few, and the wrong of all the residue.[66]

Thirty years later another writer stated the same grievance with equal force and with more precise emphasis on its political significance, referring particularly to the Merchant Adventurers' special rights in the cloth trade, but including individuals, corporations, and even the market towns in his condemnation:

[66] [R., I.], *The Trades Increase*, London, 1615, p. 52.

And it is held an undoubted principle of State, that there is nothing more pernicious and destructive to any Kingdome or Commonwealth, then Monopolies, which like Incubusses doe suck the very vitall spirits, and drive into one veine that masse of blood which should cherishe the whole body. . . .

First, it is repugnant to the Law of Nature, in regard that Wool, and the draping and merchandizing thereof . . . hath furnished this Island, and wherein she hath given every free-born Inhabitant equall interest, as matter for his industry to work upon; surely she never intended that a thin handful of men, a small contemptible number in comparison of the whole . . . should appropriate to themselves the disposing and venting of two thirds of this generall grand Commodity. . . . Secondly, it is against the Law of Nations, in regard that no Monarchy or Kingdom . . . throughout Europe has the like example. . . . Thirdly, this Incorporation is repugnant to the positive Lawes of this Land, as manifestly appears by Magna Charta, Petition of Right, Statutes of Monopolies, and severall others. . . .[67]

Roger Coke remarked bitterly that "these Companies who manage foreign Trades exclusive to other Men, are more Tyrannous and Injurious to their fellow Subjects than any of their enemies are . . . why should the Nation assist them, who have rent themselves from the Nation, and are more Enemies to them than any other?" [68]

In the eighteenth century a new theme was introduced into this chorus of indigation; not only had the rights of free-born Englishmen been sold, but the sale had corrupted the sovereign authority which had made the bargain. A pamphlet attributed to Daniel Defoe—the vigor of the style, it might be added, supports the attribution—appeared in 1701, and stated the accusation with clarity:

[67] Anon., *A Discourse consisting of Motives for the Enlargement and Freedome of Trade,* London, 1645, pp. 3-6.

[68] Coke, Roger, *A Detection,* London, 1694, pp. 43-46, unnumbered, of the Introduction, Vol. I. See also his *England's Improvements,* London, 1675, pp. 66-67 of the Epilogue.

The Grand Work which the whole Nation is now intent upon, is chusing their Representatives in Parliament, Chusing Men to Meet, and advise with the King about the most Important Affairs of the Kingdom. And while all Men ought to be fixing their Eyes upon such Men as are best Qualified to Sit in that Place of Honour, . . . Here we are plagu'd with the Impertinence of the two East India Companies, as if the Interest of either Company were to be named in a Day with the *Protestant Religion and the publick Peace.* . . . The Grand Question ask'd now, when your vote is requir'd for a Parliament Man, is not, as it should be, Is he a Man of Sense, of Religion, of Honesty and Estate? But, What Company is he for, the New, or the Old? [69]

Thirty years later this argument was elaborated into a full condemnation of the dangers of group interest and pressure politics:

But their are other Mischiefs still behind, [those of price enhancement and restriction of enterprise] which strike yet much deeper, namely, the Influence and Violence which they bring upon our Constitution. For as great Riches in private Men is dangerous to all States, so great and sudden Poverty produces equal Mischiefs in Free Governments, because it makes those who, by their Birth and Station, must be concerned in the Administration, necessitous and desperate, which will leave them the Means, and give them the Will to destroy their Country; For the Political Power will remain some Time in their Hands after their natural Power and Riches are gone, and they will ever make use of it to acquire that Wealth by Violence and Fraud, which they have lost by Folly and Extravagance; and as both of these Extreams are certainly sure of single Men, so these are more dangerous in Numbers of Men joined together, in a Political Union. . . . Now Companies bring all these Mischiefs upon us; they give great and sudden Estates to the Managers and Directors, upon the Ruin of Trade in General. . . .

[69] [Defoe, Daniel], *The Freeholders Plea against Stockjobbing Elections of Parliament Men,* London, 1701, pp. 7-8.

Giving instances of the nefarious practices of these powerful bodies, the author goes on to say that in Holland

the East India Company governs the State, and is in Effect the
State itself; and I pray God that we may never see the like
elsewhere. . . .

In fine, Monopolies are equally dangerous in Trade, in Politicks, and Religion; A free Trade, a Free Government, and a
free Liberty of Conscience, are the Rights and Blessings of
Mankind.[70]

The substance of this passage may be found, phrased with
varying degrees of eloquence, but with constant force and
sincerity, in many other writings of the eighteenth century.

Perhaps too much space has been given here to the
opponents of monopoly. What has been said earlier must
be kept in mind—this discussion divided the mercantilists
almost evenly, and for everyone who recognized and
proclaimed the evils of privilege there was an advocate
who proposed the companies as the means of ordering the
domestic activity of the nation and defending the vital
interest of her trade abroad.

In this debate both sides raised a political issue which
most mercantilist writing ignored—the question of conflicts of interest within the community. The two authors
quoted above were really asking: Whose England is this
that must be served by trade and manufacture? Does it
belong to us, the ordinary citizens, or is it the property
of the managers and directors of the great companies?
When the reply was made that national interest made
monopoly a necessary instrument of control and stimulation of enterprise, they retorted that the price was far too
heavy even if the means could secure the end, for it en-

[70] Anon., ed., *A Collection of Papers Relating to the East India Trade,*
London, 1730, pp. xi, xiii, xiv.

For lists of writers attacking monopoly on political grounds, and for
others defending by political argument, see p. 223.

tailed the sacrifice of the subject's economic freedom, and corrupted the very bodies in which were vested the sovereign power of the state. Fundamental issues of political philosophy were involved; but they were held to the specific issue of monopoly and not extended to the whole existence of the state the mercantilists envisaged.

One further aspect of the controversy must be noted. When the opponents of the companies advanced the rights of the citizen on their side of the case, it was undoubtedly the citizen merchant or the citizen manufacturer they had most often in mind. The lot of the laboring poor had failed to elicit discussion of the nature and range of national authority; but the restriction of trading opportunity did raise the mighty question of the rights of man.

V. THE MERCANTILISTS AND THEIR CONTEMPORARIES

The political aspects of monopoly, the function of Parliament, the liberties of the subject, and the powers of the king were all problems which forced the mercantilists to give some heed to the fundamental questions of political philosophy. More than this, the period in which they lived and published—if it is dated roughly from the first of the seventeenth century to the last quarter of the eighteenth—was one of intense dispute over the great issue of king versus Parliament. At the time of Cromwell's Commonwealth and again at the time of the Glorious Revolution, the gales of controversy blew a great cloud of pamphlets, broadsides, and sermons throughout the length and breadth of England; and after each event the pages rustled, lifted, and even multiplied for years after the full fury of the storm had passed. And yet, although the merchant statesman and philosopher surely must have heard the roar of the tempest—indeed, as he wrote some sheets must have been fairly snatched from his desk to whirl away upon the winds—a careful reading of his works and those of his fellows irresistibly suggests that he and they were scarcely conscious that the air was stirred at all, or that at most they noted only a passing breeze.

The mercantilists did not give much attention to the work of the political philosophers. Beyond an occasional reference to Aristotle, Plato, and Machiavelli there is almost no citation of the great names in all their works. They were not concerned with the relation of the Catholic Church to the English state, a question which exercised the political theorists, nor with what might be termed the strictly political and legal aspects of the conflict between king and Parliament. They were either ignorant of the classic names and the traditional issues, or else they ignored them deliberately—with some propriety, it must be admitted—as being irrelevant to their chief interests.

This lack of interest was fully reciprocated by the political philosophers and the jurists of the seventeenth and eighteenth centuries. There is no reference in their writings to the works of even the most celebrated of the mercantilists. The reasons for this mutual disregard may be briefly stated. Political thought was chiefly concerned with the constitutional pattern of the state, the location of sovereign power, and arguments—based frequently upon theological reasoning—justifying the possession and exercise of that power by either king or Parliament, depending on the viewpoint of the particular writer on that tremendous issue. The mercantilists, on the other hand, were interested in the practical operation of government and the practical effects of public policy. In the course of their effort to define an economic policy for the kingdom they developed conceptions of the range of government authority, the duties of the subjects, and the patterns of state organization which have been analyzed in this and the preceding chapter; but they had no real need to depend upon the conclusions or take heed of the controversies of their contemporaries. Philosophical and theological consideration of the ultimate right of either royal prerogative or parliamentary supremacy left them cold. What they wanted, and what they constructed in their writings, was a functioning government that aided a great trade abroad and managed a balanced economy at home.[71]

There were, however, two doctrines continually discussed in their time which had a relationship to some of their conceptions of the state: first, the doctrine of the divine right of kings; second, the lawyers' definition of the royal prerogative.

A. The Doctrine of the Divine Right of Kings

The brilliant study by Dr. John Neville Figgis established the view that the doctrine of the divine right of kings "was essentially a popular theory, proclaimed in the pulpit, published in the market place, witnessed on the battlefield. . . . A belief so widespread was surely the product more of practical necessity than of intellectual activity." [72] The Tudors were somewhat lacking in one of the requisites of kingly right—they had not a strictly defensible hereditary right to the throne; but the need for a single central authority led to the assertion during their reigns of a doctrine of the absolute obedience to the royal authority.[73]

The necessity of obedience to the monarch, usually put in terms of the religious difficulties arising out of the English Reformation, occupied political theorists through-

[71] For illustrative instances and further discussion of this point, see p. 223.

[72] Figgis, J. N., The Divine Right of Kings, 2nd ed., Cambridge, 1922, pp. 3-4.

[73] Ibid., pp. 93-106. For a very close and careful analysis see also Allen, J. W., A History of Political Thought in the Sixteenth Century, New York, 1928, Part II, Chs. IV and V; and McIlwain, C. H., The Political Works of James I, Cambridge, 1918, Introduction.

out the Tudor period. It remained a fundamental question during the reign of James I.[74] The statement of divine right as James himself made it, provides a striking parallel with the views of the mercantilists regarding the kingship and the extent of the state's power. In the *Trew Law of Free Monarchies* he declared:

> By the Law of Nature the King becomes a naturall Father to all his Lieges at his Coronation . . . even so is the King bound to care for all his subjects.

In the speech delivered to his first Parliament he repeated the metaphor:

> . . . the special and greatest point of difference that is betwixt a rightful King and an vsurping Tyrant is this: That whereas the proude and ambitious Tyrant doeth thinke his Kingdome and people are onely ordeined for satisfaction of his desires and vnreasonable appetites; The righteous and iust King doeth by the contrary acknowledge himselfe to bee ordeined for the procuring of the wealth and prosperitie of his people. . . . If you bee rich I cannot bee poore, if you bee happy I cannot but bee fortunate, and I protest that your welfare shall ever bee my greatest care and contentment.[75]

Such statements of the rights and duties of kings accorded with the mercantilists' confidence in the royal power; and they made frequent use of the argument that the interest of the king must be the interest of the nation.

Later defenses of the right of kings, such as Sir Robert Filmer's *Patriarcha,* likewise offered support to the mercantilist attitude. Filmer's justification of royal power on the basis of an analogy to the family fitted in with the conception of the kingdom as a household.[76]

---

[74] McIlwain, C. H., *op. cit.,* Introduction, pp. xxxiii-xxxiv.

[75] *Ibid.,* p. 55 and p. 278. Other statements in the same vein may be found in the speech to Parliament in 1605, pp. 287-289; and the speech to the Lords and Commons of the Parliament at Whitehall, pp. 307-309.

[76] Authoritative summaries of Filmer's argument may be found in Dunning, W. A., *Political Theories from Luther to Montesquieu,* New

The close-knit logic of Hobbes's *Leviathan,* with its insistence upon the importance of stability and order in government, resembled the mercantilists' regard for domestic peace as a necessary prerequisite to commercial prosperity. Their horror of disorder was fully as great as his—the state of nature was no environment for the development of industry and trade. The arguments Hobbes advanced for the monarchical form of government were all of a nature to appeal to these economic writers.[77] The statement Bolingbroke made of the powers and importance of *The Patriot King* emphasizes their favorite conception of a combination of popular assent with the exercise of royal authority. Bolingbroke likewise gave to his king large powers over the trade and commerce of the realm, in terms the mercantilists could have heartily approved.[78]

While the evidence indicates that there is an intellectual kinship between the mercantilists and the defenders of royal power, it is not permissible to suggest more than this similarity in viewpoint. It is plain, from what little has been said, that these doctrines, held during this period, would offer some support to the confidence that such men as Malynes, Temple, or Davenant expressed for the kingship as a means of establishing national control of trade and industry. This pet assumption of many mercantilists was part of the intellectual climate of their time; and though they did not make explicit reference to the arguments of the philosophers who defended the divine right of kings, they often reflected that viewpoint.

York, 1923, pp. 254-261, and Gettell, R. G., *History of Political Thought,* New York, 1924, pp. 209-210.

[77] Hobbes, Thomas, *Leviathan,* Everyman ed., pp. 98-99.

[78] Bolingbroke, Henry St. John, Viscount, *The Idea of a Patriot King,* 1738 (in *Works,* Dublin, 1793, Vol. III, pp. 51-52, 54).

The passage in which Bolingbroke discusses trade is worth attention. It is reprinted in the notes at the back of this book, p. 225.

B. *The Legal Definition of the Royal Prerogative*

The commentators on English law, throughout this same period, had been developing an interpretation of the constitution which could have been used to support the mercantilists' conception of the state. These theories were at once juristic and realistic. The lawyers wanted to describe the English constitution as it actually functioned, and from the times of Glanvil and Bracton had interpreted it as vesting the sovereignty in a king in Parliament, governing through the agency of the law, and within the law.[79] What one finds in these writings is a legal description of the king's prerogative; a statement of the legal powers of the government in which a delicate balance was maintained between Parliament and the king, never exactly defined in theory, but workable in actual practice.

Sir John Fortescue, for example, expressed this point of view very early—*The Governance of England* was written between 1471 and 1476. He argued that the king's right of sovereignty was agreed to by the people.[80] Such a description of the monarchy received a more extended statement in the works of Sir Thomas Smith, whose *De Republica Anglorum* was published in 1583. Professor J. W. Allen's analysis of the work excellently summarizes the practical point of view adopted in it:

He was asking simply how England was actually governed. He found that it was governed by the Prince, but that, normally at least, the Prince made law and imposed taxes only in Parliament. He explains that while the making of laws and the providing of money is done by the Prince in Parliament, the management of foreign relations and of official appointments is by the Prince alone. He never explicitly says that

[79] Dunning, W. A., *Political Theories from Luther to Montesquieu,* New York, 1923, pp. 197-200.

[80] Fortescue, Sir John, *The Governance of England,* 1471-76, ed. Charles Plummer, Oxford, 1885, pp. 109, 115, 127. See also Dunning, W. A., *op. cit.,* pp. 202-203.

the Prince can neither make law nor impose taxes of his own will simply. He was not, I think, prepared to say what the Prince could not do. . . . Sir Thomas never uses the word "sovereignty" and, had he been asked where sovereignty lay in England, he would have said it was in the Prince. To him "the highest and supreme authority" is that "which doth control, correct, and direct all other members of the Commonwealth." This, it may be said, is just what Elizabeth was doing.[81]

This fortunate practical combination of the king's prerogative and the people's consent through Parliament, by which the strength and stability of the realm was so well assured, was steadfastly repeated by the lawyers without much modification down to the time of Blackstone. The same convenient mixture of royal power and popular support was also a characteristic of the mercantilists' conception of the state. The practical lawyer and the merchant and man of affairs could find themselves in quite complete agreement as to the nature of the British constitution, though the strict theorist might be hard put to it to find any precise definition of the powers of prince or people.

Though the mercantilists clearly shared the views of the jurists, they made no more explicit use of them than they had of the doctrines of divine right. They cited neither the works of the lawyers nor those of the political philosophers; but it is manifest that their conception of the state was influenced by the ideas of both.

This brief reference to two important political ideas of their time shows merely that their state bore, so to speak, a strong family resemblance to these commonly discussed doctrines of sovereign power. They probably felt

[81] Allen, J. W., *A History of Political Thought in the Sixteenth Century*, New York, 1928, pp. 264-265. Another interesting work, putting forward this same conception of the relationship of king and parliament, is that of Sir John Eliot, *De Jure Maiestatis, or Political Treatise of Government*, ed. Rev. Alexander B. Grosart, privately printed, 1882. It was written about 1628.

an increased confidence in their king and his Parliament because reputable support could be found among the jurists and political philosophers for their political pattern of the realm.

VI. SUMMARY

The analysis made in the preceding chapter of the political implications of the mercantilists' economic doctrines ended by raising an important question: What was the structure of the state in which they were willing to vest so wide a grant of power? Their answer, which has been reviewed in this chapter, was largely a description of the government they saw, or thought they saw, in action. They proposed few innovations; the state was doing much; they merely wanted it to do more.

Executive power, placed in the hands of the king, seemed to them an effective instrument for the accomplishment of national economic policy. Upon this they expended some argument, advancing the view that monarchy afforded substantial guarantees of the order and stability necessary to trade, and insisting upon the fundamental harmony of interest and purpose that united the people and their prince. A few writers expressed some doubts of royal power, but most of them were quite ready to trust the monarch.

It was evident to nearly all of them that some elaboration of the administrative machinery at the king's disposal would be desirable if the full benefits of regulation and control of the national economy were to be realized. Nevertheless, their suggestions were meager. A council of trade, made up chiefly of merchants but sometimes representing other interests, was proposed almost unanimously. Such a council was usually expected to do more than offer advice; it frequently would possess considerable administrative authority and occasionally might have command of funds to carry out projects. Besides this pivotal agency, other minor bodies with specific duties to perform were advocated: banks to create and manage credit; workhouses to employ the poor and train the young; courts merchant to build up and administer a body of mercantile law. Undoubtedly they had great confidence in the existing state bureaucracy—privy council, ministers, and local justices—as being capable of carrying out the desired policies. Besides this, the specific character of their proposals seemed to make them almost self-executing and therefore proof against risks of maladministration. Most of the king's officers were family men; the nation was but a family writ large; the existing organization of the government with a few additions would serve to direct the activities of the national household.

Coupled with this confidence in executive power there existed a genuine regard for the importance of Parliament and the maintenance of the citizen's liberties. Because the mercantilists were continually preoccupied with practical problems, the fundamental difficulty of reconciling the sphere of royal prerogative with that of parliamentary authority concerned them but little. The dominance of the national interest—a magic solvent for reconciling possible conflicts among the classes of society—would serve to produce a harmonious balance under the mixed English constitution. This easy assumption of accord avoided all the problems of the location of sovereignty which harassed the political philosophers of their time.

The dispute among the mercantilists over the status of the monopolistic companies, had they followed out all its implications, would have forced upon their notice a large part of the political issues they had so lightly disregarded. The long and bitter debate over the position of the great corporations might well have revealed to them that the mutual interests of organized groups, or of the recognized classes of society, or even the presumed accord between king and Parliament, were not so widely agreed upon as they cheerfully supposed. But while the mercantilists continued to quarrel over the privileges of the companies, they never fully investigated the implications of the conflict, though they did realize that it had its political aspects. It remained a subject upon which there was disagreement among them; but the controversy never rose to the pitch where it brought the fundamental tenets of their doctrines into serious question.

If the mercantilists were to ignore the deeper issues implicit in the possibility that the interests of the corporations might run counter to the welfare of the kingdom, it is hardly to be expected that they could make much use of the political philosophy of their time. The political theorists were perpetually engaged in what must have seemed to these merchant economists an unseemly and even unpatriotic warfare over the powers of the king and Parliament, and the relationship of church and state. It is true that the doctrines of divine right, and the jurists' analysis of the royal prerogative resembled the arguments used by the mercantilists to justify confidence in executive authority exercised by a monarch. It is equally true, in the literature of mercantilism, however, that there is little or no citation of the political writers or even explicit discussion of the issues they raised. The mercantilists seem to have imbibed some of the ideas while they dodged the controversies. What they wanted was an actively functioning state which would steadily pursue the economic policies required, in their view, to build the strength of the kingdom. The Tudors had lived up to these needs admirably; the Stuarts had at least maintained centralized authority; the mixed English constitution would serve for the eighteenth century.

With the mercantilists' description of the structure of the state there is displayed the full beauty of the national household. Its domestic economy has been outlined; its business rivalries have been declared. The ties that unite the family complete the family portrait. The sanctions of parental authority have been pronounced; the consent of the members of the family is guaranteed. The members cherish their liberties; but these liberties are always subordinated to the family's interest. If perhaps the justification of the father's powers and the omnicompetence of his wisdom are taken for granted, surely no member of the kinship would be so disloyal as to point out these minor errors in an economic and political philosophy which claimed the credit for the solid fruits of domestic prosperity and the glory of Britain's power abroad.

CHAPTER V

Mercantilist Political Doctrine and
Modern Totalitarianism

THE mercantilists have suffered some injury from the scholarly conscience, industry, and skill of the economists and the historians of economic thought. Of course it is true that, since the time when Adam Smith subjected the mercantile system to the ruthless criticism which sprang from his cosmopolitan views, there have been better balanced assessments of mercantilism. Nevertheless, most students of the development of economic theory have reviewed the work of the mercantilists with the intention of tracing the growth of economic science. The method has been that of dissection and analysis. The scalpel has been used to separate the mercantilist position into its constituent parts; and under the microscope each of these parts has yielded up its merits and its faults, particularly the latter.

This technique has set forth a number of the characteristic doctrines clearly and precisely. The cardinal principle of the favorable balance of trade was the first to be examined. The high valuation attached to treasure, with its influence upon the mercantilists' conception of wealth, has been surveyed. Their ideas regarding the classic problems of economic theory have been reviewed; careful study has been made of their views of capital and interest, value and price, land and rent, population and national prosperity. Finally, their persistent advocacy of state intervention in the economic sphere, and the numerous controls they proposed for trade, manufacture, and agriculture have been analyzed and explained.

When such an analysis is made the results are of undoubted value to the economist and the historian of economic doctrines. The failure of the mercantilists to reach any conception of comparative advantage in foreign trade, and their emphasis on exports and a favorable balance, appear in clear relief. The confusion in their minds regarding the nature of wealth, their tendency to regard the precious metals as wealth itself, becomes evident. The fact that they arrived at no satisfactory definition of capital explains their willingness to regulate the interest rate by law; their insistence upon a bare subsistence theory of wages arises from an incomplete examination, on their part, of the costs of production; their readiness to regulate the quality, prices, and methods of manufacture of commodities is the result of very serious confusions about the economic concept of exchange value. The economist of the present day points out that this is a very rudimentary system of economics; and he is justified in doing so. It was rough; it was confused; it was incomplete.

But such a method of criticism is exposed to two definite risks. First of all, there is the constant temptation, to which earlier historians of economic thought yielded, to oversimplify the mercantilists' position and describe it merely as a tariff policy, animated by the desire to secure the precious metals by the maintenance of a favorable balance of trade. The second temptation has already been suggested. If mercantilism is dissected into its constituent doctrines, each particular reveals itself immediately as bad economics by modern standards. It then becomes almost too easy to point out the fallacies in the system, and to show the blunders in the state policies proposed. The tariffs exhibit the fallacies which laissez-faire economists have condemned in all schemes of protection; and the colonial policies come in for the same sort of criticism. The dangers of state intervention in the domestic economy are readily made manifest; capital and labor may be seriously misdirected if the regulating action of the market is obstructed. A blind faith in a large and rapidly increasing population is as alarming to the expert, who is trying to work out a formula for a desirable optimum, as it was to the Malthusian, who feared increasing misery as numbers pressed upon the means of subsistence. Measured by the standards of the twentieth, or even the nineteenth century, these earnest merchants diminish to the status of men who knew there ought to be a science of economics, but were unable to do more than open the discussion of its basic principles.

If the students of economic thought have been too harsh in condemning the mercantilists because they were not scientific economists, students of politics have committed a more serious error in ignoring them upon the assumption that, whether they were scientific or not, they were economists. Historians of political theory have quite consistently disregarded mercantilism; because the predominant concern of the system with the economic activities of the state seemed to justify its exclusion from the story of political ideas. It is true, as the preceding chapter shows, that the mercantile system, while it carried a number of important political implications as an integral part of its whole attitude, gave scant attention to the strictly political issues of the time, which centered round the relation of church and state, the powers of the monarch, and, during the Puritan Revolution, the declaration of democratic theory. The classic problems of politics—the nature of the state, the justification of its powers, the structure of its government, even the rights of its citizens—received relatively little notice from these merchant-philosophers. It is easy to understand why the political scientist, occupied in tracing the growth of these political ideas, has ignored the mercantilists as lying outside the field of his inquiry.

A satisfactory estimate of mercantilism must give due weight to both its political and economic aspects. If it is recognized that the economic proposals of the mercantilists were powerfully influenced by political considerations, their economic doctrines become much more intelligible; especially when they are viewed in relation to the dominant factors of the historical situation in which they arose. Recent studies, notably Heckscher's extensive work and Furniss' earlier but closely knit analysis, approach the system from such a standpoint.

Regarded as economic strategy, aimed at the achievement of political objectives in a world of competing national states, the policies of mercantilism exhibit more logical consistency than many economists have been willing to concede to them. The doctrine of the favorable balance of trade, and the tariffs, bounties, and prohibitions which were proposed to secure an excess of exports over imports, regain their original meaning as instruments of national power. Mere treasure, or treasure as a store of value, had real political significance; and the programs were framed to take account of that political objective. The colonial policy and the navigation acts were designed to stimulate shipping and provide a fleet; as such they have a practicability and purpose which they can scarcely show if they are analyzed merely as a stage in the development of economic science.

The domestic program likewise becomes more intelligible when its political aspect is taken into consideration. The control of the labor force, the regulation of manufacture, and the proposals to fix a legal rate of interest were all designed to build a national economy which would be strong in competition with others. The encouragement of new industries, the training of laborers, the encouragement of a large population, the provision of subsistence for this population by supporting enclosures and corn laws as means for reorganizing agriculture, were also to contribute to this planned domestic economy. The proponents of the system were willing to go the logical length of directing the nation's consumption habits in order to conserve and increase its wealth. The mercantilists were prepared to support such programs even if they should prove to be expensive; if freights and wheat prices rose they were still willing to continue the navigation laws and the bounties on grain exports.

These practical proposals, in all their variety, were knit together and given coherence by the political objectives. Control of the domestic economy aided foreign trade by directing the forces of the community to the production of its most salable commodities; sumptuary laws husbanded its wealth; colonies contributed to national self-sufficiency.

Though national strength was the most clearly recognizable purpose, mercantilism cannot be regarded as purely and simply a system of power. It was also a system of welfare. The economic activity of the commonwealth was *mobilized* for international rivalry; but at the same time it was *ordered* and *balanced* for the prosperity, employment, and security of its members and classes of members. The poor were many and their living was scant, but it was imperative that they should have employment, and some of the mercantilists even favored high wages. The rich were to accept responsibility in their spending, if sumptuary laws could be enforced. The merchant, the manufacturer, the lender, and the landlord were subject to state supervision which ran the whole gamut from standardization of goods to control of prices. Invention and enterprise were encouraged by subsidies, tariffs, and monopolies. The interests of the state fortunately coincided with the welfare of its citizens; the Prince and his subjects were to be a strong and disciplined, united and happy family.

Such an interpretation must not be regarded as an attempt to rehabilitate the mercantilists in the eyes of the modern critic. All their economic plans remain open to the criticism of the economist; but the fallacies are not so easily condemned when the ideal of state-making by both economic and political means is given its proper weight. The system is properly exposed to criticism in terms of individualist economics; but the parts of the system, when measured by the objectives they were intended to accomplish, seem much less confused and contradictory.

The most severe criticism of mercantilism should be aimed not so much at its economics as at its politics. It might be said that its advocates were guilty of no more than venial errors in their economic doctrines, but in their political theories they committed major crimes.

The most serious charge which the political philosopher can bring against them is directed at the most fundamental assumption of their whole system. One basic political implication exists in the work of all these writers; they were willing to extend greatly the powers of the state. It is a presumption which both makes and mars their conception of an ordered society; for they never investigated it to discover if it were justifiable. It is revealed by the lengths they were willing to go in allowing the state to control the economic structure. It is displayed in the pattern of the state in which they were ready to vest these powers; a pattern which made use of the powers of the monarch and assumed that the assent of the subjects could almost always be secured. In brief, they asserted the power of the state without investigating its nature or its sanctions.

Nor can they be freed from responsibility for this omission, for they encountered the important issues, veiled only slightly, in the problem of the monopolistic companies. There they were confronted with the question of who owned and managed the powers and privileges of government authority. Both the opponents and the advocates of the great companies realized that the harmony of interests was marred by discords; but even the critics were unwilling to pursue the discussion to its ultimate implications, or failed to realize the gravity of its meaning.

Making a detour round the deep issues implicit in monopoly, they took the state as it stood for granted. The monarch could be relied upon to safeguard the interests of the realm; the Parliament, while it was important, was usually an agency for publishing the popular consent. The duties of the classes were subordinated to the interests of the nation; and what is worse, those duties were unequally allotted. The lower classes bore the burden of all the work; they were guaranteed employment and subsistence, but little more. This attitude was not surprising. The state the mercantilists endowed with these great powers had been defended and supported by reputable political philosophers on other than economic grounds; there seemed no real necessity for examining its nature or defending its authority.

This initial assumption wore still another aspect. It was the strength of the state that was their chief concern; and from this strength the welfare of the members of the state was to follow. But this competitive power against other nations was attained by laying arduous duties upon some citizens, and granting privileges to others. The companies, the manufacturers, the merchants, and the merchant fleet were to be aided; the laborer and sometimes the landlord were asked to make sacrifices. The merchant princes were admitted to the councils of trade; the politically powerless were always in danger of exploitation. The same argument which sanctioned inequality of duties could be used to justify an unequal distribution of benefits.

Finally, this assumption led to a ferocious foreign policy in the relationships among states. Rivalry took the form of economic competition and political conflict; state-making in each state led to constant struggle between states. However little the mercantilists might like the possibility of a "wild state of nature" within the commonwealth, they expected and prepared for just such a condition in the community of nations. Their ideal state sold to all and bought from none, and freely used colonial aggrandizement, military and naval power, manufacturing skill, commercial connection, in fact, every means at its disposal, in order to come in first in the race with other nations.

Perhaps the mercantilists' interest in building a powerful state could be pleaded as extenuation for their failure to scrutinize the nature and character of the state they made. Practical merchants and manufacturers might well be more concerned with policies of action rather than questions of philosophical right. Curiously enough, they are open to a serious practical criticism. They dismissed very casually one of the most important problems of their program of state control; the continuous and urgent necessity of efficient administration.

They took for granted the capabilities of the government almost as readily as they had assumed the right of the state to extend its powers. They made only the most meager provision for machinery to carry out their projects. The sketchy proposals for councils of trade, for the establishment of banks, and for the creation of workhouses exhausted the suggestions they had to offer for implementing their policies. There is a plausible explanation for this; the objectives they set had a deceptive simplicity. Probably their purposes seemed in their eyes sufficiently specific to be executed by the existing government with only slight additions to its mechanism.

This easy confidence that the state could find the means to accomplish the desired ends, seems more astonishing when the mercantilists' attention to particular problems is recalled. They consistently supported schemes for the increase of population when their only knowledge of the population of England in their time was based on their own wild guesses. They proposed tariffs to secure a favorable balance of trade while they disputed among themselves the method by which that balance was to be computed. The granting of monopolies was cheerfully envisaged by many of the writers, though the effect of monopoly price upon the consuming population could not be satisfactorily calculated, and was, besides, one of the most hotly debated features of their system. The controls of wages, prices, and the quality of goods were vested in the justices of the peace, though it was known that the justices were scarcely competent to exercise such powers. The confidence in the existing structure of the state, manifest in their willingness to invest it with extensive powers, led the mercantilists to the belief that the government could successfully administer the varied tasks entailed in that broad grant of authority.

A further proof of their casual attitude toward the problems of administration is found in their proposals to entrust the performance of important public functions to individuals or private corporations. So important a part of their general scheme as the development of colonies was handed over to the management of the chartered companies, subjected to fluctuating and uncertain public control. Many of the projects for putting the indigent poor to work were to be handled by companies of capitalists who set up workhouses. Frequently the means of encouraging new manufactures was a grant of monopoly, or a subsidy; and the bargaining for such privileges very properly shocked the Puritan critics of the Stuart kings.

To summarize briefly, then, there are two fundamental criticisms of mercantilist political doctrine. The first and more serious charge is that they proposed a great extension of the powers of the state without any adequate analysis of its nature or any carefully reasoned justification for the grant of authority. Though the problem of monopoly very nearly forced the issues upon their notice, they failed to go behind the familiar facade of "the mixed English constitution." This resulted in a real risk of exploitation of the politically powerless; and therefore an unequal distribution of benefits and privileges in their commonwealth. Omnipotence in domestic affairs led to anarchy in international relations. There was, so to speak, a direct ratio between the degree of organization of the home economy and the ferocity of foreign policy. States competing so strenuously in peacetime, readily resorted to war in the national interest. The second criticism is important, but carries only practical, not moral or philosophical implications. The mercantilists assumed that the state which possessed such power would be able to administer the manifold and complicated functions required by their program. The specific character of their proposals concealed from them the problems of performance. Put in a sentence, the assertion of power carried for these merchant statesmen the presumptions both of right and of competence.

This commonwealth of merchant princes irresistibly suggests comparisons and contrasts with the totalitarian states of the present day. It is really impossible to conclude a discussion of mercantilist political doctrine without remarking that the Fascist, Nazi, and Soviet states are instances of neo-mercantilism, equipped with elaborate streamlined bureaucracies and the intense propaganda of modern nationalism. Though the mercantilists would surely recoil from acknowledging these dictatorships as descendants of the state they created, there are a few striking family traits which they would be embarrassed to deny.

The most unmistakable of the family features is immediately recognizable in both the mercantilists' state and the twentieth-century dictatorship, the aggressiveness of each toward the other states of their world. Fascist, Nazi, and Soviet policies of national self-sufficiency may be compared to the tariffs, the navigation laws, and the colonial system which were built upon the doctrine of the favorable balance of trade. Of course, the old duties, bounties and prohibitions seem crude compared to the marvelously intricate machinery of quotas, clearing agreements, and exchange controls devised by Dr. Schacht and his successors in Germany; and the demands for colonies, for *lebensraum,* and for trading privileges, in satellite states like the Balkans, are much more elaborate than the policies of the mercantilists toward the plantations. The assertion of the exclusive and uninhibited sovereignty of the state is a fundamental element common to both philosophies; and an international anarchy that may break out into open warfare at any moment has been the result of such irreconcilable claims. Though technique and structure may differ as times change, the perils of conflict between aggressive nations remain the same in any century. What is worse, peace is costly in such a world, for the effort to establish and maintain a self-sufficient economy, which in the seventeenth and eighteenth centuries called for higher shipping costs, as Samuel Fortrey admitted, now requires the exorbitant production costs of the *ersatz* industries or the high level of grain prices set by the "Battle of the Wheat."

The management of foreign trade to secure national advantage in a relentless competition between states entails, logically and practically, the mobilization of domestic activity. The controls proposed by the mercantilists over labor, prices, standards of manufacture, and the use of capital, reappear in the regimentation of workers, the rationing of raw materials, and the manipulation of credit in Germany, Italy, and Russia. The methods are much more complicated, taking advantage of the development of economic science, but the intentions are in essence identical. Whenever the interest of the nation is recognizable, then let the power of the state be felt in order to direct the productive power of the community into the channels contributing to national strength. The elaborate mechanism of the Russian Gosplan, or the intricate machinery of the corporative state, are but the seventeenth-century council of trade, or national bank, with powers covering a wider range of functions and possessing a more complex apparatus of supervision. The control of national consumption, an ideal the mercantilists had advocated, but which the admitted imperfections of sumptuary legislation had left unrealized, has been actually achieved for both rich and poor in the dictatorships by the ration card and the queue. The assignment of service to the classes has had added to it the discriminations against the Jews and the political dissenters.

Tempting as these analogies are, the similarities of policy and practice should not be pressed too far. The methods of totalitarian control are employed in a very different technological setting, and display a revolutionary intensity, that would be alien to the mercantile system. Enough has been said, however, to point out the basic resemblance of one to the other, the assertion of the exclusive rights of the national community in its dealings with the world outside, and the extensive authority of the state in the domestic economy. Fascist, Nazi, and Soviet dictatorships have revived and intensified the ideal of political and economic state-making.

It has already been suggested that this ideological kinship in purpose might be accompanied by similarities in the pattern of the state. Confidence in executive power is expressed by both the advocates for mercantilism and the propagandists for dictatorship; but even the most enthusiastic supporter of the Prince would resent the sight of him tricked out in the extravagant authority of *Il Duce* or *Der Fuehrer*. The merchant philosopher was willing to argue, in commonsense terms, that there was an obvious and substantial identity of interests between the ruler and his loyal subjects, which made executive authority worthy of trust while it was prompt and effective in getting things done. But he would balk at subscribing to a modern mysticism which claimed that the Leader embodied in his person the national spirit, or the racial genius, or the full intellectual comprehension of the design of a Marxian millennium. Nevertheless, both mercantilism and totalitarianism must vest a great authority in the executive; for the rapid accomplishment of extensive programs cannot be achieved without the concentration of power.

Again, while popular assent was and is an essential condition for the realization of the objectives of a planned national economy, no mercantilist would be ready to see his Parliament degenerate into a mere cheering section. Nor would he be satisfied with a series of corporative councils or soviets, unless such bodies possessed some small degree of right to be consulted and power to advise. He would, of course, be amazed at the fanfare of propaganda; though he was himself an able and not too scrupulous pamphleteer. But much as in the case of executive authority, the mercantilist would scarcely be able to deny the tell-tale family resemblance between his state and the modern dictatorship. In both it is assumed that the broad declaration of national interest will secure public assent; representative bodies will therefore automatically reflect support for government policy.

If this power of the executive and the presumption of consent is once granted, groups that lack effective political influence constantly stand in peril of exploitation. The mercantilists asked the poor to accept a poor living and heavy tasks; the modern dictatorship holds down wages and lengthens hours by means of an elaborate labor or-

ganization and a system of labor courts. At least the mercantilist had no prejudices against alien racial or national
groups; it has been the leaders of the one-party state who
have revived medieval discriminations against the Jews
and other racial or national minorities. In both systems,
however, the danger of inequality of duty and benefit is
always present; for the superior claims of the state can be
used to justify both, and even the communist society in
Russia cannot be exempted from this charge.

One criticism of the mercantilists' state, the easy assumption of competence and consequent disregard for problems of administration, cannot be leveled at the totalitarian state. There, in fact, an opposite complaint may
be made, for there seems to be no activity so trivial as not
to employ an army of government and party bureaucrats.
From the recreational activities of laborers to the cere-
monies of religious observance the most minute detail is
given close attention, and appropriate organizations pro-
liferate from state and party. The merchant of the eighteenth century was, in that simple era, innocent of the arts
of advertising and publicity, and would be dumbfounded
by the terrifying ballyhoo of national propaganda used
today.

A comparison of the underlying ideas, and even the
essentials of structure, in the state as conceived and defended by the advocates of the mercantile system in the
eighteenth century, and the totalitarian state of the twentieth, yields some instructive analogies. The broad assertion of sovereignty, the international anarchy, the risks of
exploitation of the classes without political influence, appear in both. Even the structure proposed for the state,
expressing reliance upon executive power and presuming
popular consent, is recognizably similar in the two systems. The combination of political and economic objectives, when animated by an uncritical emphasis on national patriotism, seems to create dangers to the world and

to the individual, regardless of the century in which it occurs.

One more observation is suggested by the present-day renaissance of nationalism and state authority. The revival of economic nationalism, embittering international affairs and fully controlling domestic economy, reduces laisser-faire to a viewpoint held for but a brief interlude between two periods of rampant devotion to the state and the nation. After all, the acceptance of laissez-faire economics was based on the attractive conceptions of division of labor, market determination of exchange value, and the effectiveness of these forces in apportioning the use of labor and capital in productive activity. These principles, when presented by the skillful advocacy of Adam Smith or the rigid logic of Ricardo, offered a method superior to that of extensive state control for increasing the wealth of nations, particularly that of the home country. Needless to say, the freedom of action granted to individual enterprise was of vital importance to the invention and use of new techniques, and to the expanding activity of the Industrial Revolution.

The most ardent defender of classical economics must admit, however, that laisser-faire was always as much a myth as it was a reality. From the very beginning of industrial change it has been possible for monopoly advantage or group interest to defeat, partially at least, the beneficent control of the invisible hand of self-interest, which was expected to guide economic action intelligently, and distribute benefits fairly. Moreover, humanitarian concern over the labor of women and children, and recognition of the public interest and need for government intervention in such a field as transport, have led to policies that demonstrated that the self-regulating character of a society operating under economic laws, could not always be depended upon to care for the general welfare. The action of groups and the action of government led to a growing rigidity of prices and wages which impeded the ready flow of the forces of production in response to market demand. While this was happening at home in all industrialized nations, the policies of governments toward international trade—despite English adoption of free trade in the latter half of the nineteenth century—made illusory the cosmopolitan assumptions of individualist economics so far as exchange of goods and services across national boundaries was concerned. Mercantilism persisted, so to speak, in the forms of protectionism; and regulation of the home economy proposed by reformers anxious to mitigate abuses, restricted the activity of individual enterprise.

The most real difficulty with laisser-faire as a practical policy was probably political rather than economic. It is difficult to rouse enthusiastic support for such abstract ideas as the maintenance of a free competitive market, determination of exchange value through the pricing system, the organization of production by allowing capital and labor to flow unimpeded in search of profit and employment. For a time such ideas enjoyed public approval because they seemed to be logically linked to the rise of democratic political theory, with its emphasis upon individual liberty and civil and political equality. Economic man, at best a rather dismal and selfish fellow, shared the popularity of his twin, political man, an engaging reformer, who promised improvement in the lot of the great majority of people.

As the Industrial Revolution advanced from one technical triumph to the next, large groups of people became dependent for their livelihood and comfort on the continuous activity of enterprise organized on a great scale. The opportunities open to individual initiative, however active and industrious, were restricted, or seemed to be, by the overwhelming importance of corporate activity with huge capital resources. The way was then open for Fascist, Nazi, or Communist leadership to mobilize a mass following by promising that the community, the state, the nation, or even the race, would take charge of the whole economy and take care of all the citizens. These leaders were able to make use of a remarkably enduring sentiment of ancient origin, loyalty to the group of which all are members, whether it be family, tribe, or nation.

In this last respect the totalitarian state offers, as did the mercantilists, a system of welfare as well as a system of power. It promises, at least, a secure place in the society to all the members of the national family. It rallies large numbers of its citizens to its support by a program of education and recreation; and it inculcates in them a feeling of participation in a great national effort while it holds out hope of improvement in the standard of living. The Italian labor syndicates, the Nazi Labor Front, and the Soviet trade unions constitute a system of social insurance and presumed representation of workers, organized and animated by the party, and linked to the party program. Besides these establishments there are the labor courts and the mechanisms of price control and rationing, which are widely publicized as means of protecting and improving the lot of the common man. The extent to which the goods promised have actually been delivered is actually little. Comparisons of real and money wages over periods of time and from country to country are admittedly difficult and likely to be misleading; but there seems to be fairly substantial evidence to show that the situation of the working man in the totalitarian state has not improved, and probably has deteriorated. The colored spotlights of the propaganda campaigns obscure the hard facts of all the three- and four- and five-year plans.

The new mercantilism, however, has evoked support by resort to an old mysticism. The grandeur that was Rome has been revived to infuse an ardent sense of patriotic devotion to a state that is Fascismo; the legend of an Aryan race has been employed to create an active contemporary consciousness of a primeval Teutonic kinship; the promise of a Communist millennium can outweigh for years the creature comforts of cosmetics and silk stockings. The mercantilists' metaphor of the national household has reappeared as a powerful engine of statecraft; and the ties of blood and doctrine suffice to justify the new and bitter sacrifices demanded by the clan. Small wonder that the blare of the trumpets and the marching rhythm of the parades can overwhelm the cool calculation of marginal increments of utility that guided the sober conduct of economic man!

It is this readiness to assert the claims of the state that once led the mercantilists, and now prompts the dictators, to create a deadly anarchy in international affairs and a ruthless inequality at home. The domestic aspect of uncritical patriotism produces a grim exploitation of the groups and classes who are not in possession of political influence; while the aggressive nature of national foreign policy subjects them to the perils of a dangerous world. Yet, when the work of the mercantilists is reviewed, or the doctrines of the totalitarian state are objectively analyzed, it is easy to see that their leaders, whether they lived in the eighteenth century or now, have laid hold of one fundamental social fact, the interdependence of economic and political phenomena. It is in this respect that the mercantilists measure up well if compared to their contemporaries, the English political philosophers; for these merchants and manufacturers had a firm grip upon reality, and gave less attention to the refinements of theological and theoretical doctrine. They dealt with both the political and economic affairs of their time.

A final lesson may be read, then, in both the political doctrines of the mercantile system and the excesses of twentieth-century dictatorship. The democratic state must devise methods for assuring some of the benefits of collective action, while it safeguards the genuine social values of freedom of speech and criticism, and a maximum sphere of liberty for individual action. In meeting these problems, the separation of economic and political theory, which occurred during the nineteenth century, has done some injury to the social sciences. If the world is to be made safe and happy, the economists and political scientists must revive and improve the study which the mercantilists began—the art and science of political economy.

Bibliographical Notes

The following notes, as explained in the preface, are placed here at the back of the book to avoid overloading the pages of the text with lengthy footnotes. These notes are referred to by the footnotes in the text, and occur here in the sequence in which those references are made. Each note here is preceded by page number, note number, and chapter number, so that its reference is clear. For example: p. 2, n. 1, I, given at the beginning of the first note below, means the reference is found at page 2 of the text, footnote 1 on that page, in Chapter I. The following notes are numbered accordingly.

p. 2, n. 1, I.
The scholarly literature on the subject of mercantilism displays a very interesting cycle of opinion. Adam Smith's criticism of the mercantile system in the fourth book of *The Wealth of Nations* established its nature for a long time as essentially a gold-getting and gold-keeping commercial policy. Perhaps one of the most impressive tributes to the power of thought and the energy of style of the great Scottish philosopher lies in the significant fact that his errors, as well as his principal doctrines, perpetuated themselves in the thinking of succeeding scholars. That his critique of mercantilism stood as well for an accurate description of the system is evidenced by such works as Ingram, J. K., *A History of Political Economy,* revised edition, London, 1905 (first published in 1888), pp. 34-35; Blanqui, J. A., *A History of Political Economy in Europe,* translated from the 9th French edition by Emily J. Leonard, New York, 1882, pp. 308-309, 312; Eisenhart, H., *Geschichte der Nationalökonomie,* Jena, 1891, pp. 15-25; Espinas, A. V., *Histoire des Doctrines Économiques,* Paris, 1891, pp. 137-138; Cossa, L., *An Introduction to the Study of Political Economy,* translated by Louis Dyer, London, 1893, pp. 194-195, 210; Dubois, A., *Précis de l'Histoire des Doctrines Économique dans leurs Rapports avec les Faits et avec les In-*

195

stitutions, Paris, 1903, in the definition of "le mercantilisme pur" and "le mercantilisme dégradé," p. 217; Rambaud, J., *Histoire des Doctrines Économiques,* Paris, 1909, pp. 104-143.

Naturally enough, it was the work of the economic historians which imposed extensive modification on such a picture of the mercantilist system. When the practice of national states in the period was investigated it soon became clear that a more inclusive description must be found, which took into account other aspects than the desire for treasure and the favorable balance of trade. The first edition of Archdeacon Cunningham's *Growth of English Industry and Commerce* appeared in 1882, and established a much more accurate analysis of the range of mercantilist policy. Two years earlier Edmund Freiherr von Heyking in his *Geschichte der Handelsbilanztheorie* had connected the rise of the theory with the rise of the nationalist state. Professor Gustav Schmoller's classic essay, *The Mercantile System and its Historical Significance,* was translated by Sir William Ashley in 1895, and after that the clearly nationalist character and the wide scope of mercantilist economic policy was accepted by the historians of economic theory. Some works which adopt this general interpretation are: von Erdberg-Krcenciewski, R., *Johann Joachim Becher, ein Beitrag zur Geschichte der Nationalökonomie* (In *Staatswissenschaftlichen Studien von Elster,* 6 Band, 2 Heft, pp. 217-357, Jena, 1896); Dühring, E., *Kritische Geschichte der Nationalökonomie und des Socialismus von ihren Anfang bis zur Gegenwart,* Leipzig, 1900; Schacht, H.G.H., *Der Theoretische Gehalt des Englischen Merkantilismus,* Berlin, 1900. More recent accounts of the development of economic thought have sustained this broad interpretation: Oncken, A., *Geschichte der Nationalökonomie,* Leipzig, 1922; Gonnard, R., *Histoire des Doctrines Économiques,* Paris, 1924; Haney, L. H., *History of Economic Thought,* revised edition, 1924.

In the past few years there have appeared some studies of the mercantile system which have added greatly to our knowledge of the doctrines. The first of these is E. S. Furniss' admirable study, *The Position of the Laborer in a System of Nationalism,* Boston, 1920, which gives a brilliant analysis of the labor doctrines held by these writers, with ample documentation. The outlines of the whole system are made clear as well as the full import of the theories of the place of labor in the national economy. The most comprehensive and extensive survey of mercantilism in Europe is made in Professor Heckscher's two volumes, *Mercantilism,* translated into English by Mendel Shapiro, London, 1935. This is a fine work of scholarship. Professor E. A. J. Johnson, in his *Predecessors of Adam Smith,* New York, 1937, carefully analyzes the work of a number of the most distinguished of the British mercantilists, and M. Beer's *Early British Economics,* London, 1938, makes a survey of the development of economic ideas from their medieval origins to the time of Adam Smith with insight and careful documentation, though the work is compact. Professor Viner made a careful analysis of the foreign trade theories, illustrated by admirably chosen quotations, in an article published in two issues of the *Journal of Political Economy,* June and August, 1930, Vol. XXXVIII, 249-301, 404-457, under the title "Early English Theories of Trade before Adam Smith."

As their titles imply, however, these studies are concerned with the development of economic theory. While every study of the mercantile system must deal with its political and nationalist character, the political ideas have never been carefully analyzed. Professor Heckscher devotes two sections of his second volume (Part II, "Mercantilism as a System of Power," Vol. II, pp. 13-49, and Part V, "Mercantilism as a Conception of Society," Vol. II, pp. 269-324) to an examination of other aspects than the purely economic ideas, but he does not deal closely with the mercantilist conception of the state.

p. 25, n. 15, II.

Some of the important and curious writings, in addition to those already cited, which declare the doctrine, are as follows, in roughly chronological order: [Bennett, Edward], *A Treatise divided into three parts . . . touching . . . Tobacco,* [1620]; Robinson, Henry, *England's Safety in Trades Encrease,* London, 1641; Maddison, Ralph Kt., *Great Britain's Remembrancer, Looking In and Out,* London, 1655; Fortrey, Samuel,

England's Interest and Improvement, London, 1673 (in Mc-Culloch, J. R., *Early English Tracts on Commerce,* London, 1856); Anon., *The East India Trade a most Profitable Trade to the Kingdom,* London, 1677; Anon., *Dialogue between Content and Complaint,* London, 1677 (in McCulloch, J. R., *op. cit.*); [B., J.], *An Account of the French Usurpation upon the Trade of England,* London, 1679; Child, Sir Josiah, *Trade and the Interest of Money Considered,* London, [1668] and *Discourses of Trade,* London, 1690; Clement, Simon, *A Discourse of the General Notions of Money, Trade, and Exchanges,* London, 1695; Locke, John, *Considerations on the Consequences of Lowering the Interest,* London, 1692, and *Further Considerations,* London, 1695; Anon., *Aggravvii Venetiani,* London, 1697, an amusing account of the losses of the trade with Venice and her island of Zant; Davenant, Charles, *An Essay on the Probable Methods of making the People Gainers in the Balance of Trade,* London, 1699; Cary, John, *An Essay on the State of England, in relation to its Trade,* etc., London and Bristol, 1695, and *An Essay towards Regulating the Trade, and Employing the Poor, of this Kingdom,* London, 1717; Paxton, P. (M.D.), *A Discourse concerning the Nature, Advantage, and Improvement of Trade,* London, 1704; King, Charles, compiler, *The British Merchant,* London, 1713; Wood, William, *A Survey of Trade,* second edition, London, 1719; Defoe, Daniel, *A Plan of the English Commerce,* London, 1728, and numerous other works; Gee, Joshua, *Trade and Navigation of Great Britain Considered,* London, 1731; Berkeley, George, *The Querist,* London, 1734-36, edited by J. H. Hollander, Baltimore, Johns Hopkins University Press, 1910; Vanderlint, Jacob, *Money Answers All Things,* London, 1734, edited by J. H. Hollander, Baltimore, Johns Hopkins University Press, 1914; Decker, Sir Matthew, *Essay on the Decline of the Foreign Trade,* London, 1739; Anon., *A Speech delivered in Parliament by a person of Honor, wherein is shown the cause and cure of the decay of Trade,* London, 1739; Postlethwayt, Malachy, *Dissertation upon the Plan of the Universal Dictionary of Trade and Commerce,* London, 1749 (attributed to him, but not with complete certainty) and *Great Britain's Commercial Interest Explained and Improved,* London, 1759, and *Dictionary of Commerce,* London, 1760-74, many editions, and *Britain's True System,* London, 1757; Law, John, *Money and Trade,* Glasgow, 1750; [Harris, Joseph], *An Essay upon Money and Coins,* London, 1757; Mildmay, Sir William, *The Laws and Policy of England, Relating to Trade,* London, 1765; Mortimer, Thomas, *The Elements of Commerce, Politics, and Finances,* London, 1772; [Young, Arthur], *Political Essays concerning the Present State of the British Empire,* London, 1772.

This is by no means an exhaustive list, but it indicates the persistence of the doctrine throughout the seventeenth and eighteenth centuries, and contains most of the important and interesting items.

p. 33, n. 34, II.

Some of the other works by various authors putting forward this same type of argument, and where it is extended to other commodities than wool the fact is indicated, follow in roughly chronological order:

Anon., *Leather: A Discourse,* London, 1629, argues for leather as its title implies; Robinson, Henry, *Briefe Considerations concerning the Advancement of Trade and Navigation,* London, 1649; [Haines, Richard], *The Prevention of Poverty,* London, 1674, linen as well as wool; Anon., *The Proverb Crossed,* London, 1677; [Carter, W.], *The Usurpations of France upon the Trade of the Woollen Manufacturers of England,* London, 1696; [Cox, Sir Richard], *Some thoughts on the Bill . . . for prohibiting the exportation of the Woolen Manufacture of Ireland to foreign ports,* London, 1698; [Blanch, John], *The Beaux Merchant,* London, 1714; [Forman, C.], *The Importance of the Ostend Company Consider'd,* London, 2nd ed., 1726; D'Anvers, Caleb, *The Craftsman,* a periodical, Vol. I, no. 15, Jan. 23, 1727; [Defoe, Daniel], *An Humble Proposal to the People of England,* London, 1729; Anon., *Remarks on the English Woollen Manufacture,* London, 1730; Anon., *Some Thoughts on the Woollen Manufacture,* London, 1731; [Lindsay, Patrick], *Reasons for encouraging the Linnen Manufacture,* London, 1735, deals with linen as the title implies; Anon., *A Letter from a Merchant who has left off trade,* London, 1738, deals with linen; Anon., *A Speech delivered in Parliament by a person of Honor,* London, 1739, deals with staples as well as wool; Anon., *Dissertation on the Present Conjuncture,* London, 1739; London, John of Tiverton, *Some Considerations on the Importance of the Woollen Manufactures,* London, 1740; Smith, John, *A Review of the Manufacturer's Complaints against the Wool Grower,* London, 1753; Dyer, John, *The Fleece,* London, 1757; Campbell, John, *A Political Survey of Great Britain,* London, 1774, two immense volumes, Book VI, Ch. IV, deals with the encouragement of all manufactures.

p. 36, n. 43, II.

Some recommendations for establishing the fishing trade, in addition to those cited, follow in roughly chronological order:

[R., I.], *The Trades Increase,* London, 1615; Malynes, Gerard de, *Consuetudo, vel, Lex Mercatoria, or the Antient Law Merchant,* London, 1636, ch. xlvii; Jenner, Thomas, *London's Blame, if not its Shame,* [London], 1651; [Bland, John], *Trade Revived,* London, 1659, pp. 8 et seq.; Anon., ΙΧΘΥΟΘΗΡΑ *or the Royal Trade of Fishing,* London, 1661-62; L'Estrange, Sir Roger, *A Discourse of the Fishery,* London, 1674; Collins, John, *Salt and Fishery,* London, 1682; [Chamberlin, Hugh and Dalby Thomas (?)], *A Proposal for encouraging of Persons . . . for the erecting and managing of Trade by a General Fishery,* London, ca. 1695; [Chamberlin, Hugh], *A Supplement to the proposal for a general Fishery,* London, ca. 1695; Killigrew, William, *An Essay upon the Necessity of raising the Value of Twenty Millions of Pounds,* London, 1695 (?); Elking, Henry, *A View of the Greenland Trade and the Whale Fishery,* London, 1722 (in McCulloch, J. R., *A Select Collection of Scarce and Valuable Economic Tracts,* London, 1859, pp. 63-103); Dobbs, Arthur, *An Essay on the Trade and Improvement of Ireland,* Dublin, 1729-31, pp. 105-137; [Little, Otis], *The State of Trade in the Northern Colonies Considered,* London, 1748.

Besides these items similar proposals are to be found in the work of a number of more celebrated writers such as John

Cary, Charles Davenant, Joshua Gee, John Pollexfen, Malachy Postlethwayt, Henry Robinson, and Sir William Temple.

p. 39, n. 54, II.

Other works demanding controls of standards and prices follow in roughly chronological order:

Robinson, Henry, *England's Safety in Trade's Encrease,* London, 1641, pp. 17-18; Anon., *Leather: A Discourse,* London, 1629; S., W. Gent., *The Golden Fleece,* London, 1656, especially Ch. XIV; Anon., *England's Glory by the Benefit of Wool,* London, 1669; Carter, W., *England's Interest by Trade Asserted,* London, 1671, pp. 35-36; Coke, Roger, *A Treatise . . . that the Church and State of England are in equal danger with the trade of it,* London, 1671, pp. 87-90 of the Epilogue to the first treatise. Interesting because he is more of a cosmopolitan economist than a mercantilist, but still he favors these controls of standards. (This work is hereafter cited as Coke, Roger, *Treatise.*) Vickaris, A., *An Essay for the Regulating of the Coyn,* London, 1696, p. 2; Pollexfen, John, *England and East India inconsistent in their Maufactures,* London, 1697, p. 52; Davenant, Charles, *Discourse of the Public Revenues,* London, 1698 (in *Works,* Vol. I, pp. 422 et seq.); Anon., *A Dialogue between Mr. Smith, M. Ragouse,* etc., London, 1701, pp. 3-4; Povey, Charles, *The Unhappiness of England,* London, 1701; Paterson, William, *Proposals for a Council of Trade,* Edinburgh, 1701, p. 15; Anon., *A Discourse on Trade, more particularly on Sugar and Tobacco,* London, 1733, pp. 20-22; [Postlethwayt, Malachy], *Dissertation upon the plan of the Universal Dictionary of Trade and Commerce,* London, 1749.

p. 52, n. 85, II.

For similar statements of interest in agriculture see the following:

[Child, Sir Josiah], *A Short Addition to the Observations concerning Trade and the Interest of Money,* London, 1668; [Bethel, Slingsby], *The World's Mistake in Oliver Cromwell,* London, 1668; Davenant, Charles, *An Essay upon the Probable Methods of making a People Gainers in the Ballance of*

Trade, 2nd ed., London, 1700; Paxton; P., *A Discourse concerning the Nature, Advantage and Improvement of Trade,* London, 1704, especially pp. 10-11, 80, but he condemns enclosures; Dobbs, Arthur, *An Essay upon the Trade and Improvement of Ireland,* Dublin, 1729-31, pp. 79-92; Decker, Sir Matthew, *An Essay on the Decline of the Foreign Trade,* London, 1739; Tucker, Josiah, *The Elements of Commerce, and Theory of Taxes,* Bristol, 1755, pp. 44-75.

p. 57, n. 94, II.

Nearly all the mercantilists, if they deal with the subject of shipping and navigation, advance the political argument for the navigation acts, but some of the strong statements of the case follow, in roughly chronological order:

Hitchcock, Robert, *A Pollitique Platt,* London, 1580; Anon., *A Briefe Note of the Benefits that grow to this Realme by the Observation of Fish Daies,* London, 1595; Sharpe, Edward, *Britaine's Busse,* London, 1615; Evelyn, John, *Navigation and Commerce, their Original and Progress,* London, 1674 (in McCulloch, J. R., *A Select Collection of Scarce and Valuable Tracts on Commerce,* London, 1859, pp. 29-103); Maydman, Henry, *Naval Speculations and Maritime Politicks,* London, 1691, especially pp. 239-300; [Harris, Sir Walter], *Remarks on the Trade of England and Ireland,* London, 1691; Clement, Simon, *A Discourse of the General Notions of Money, Trade, and Exchanges,* London, 1695; Brewster, Sir Francis, *New Essays on Trade,* London, 1702; Wood, William, *A Survey of Trade,* 2nd ed., London, 1719, especially pp. 136-7; Elking, Henry, *A View of the Greenland Trade,* London, 1722 (in McCulloch, *op. cit.,* pp. 63-103); [Hall, F.], *Importance of the British Plantations in America,* London, 1731; [Lyttelton, George], *Considerations upon the Present State of Our Affairs,* London, 1739; Perrin, William, *Present State of the British and French Sugar Colonies,* London, 1740, an interesting argument, in strict mercantilist terms, for relaxing somewhat the navigation laws; Horsley, William, *A Treatise on Maritime Affairs,* London, 1744; Anon., *Considerations on the Utility and Necessity of a Marine in every Trading Country,* London, 1756; Postlethwayt,

Malachy, *Great Britain's Commercial Interest Explained and Improved,* 2nd ed., London, 1759, Vol. II, Dissertation xxviii, and *Dictionary of Trade and Commerce,* 4th ed., London, 1774, under title "Colonies"; [Sheffield, John Baker H., First Earl of], *Observations on the Commerce of the American States,* London, 1783; Sheffield, John Baker H., First Earl of, *Strictures on the Necessity of Inviolably Maintaining the Navigation and Colonial System of Great Britain,* London, 1804.

These citations could be multiplied indefinitely, but the above items are all defenses of the system, and can be taken as additions to the works of Mun, Temple, Fortrey, Steuart, and other classical expressions of the argument.

p. 58, n. 96, II.

Besides the works cited in the preceding Note, the statement of the economic argument was made by Mun; Berkeley, George, *Essay Towards preventing the Ruin of Great Britain,* London, 1721 (in *Works,* ed. by Alex. Campbell Fraser, Oxford, 1871, Vol. III, pp. 193-211); Gee, Joshua, *Trade and Navigation,* 3rd. ed., London, 1731, Ch. XXV; Davenant, Charles, *Discourses on the Public Revenues and on Trade,* London, 1698 (in *Works,* ed. by Sir Charles Whitworth, London, 1771, Vol. II, pp. 10-29).

p. 59, n. 101, II.

Some other expressions of the general argument on colonies, as an extension of the economy of the realm, follow in chronological order:

Malynes, Gerard de, *The Center of the Circle of Commerce,* London, 1623, Ch. xlvi; Cary, John, *A Discourse concerning the Trade of Ireland and Scotland,* London, 1696, especially pp. 5-6; Anon., *An Essay upon the Government of the English Plantations,* London, 1701; [Oldmixon, John], *The British Empire in America,* London, 1708, 2 Vols., especially the introduction to Vol. I; Anon., *Some Considerations on the late Mismanagement of the South Sea Stock,* London, [1720], pp. 19-23; Anon., *Directions to judge whether a Nation be in a Thriving Condition,* London, 1729; *The Craftsman* (a periodical, published 1726-33), London, no. 130, Dec. 28, 1728, and no. 133, Jan. 18, 1733; Anon. ed., *Select Tracts relating to the Colonies,* London, [1732]; Anon., *A Speech . . . by a person of Honor . . .* London, 1739; Ashley, John, *Memoirs and Considerations concerning the Trade and Revenues of the British Colonies,* London, 1740; Pownall, Thomas, *The Administration of the Colonies,* London, 1765, especially pp. 200-202; Mortimer, Thomas, *The Elements of Commerce,* London, 1772, especially pp. 150-158.

All the above works state the general argument for colonies, but every discussion of the colonies also states the general concept of incorporating the plantations into the British national economy, so the reader is referred to all the citations regarding colonies.

p. 60, n. 102, II.

Some other statements of the advantage of the colonies as a means of taking care of population follow: [Vaughan, William], *The Golden Fleece,* London, 1626, especially Part III, p. 13; Robinson, Henry, *England's Safety in Trades Encrease,* London, 1641, p. 13; Anon. ed., *Select Tracts relating to Colonies,* London, [1732]; Anon., *Miscellaneous Reflections on the Peace,* London, 1749; [Ignotus], *Thoughts on Trade in General,* London, 1763.

p. 61, n. 104, II.

The fear of depopulating England by emigration to the colonies had been expressed by Coke, Roger, *Treatise,* London, 1671, pp. 1-36; and the necessity for a large population had been stressed by many writers, Paxton, P., *A Discourse concerning the Nature, Advantage and Improvement of Trade,* London, 1704, pp. 45-68, might be mentioned as an instance.

Writings in which the fear of depopulation is recognized as a commonly expressed viewpoint, and in which the counter argument of the imperial economy is developed to refute such alarm follow:

[Littleton, Edward], *The Groans of the Plantations,* London, 1689, pp. 28-31; Cary, John, *An Essay on the State of*

England, Bristol, 1695, pp. 67-68; Ferguson, Robert, *A Just and Modest Vindication of the Scots Design,* London, 1699; Wood, William, *A Survey of Trade,* 2nd ed., London, 1719, pp. 136-138; [Martyn, Benjamin], *Reasons for establishing the Colony of Georgia,* London, 1733; [Campbell, John], *Candid and Impartial Considerations on the Nature of the Sugar Trade,* London, 1763.

p. 62, n. 106, II.

Nearly every author dealing with the subject of the trade with the colonies emphasizes the importance of the market for British goods there, but some of the more decisive statements occur in the following:

[Littleton, Edward], *The Groans of the Plantations,* London, 1689, pp. 26-28; Davenant, Charles, *An Essay upon the East India Trade,* London, 1697, and *Discourse of the Public Revenues,* London, 1698 (both in *Works,* ed. Sir Charles Whitworth, London, 1771, Vol. I); Defoe, Daniel, *A Plan of the English Commerce,* London, 1728 (reprinted, Oxford, 1928); Gee, Joshua, *Trade and Navigation,* 3rd ed., London, 1731, especially Ch. XXXI; Keith, Sir William, Bart., *A Collection of Papers,* 2nd ed., London, 1749; Postlethwayt, Malachy, *Great Britain's Commercial Interest Explained and Improved,* 2nd ed., London, 1759; [Campbell, John], *Candid and Impartial Considerations on the Nature of the Sugar Trade,* London, 1763; [Grenville, George], *The Regulations lately made concerning the Colonies,* London, 1765; Ray, Nicholas, *The Importance of the Colonies of North America,* London, 1766; Anon., *American Husbandry,* London, 1775.

p. 63, n. 108, II.

The argument for controlling colonial manufacture so that their complementary relationship with the mother country would be maintained is a commonplace of the mercantilist literature. Some statements of it follow:

Child, Sir Josiah, *Trade and the Interest of Money Considered,* London, 1669, Ch. X; Cary, John, *An Essay on the State of England,* Bristol, 1695, especially p. 71; Anon., *Some Reasons for a Farther Encouragement of Bringing Naval Stores from America* [London, 1713]; Wood, William, *A Survey of Trade,* London, 1719, pp. 136-148; Anon., *A Letter to a Member of Parliament, concerning the Naval Stores Bill,* London, 1720; [Hall, F.], *The Importance of the British Plantations in America,* London, 1731; [Bennett, John], *The National Merchant,* London [1736]; Keith, Sir William, Bart., *The History of the British Plantations,* London, 1738; [Little, Otis], *The State of Trade in the Northern Colonies Considered,* London, 1748; [McCulloch, William T.], *A Miscellaneous Essay concerning the Courses pursued by Great Britain in the Affairs of her Colonies,* London, 1755, especially pp. 82-102; Anon., *An Examination into the Value of Canada and Guadeloupe,* London, 1761; Massie, J., *General Propositions relating to Colonies,* [London, 1761]; Anon., *An Essay on the Trade of the Northern Colonies,* London, 1764; Mildmay, Sir William, *The Laws and Policy of England, Relating to Trade,* London, 1765, especially pp. 33-88; Pownall, Thomas, *The Administration of the Colonies,* London, 1765, especially pp. 200-202; [Fothergill, John], *Considerations relative to the North American Colonies,* London, 1765, asking for moderation in the policy, but asserting the fundamental viewpoint nevertheless; Anon., *The True Interest of Great Britain with respect of her American Colonies,* London, 1766; [Mitchell, John], *The Present State of Great Britain and North America,* London, 1767; Anon., *The Importance of the British Dominions in India,* London, 1770; [Young, Arthur], *Political Essays concerning the Present State of the British Empire,* London, 1772, especially pp. 328-343; Campbell, John, *A Political Survey of Great Britain,* London, 1774, especially Book V, Ch. VI; [Knox, William], *The Interest of the Merchants and Manufacturers of Great Britain,* London, 1774.

There are occasional notes of disagreement in this chorus of empire economists, like the liberal views of [Bollan, William], *The Mutual Interest of Great Britain and America,* London, 1765.

The relative merits of the sugar colonies of the West Indies and the commercial and industrial nature of the northern colonies, coupled with the question of the trade between the colonies, occasionally led to little outbursts of argument over the imperial system, with slightly unseemly demonstrations by the interest groups involved. Following are some samples of these conflicts of interest within the empire:

Anon., *The Importance of the Sugar Colonies to Great Britain Stated,* London, 1731; Anon., *Considerations on the Bill now depending in Parliament concerning the British Sugar Colonies in America,* London, 1731; Anon., *A Comparison between the British Sugar Colonies and New England,* London [1732]; Anon., *A Supplement to the Detection of the Present Sugar Plantations,* London, 1733; Anon., *The Case of the British Northern Colonies,* [London, 1745]; [B., M.], *A Letter to the West India Merchants,* London, 1751.

p. 69, n. 127, II.

Some of the principal critics of duties, bounties, and prohibitions follow:

Robinson, Henry, *England's Safety in Trades Encrease,* London, 1641, pp. 8-12, and *Briefe Considerations concerning the Advancement of Trade and Navigation,* London, 1649; Child, Sir Josiah, *Trade and the Interest of Money Considered,* London, 1669; [Bethel, Slingsby], *The Present Interest of England Stated,* London, 1671; [Petty, Sir William], *A Treatise of Taxes and Contributions,* London, 1679; [Petyt, William], *Britannia Languens,* London, 1680; K., C., *Some Seasonable and Modest Thoughts,* London, 1696; Davenant, Charles, *Essay on Ways and Means,* London, 1695 (in *Works,* ed., Sir Charles Whitworth, London, 1771, Vol. I, p. 30), *An Essay upon the East India Trade,* London, 1697 (in *Works,* I, pp. 98-99), and *Report to the Honourable the Commissioners,* London, 1712 (in *Works,* Vol. V, pp. 378-9, 387-88); [Cox, Sir Richard], *Some Thoughts on the Bill . . . for prohibiting the exportation of the Woolen Manufacture of Ireland,* London, 1698; Paxton, P., *A Discourse concerning the Nature, Advantage, and Improvement of Trade,* London, 1704, pp. 13-14; Anon., *A Discourse on Trade more particularly Sugar and Tobacco,* London, 1733; Anon., *Reflections and Considerations . . . on Foreign Linens,* London, 1738; Vanderlint, Jacob, *Money Answers All Things,* London, 1734; Decker,

Sir Matthew, *Essay on the Decline of the Foreign Trade*, London, 1739; [Richardson, William], *Essay on the Causes of the Decline of the Foreign Trade*, London, 1744; Anon., *Considerations Relating to the Laying any Additional Duty on Sugar from the British Plantations*, London, 1747; Anon., *The State of the Sugar Trade*, London, 1747; Tucker, Josiah, *The Elements of Commerce*, Bristol, 1755; [Whately, George], *Principles of Trade*, London, 1774.

Very few of the above propose any more than a modification of some part of the tariff policies; almost all of them believe in the general scheme of tariffs.

p. 70, n. 130, II.

The critics of the restrictive aspects of the colonial policy are more numerous:

[Petyt, William], *Britannia Languens*, London, 1680, section XI; Anon., *Remarks upon a book entitled "The Present State of the Sugar Colonies, Considered,"* London, 1731; Keith, Sir William Bart., *The History of the British Plantations in America*, London, 1738, especially p. 13; Decker, Sir Matthew, *Essay on the Decline of the Foreign Trade*, London, 1739; Ashley, John, *Memoirs and Considerations concerning the Trade and Revenues of the British Colonies in America*, London, 1740; Anon., *Considerations against laying any new duty on Sugar*, London, 1744; Anon., *A Letter to a Member of Parliament on the importance of the American Colonies*, London, 1757; [Bollan, William], *The Mutual Interest of Great Britain and the American Colonies Considered*, London, 1765; Ray, Nicholas, *The Importance of the Colonies of North America and the Interest of Great Britain*, London, 1766; Anon., *The True Interest of Great Britain with respect of her American Colonies*, London, 1766. Finally there must be mentioned in this connection the works of Josiah Tucker, but he comes very close to being a laissez-faire economist, rather than a mercantilist. However, there is a good deal of mercantilism in his views, and the following works should be noted for their criticism of colonial policy: *The True Interest of Great Britain set forth in Regard to the Colonies* (in *Four Tracts on Political and Commercial Subjects,* London, 1774) and *An Humble Address and Earnest Appeal,* London, 1775.

p. 71, n. 132, II.

The advocates of a national bank, besides the great protagonist of the bank, William Paterson, are the following:

Anon., *An Humble Proposal whereby His Majesty may Raise and Extend his Credit to the annual value of his Revenue,* London, 1673-74; [Turner, Thomas], *The Joyful News of opening the Exchequer to the Goldsmiths of Lombard Street and their Creditors,* London, 1677, not exactly relevant, but an interesting item; Houghton, Thomas, *A Book of Funds,* London, 1696; Murray, Robert, *Proposal for a National Bank,* London, 1695-96, and *A Proposal for the more easie Advancing to the Crown any fixed sum of Money,* [London, 1696]; Anon., *A Letter to a Member of the Honourable House of Commons; in Answer to Three Queries,* London, 1697; Anon., *A Letter to a Friend, concerning the Credit of the Nation,* London, 1697; Brewster, Sir Francis, *New Essays on Trade,* London, 1702, the protests of a hard money mercantilist against all the paper money schemes; Anon., *The Vindication and Advancement of our National Constitution and Credit,* London, 1710, a severe criticism of the bank, but a defense of paper money schemes brought under more governmental control, especially p. 73 *ff;* Mackworth, Sir Humphrey, *A Proposal for the Payment of the Publick Debts,* London [1720] and *An Answer to the Several Queries relating to a Proposal for Payment of the Publick Debts,* London, 1720; [G., T.], *Two Proposals for raising £1,250,000 for the current service of the year 1729,* London, 1729.

Some of the conspicuous proposals for a landbank scheme are as follows:

Cradocke, Francis, *Wealth Discovered,* London, 1661; Briscoe, John, *An Explanatory Dialogue of a Late Treatise, intituled a Discourse on the Late Funds of the Million-Act,* London, 1694, and *Proposals for Raising Money for a National Land-Bank,* London, 1695; [Briscoe, John], *A Discourse on the Late Funds of the Million-Act,* 2nd ed., London, 1694; [Chamberlin, Hugh, and Thomas, Dalby], *A Proposal for encouraging of Persons, to subscribe toward a Common Stock,* London, 1695; [Chamberlin, Hugh], *A Supplement to the Proposal for a General Fishery,* London, 1695; Killigrew, William, *An Essay upon the Necessity of Raising the Value of Twenty Millions of Pounds,* London, 1695, and *A Proposal, shewing how this Nation may be vast gainers by all the sums of Money, given to the Crown,* London [1633]?; Cary, John, *An Essay Towards the Settlement of a National Credit,* London, 1696; Asgill, John, *Several Assertions Proved, in order to Create another Species of Money than Gold and Silver,* London, 1696; Anon., *Proposals for Restoring Credit, for making the Bank of England more Useful and Profitable,* London, 1721; Anon., *An Honest Scheme for Improving the Trade and Credit of the Nation,* London, 1729.

Some of the writings which deal more strictly with the coinage are interesting in this connection, for in most of them the same views of the national interest are expressed:

Anon., *The Use and Abuses of Money,* London, 1671, a proposal for alloying the coin, because it is over-valued; Blackwell, John, *An Essay towards carrying on the Present War against France,* London, 1695, arguments for improving the clipped coins; Anon., *A Review of the Universal Remedy for All Diseases incident to Coin,* London, 1696; Anon., *Some Considerations about the Raising of Coin,* London, 1696; J., R., *A Letter of advice to a Friend about the Currency of Clipt Money,* London, 1696; Anon., *A Proposal for the Raising of the Silver Coin of England,* London, 1696; Vickaris, A., *An Essay for the Regulating of the Coin,* London, 1696; [Prat, Samuel, Dean of Rochester], *Regulating the Silver Coin,* London, 1696; Hodges, William, *The Groans of the Poor,* London, 1696.

p. 81, n. 7, III.

Some other examples of the assertion of the power of the state, in addition to the foregoing, are: Malynes, Gerard de., *England's View, in the Unmasking of two Paradoxes,* London, 1603, pp. 138-174, gives a long list of the state's duties of management of trade; Dalton, M., *The County Justice,* London,

1655, a handbook for the J. P. instructing him in his manifold duties, first issued in 1618, and while not directly relevant here, its obvious tone of approval for all his economic tasks is suggestive; Robinson, Henry, *England's Safety in Trades Encrease*, London, 1641; [Bland, John], *Trade Revived, or a Way Proposed to Restore, Increase, Inrich, Strengthen and Preserve the Decayed and even Dying Trade of this our English Nation*, London, 1659, pp. 8 et seq.; Yarranton, Andrew, *England's Improvement on Sea and Land*, London, 1678, sets forth an extensive program of state regulation; [Harris, Sir Walter], *Remarks on the Trade of England and Ireland*, London, 1691; Anon., *Directions to Judge whether a Nation be in a Thriving Condition, and how to advance the Wealth and Power of Great Britain*, London, 1728; [Bennett, John], *The National Merchant; or Discourses on Commerce and Colonies*, London, [1736]; Postlethwayt, Malachy, *A Short State of the Progress of the French Trade and Navigation*, London, 1756, praising the French government's management of trade as a lesson to England; Mildmay, Sir William, *The Laws and Policy of England, Relating to Trade*, London, 1765, pp. 23-50; Anon., *Political Speculations; or, an Attempt to discover the Causes for the Dearness of Provisions*, London, 1767.

p. 89, n. 17, III.

Other statements of the faith in numbers of people, and of the necessity, in some way or another, of enlisting the authority of the state to encourage population growth, follow:

S., W. Gent., *The Golden Fleece*, London, 1656, pp. 79-78, misnumbered; Coke, Roger, *Treatise*, London, 1671, petitions 2-5 in pp. 16-17, unnumbered, of the preface; Anon., *The Grand Concern of England Explained*, London, 1673, p. 13; Ferguson, Robert, *A Just and Modest Vindication of the Scots Design*, London, 1699, pp. 17-18; Wood, William, *A Survey of Trade*, London, 1719, p. 306; [Hay, William], *Remarks on the Laws relating to the Poor*, London, 1735, pp. 22-23; Tucker, Josiah, *Reflections on the Expediency of a Law for the Naturalization of Foreign Protestants*, London,

1751, pp. 16, 19; North, Roger, *A Discourse of the Poor,* London, 1753, p. 78; [Ignotus], *Thoughts on Trade in General,* London, 1763; Craufurd, George, Esq., *An Essay on the Actual Resources for re-establishing the Finances of Great Britain,* London, 1785, p. 10.

p. 91, n. 22, III.

Similar condemnations of idleness and desire for some machinery for enforcing industry may be found in: Hitchcock, Robert, *A Pollitique Platt, for the Honour of the Prince,* London, 1580; [Decker, Thomas], *Grievous Grones for the Poor,* London, 1621; Fielding, Henry, *An Enquiry into the Causes of the Late Increase of Robbers,* London, 1751, the result of the famous author's experience as a magistrate; Townsend, Joseph, *Dissertation on the Poor Laws,* London, 1786.

Similar views were expressed by nearly every author who put forward a workhouse scheme, which were very numerous.

p. 92, n. 24, III.

Similar statements of the sin of idleness and the obligation to work for low wages are found in the following:

[Scott, Thomas], *The Belgicke Pismire,* London, 1622; Anon., *The Use and Abuses of Money,* London, 1671; Coke, Roger, *Treatise,* London, 1671, pp. 74 et seq., and *A Detection,* London, 1694, pp. 47-48, unnumbered, of the Introduction; Anon; *The Ancient Trades Repaired,* London, 1678, p. 8; Dunning, Richard, Gent., *A Plain and Easie Method,* London, 1686; Asgill, John, *Several Assertions Proved,* London, 1696, pp. 74-75; Anon., *Two Discourses concerning the Affairs of Scotland,* Edinburgh, 1698, pp. 28-31 of the second discourse; Paxton, P. (M.D.), *A Discourse concerning the Nature, Advantage and Improvement of Trade,* London, 1704, pp. 5-13; Anon., *The Consequences of a Law for Reducing the Dutys upon French Wines,* London, 1713, pp. 6-7; Anon., *General Maxims in Trade,* London, 1713, pp. 10-12; [Richardson, William], *Essay on the Causes of the Decline of the Foreign Trade,* London, 1744, pp. 57-59.

p. 95, n. 30, III.

Other statements of high wage doctrines in addition to those cited above are:

Cary, John, *A Discourse concerning the East-India Trade,* Bristol, 1695, pp. 5, 10; S., T., *Reasons Humbly Offered for . . . hindering the Consumption of East-India Silks,* London, 1697; T., T., Merchant, *Some General Considerations offered relating to our present Trade,* London, 1698, pp. 5-7; Mortimer, Thomas, *The Elements of Commerce, Politics, and Finances,* London, 1772, pp. 77-101.

p. 95, n. 31, III.

The literature throughout the period teems with proposals for workhouse schemes, which are to serve the purpose of training workers, discouraging idleness, often keep wages down, and keep the population employed. Instances follow, in chronological order:

Child, Sir Josiah, *Trade and the Interest of Money Considered,* London, 1669; [Haines, Richard], *The Prevention of Poverty,* London, [1674]; Haines, Richard, *Proposals for building in every County a Working Alms-House or Hospital,* London, 1677, *A Breviat of Some Proposals,* London, 1679, and *England's Weal and Prosperity Proposed,* London, 1681; [Firmin, Thomas], *Some Proposals for the Employing of the Poor,* London, 1678; Anon., *Proposals for promoting the Woollen Manufactury,* London, 1679; Coke, Roger, *A Detection,* London, 1694, Vol. II, p. 495; Cary, John, *An Essay on the State of England,* Bristol, 1695, pp. 157-162; Bellers, John, *Proposals for raising a Colledge of Industry,* London, 1696; [Bellers, John], *A Supplement to the Proposal,* London, 1696; Temple, Sir William, *Of Popular Discontents,* circa, 1680-? (in *Works,* London, 1814, pp. 52-53, the editor, Swift, in a note, refuses to date the work, but it must have been written before Temple's death in 1700); Nourse, Timothy, *Campania Foelix,* London, 1700, Ch. XIV; Povey, Charles, *The Unhappiness of England as to its Trade by Sea and Land,* London, 1701; Berkeley, George, *An Essay towards Preventing the Ruin of Great Britain,* 1721 (in *Works,* ed. Alexander Campbell Fraser, Oxford, 1871, Vol. III, pp. 197-198); Dobbs, Arthur, *An*

Essay on the Trade and Improvement of Ireland, London, 1729-31, pp. 45-57; [Hay, William], *Remarks on the Laws relating to the Poor,* London, 1735; Cox, Sir Richard, *A Letter from Sir Richard Cox, Bart. to Thomas Prior, Esq.,* London, 1749; Anon., *Considerations, humbly offered Parliament, relative to a bill for promoting Industry,* London, 1758; Burn, Richard, *The History of the Poor Laws,* London, 1764; Anon., *A Scheme for the better Relief and Employment of the Poor,* London, 1765; Anon., *An Examination of the Alteration in the Poor Laws, proposed by Dr. Burn,* London, 1766; [Potter, Robert], *Observations on the Poor Laws,* London, 1775, one of the few humanitarian expressions on the subject.

p. 100, n. 38, III.

The arguments for sumptuary legislation, put upon any one or all of the grounds discussed in the text, in addition to those cited, follow in chronological order:

[Vaughan, William], *The Golden Fleece,* London, 1626, Part II; Anon., *The Grand Concern of England Explained,* London, 1673, Chs. VI, VII, VIII, especially p. 50; Philo-Anglicus, Gent., *Bread for the Poor,* London, 1678, p. 6; Anon., *The Ancient Trades Decayed, Repaired Again,* London, 1678, Sections VII and VIII; Hodges, William, *The Groans of the Poor,* London, 1696, p. 4; [M., J.], *To the Honourable Knights . . . of the House of Commons, Proposals most humbly offered . . .* London, 1696, more a taxing scheme than a sumptuary law; Pollexfen, John, *England and East-India Inconsistent in their Manufactures,* London, 1697, pp. 46-49; Nourse, Timothy, *Campania Foelix,* London, 1700, Ch. XIV; Anon., *The Circumstances of Scotland Consider'd,* Edinburgh, 1705, p. 23; Paxton, P. (M.D.), *A Discourse concerning the Nature, Advantage, and Improvement of Trade,* London, 1704, pp. 68-80, not orthodox because he inclines to a laissez-faire analysis, but nevertheless interesting; [Defoe, Daniel], *A Brief State of the Question,* London, 1719, pp. 12-21, 39; Anon., *Considerations on the Present State of the Nation,* London, 1720, p. 27; [Gordon, Thomas], *Three Political Letters to a Noble Lord,* London, 1721, p. 7; [Bennett, John], *The National Merchant,* London, [1736]; Anon., *Seasonable*

Observations on the Present Fatal Declension of the Commerce of England, London, 1737; [Richardson, William], *Essay on the Causes of the Decline of the Foreign Trade,* London, 1744, sometimes attributed to Sir Matthew Decker, is laisser-faire in much of the analysis, but still asks for sumptuary laws; Anon., *Political Speculations; or, an Attempt to discover the Causes of the Dearness of Provisions,* London, 1767, Part I; Anon., *An Infallible Remedy for the High Prices of Provisions,* London, 1768, pp. 29-31. See also Notes 86-91 on Chapter II, *supra.*

One of the few writers to express doubts on the efficacy of administration of such laws was [Harris, Joseph], *An Essay upon Money and Coins,* London, 1757, pp. 29-30.

E. S. Furniss gives an interesting discussion of the duty of the gentry to furnish an example to the laboring classes in his *Position of the Laborer in a System of Nationalism,* p. 56.

p. 104, n. 44, III.

Other expressions of the importance of the merchant and manufacturer, often declaring the necessity of state regulation of their activities, follow:

[Milles, Thomas], *The Customers Replie,* London, 1604; Anon., *Leather: A Discourse,* London, 1629; [Bethel, Slingsby], *The Present Interest of England Stated,* London, 1671, pp. 8-10; Anon., *The East-India-Trade a most Profitable Trade to the Kingdom,* London, 1677, pp. 3-4; Philo-Anglicus, Gent., *Bread for the Poor,* London, 1678, p. 6; Anon., *The Ancient Trades Decayed, Repaired Again,* London, 1678; Child, Sir Josiah, *A Treatise wherein is demonstrated, I. That the East India Trade is the most National of all Foreign Trades,* London, 1681, pp. 1-2; Anon., *Considerations requiring greater Care for Trade in England,* London, 1695; Pollexfen, John, *England and East India inconsistent in their Manufactures,* London, 1697, pp. 46-49; Davenant, Charles, *An Essay upon the Probable Methods of making a People Gainers in the Ballance of Trade,* London, 2nd ed., 1700, p. 173 (first published in 1699); King, Charles, compiler, *The British Merchant,* London, 2nd ed., 1743, Vol. I, p. 31 (first issued as a weekly, 1713-14); Gee, Joshua, *Trade and Navigation of*

Great Britain Considered, 3rd ed., London, 1731, p. 136 (first published 1729); Postlethwayt, Malachy, *Great Britain's Commercial Interest Explained and Improved,* 2nd ed., London, 1759, Vol. II, p. 368 (first published 1757).

See also the discussion of councils of trade in the text, Ch. IV.

p. 111, n. 53, III.

Other expressions of a harmony of interest, in addition to those cited, though more specific in intent, are: Anon., *The Proverb Crossed,* London, 1677, p. 7; Cary, John, *An Essay on the State of England,* London, 1695, pp. 149-150, while he is arguing for high wages; Bellers, John, *Proposals for raising a Colledge of Industry,* London, 1696, p. 20; T., T., Merchant, *Some General Considerations offered relating to our Present Trade,* London, 1698, pp. 5-7, also arguing for high wages; Anon., *Reasons offered against the Continuance of the Bank,* London, 1707, p. 9.

p. 115, n. 59, III.

Other general expressions of the rivalry of states, and its likelihood to result in war, follow:

[Bethel, Slingsby], *The World's Mistake in Oliver Cromwell,* London, 1668, especially p. 8; Temple, Sir William, *Observations upon the United Provinces of the Netherlands,* London, 1673 (in *Works,* London, 1814, Vol. I, pp. 180-181); Maydman, Henry, *Naval Speculations and Maritime Politicks,* London, 1691; Cary, John, *An Essay on the State of England,* Bristol, 1695, pp. 49-129; Anon., *A Dialogue between Mr. Smith, Monsieur Ragouse, Menheir Dorveil and Mr. Manoel Texiera, in a Walk to Newington,* London, 1701, pp. 24-30; Anon., *The Important Question Discussed,* London [1746]; Anon., *The State of the Nation Considered in a Letter to a M. P.,* London, [1747] especially p. 10.

See also the many advocates of policies of rivalry toward the French, Dutch, and Spanish, Notes 66-68, below.

p. 119, n. 66, III.

Other demands for action against France follow in chronological order:

Carter, William, *England's Interest by Trade Asserted,* London, 1671, also attacks the Dutch; Anon., *The Ancient Trades Decayed, Repaired Again,* London, 1678, also attacks the Dutch; Anon., *The Present State of Christendome and the Interest of England with regard to France,* London, 1678; [B., J.], *An Account of the French Usurpations upon the Trade of England,* London, 1679, especially p. 6; Collins, John, *Salt and Fishery,* London, 1682; [Bethel, Slingsby], *Observations on a Letter written by the Duke of Buckingham to Sir Thomas Osborn,* London, 1689; Anon., *Considerations requiring greater Care for Trade,* London, 1695; Cary, John, *An Essay on the State of England,* Bristol, 1695, pp. 128-129; [Carter, William], *The Usurpations of France upon the Trade of the Woollen Manufacture of England,* London, 1696, especially p. 2; Davenant, Charles, *Discourses of the Public Revenues,* London, 1698 (in *Works,* London, 1771, Vol. I, pp. 394-408); Anon., *The Interests of the Several Princes and States of Europe Consider'd, with respect to the Succession of the Crown of Spain,* London, 1698; [Defoe, Daniel], *The Two Great Questions Considered,* London, 1700; [Stepney, G.], *An Essay upon the Present Interest of England,* London, 1701; Anon., *The Dutch Barrier Our's,* London, 1712; Anon., *The Consequences of a Law for Reducing the Dutys upon French Wines,* London, 1713; Anon., *General Maxims in Trade, particularly applied to the Commerce between Great Britain and France,* London, 1713; Anon., *A Letter to a West-Country Clothier,* London, 1713; Anon., *Seasonable Observations on the Present Fatal Declension of the Commerce of England,* London, 1737; Perrin, William, *The Present State of the British and French Sugar Colonies,* London, 1740; [Morris, Corbyn], *An Essay towards deciding the Important Question,* London, [1747]; Keith, Sir William, Bart., *A Collection of Papers and other Tracts,* 2nd ed., London, 1749; Anon., *The Important Question concerning Invasions,* London, 1755; Postlethwayt, Malachy, *A Short State of the Progress of the French Trade and Navigation,* London, 1756, *Great-Britain's True System,* London, 1757, letters X and XI, and *Dictionary of Trade and Commerce,* 4th ed., London, 1774, preliminary discourse II; [Williamson, Peter], *Occasional Reflections on the Importance of the War in America,* London, 1758; Anon., *The Comparative Importance of our Acquisitions from France in America,* London, 1762.

To this list must be added the long debate between Daniel Defoe in his *Mercator* and Charles King with his associates in *The British Merchant* during 1713 and 1714.

It might be added that the above identifications of France as an enemy are in most cases general declarations concerning the rivalry of the states in Europe as well.

p. 119, n. 67, III.

Other attacks on the Dutch are:

[Bethel, Slingsby], *The World's Mistake in Oliver Cromwell,* London, 1668; Carter, William, *England's Interest by Trade Asserted,* London, 1671, also attacks France; De Britaine, William, *The Dutch Usurpation,* London, 1672; [De Britaine, William], *The Interest of England in the Present War with Holland,* London, 1672; [Stubbs, Henry], *A Justification of the Present War against the United Netherlands,* London, 1672; Stubbs, Henry, *A Further Justification of the Present War against the United Netherlands,* London, 1673; Anon., *The Ancient Trades Decayed, Repaired Again,* London, 1678, also attacks the French; Yarranton, Andrew, *England's Improvement by Sea and Land,* London, 1678.

p. 119, n. 68, III.

The writings identifying Spain as an enemy:

Hagthorpe, John, Gent., *Englands-Exchequer,* London, 1625, pp. 15 et seq.; [Ferguson, Charles], *A Letter Address'd to every Honest Man in Britain,* London, 1738; [Lyttelton, George], *Considerations upon the present State of our Affairs, at Home and Abroad,* London, 1739, and *Farther Considerations on the present State of Affairs at Home and Abroad,* London, 1759; Anon., *Dissertation on the Present Conjuncture,* London, 1739.

p. 140, n. 35, IV.

Other proposals for councils of trade follow in chronological order:

Roberts, Lewis, *The Treasure of Traffike*, London, 1641 (in McCulloch, J. R., *Early English Tracts on Commerce*, London, 1856, pp. 90-113); Robinson, Henry, *England's Safety in Trades Encrease*, London, 1641, p. 46; Parker, Henry, *Of a Free Trade*, London, 1648, p. 36; Raleigh, Sir Walter, *Observations touching Trade and Commerce* (in McCulloch, J. R., *Early English Tracts on Commerce*, London, 1856, pp. 250-274); [Bethel, Slingsby], *The Present Interest of England Stated*, London, 1671, p. 10, a proposal for courts merchant; Collins, John, *A Plea for the Bringing in of Irish Cattel*, London, 1680, pp. 29-30; Vickaris, A., *An Essay for regulating of the Coyn*, London, 1696, pp. 1-2; Davenant, Charles, *Discourses of the Public Revenues and on Trade*, London, 1698 (in *Works*, ed. Sir Charles Whitworth, London, 1771, Vol. I, pp. 422 et seq.); T., T., Merchant, *Some General Considerations offered relating to our present Trade*, London, 1698, the concluding pages; Povey, Charles, *The Unhappiness of England as to its Trade by Sea and Land*, London, 1701, pp. 15-33, councils in the various cities; Anon., *The Present State of the British and French Trade to Africa considered and compared*, London, 1745, pp. 25-26; [McCulloch, William T.], *The Wisdom and Policy of the French in the Construction of their Great Offices*, London, 1755, pp. 75-79.

p. 141, n. 37, IV.

Other discussions of the need of a national bank follow in chronological order:

Robinson, Henry, *England's Safety in Trades Encrease*, London, 1641, pp. 34-42; Benbrigge, John, *Usura Accommadata*, London, 1646; Maddison, Ralph, Kt., *Great Britain's Remembrancer Looking In and Out*, London, 1655, pp. 25 et seq.; Cradocke, Francis, *Wealth Discovered*, London, 1661; Anon., *An Humble Proposal whereby His Majesty may Raise and Extend his Credit*, London, 1673-74; [Briscoe, John], *A Discourse on the Late Funds of the Million-Act*, London, 1694; Anon., *An Essay upon the Necessity of Raising the Value of Twenty Millions of Pounds*, London, 1695-?; Murray, Robert, *Proposal for a National Bank*, London, 1695-6, and *A Proposal for the more easie Advancing to the Crown any fixed*

Sum of Money, London, [1696]; Anon., *A Letter to a Friend, concerning Credit,* London, 1697; Anon., *A Letter to a Friend, concerning the Credit of the Nation; and with Relation to the Present Bank of England,* London, 1697; H., P., *The Bank of England, and their Present Method of Paying,* London, 1697; Anon., *Reasons offered against the Continuance of the Bank,* London, 1707; Anon., *The Vindication and Advancement of our National Constitution and Credit,* London, 1710; Anon., *An Honest Scheme, for improving the Trade and Credit of the Nation,* London, 1739; Berkeley, George, *The Querist,* London, 1734-36, ed. J. H. Hollander, Baltimore, 1910, Part I, questions 199-208, and all of Part II.

p. 153, n. 54, IV.

Other works in the eighteenth century, placing a similar emphasis on the "mixt elements" of the British Constitution, frequently decrying party strife and asking for more power and leadership in the kingship, follow:

[Drake, Sir James], *The History of the Last Parliament,* London, 1702; Anon., *The Vindication and Advancement of our National Constitution and Credit,* London, 1710, especially the introductory essay; Anon., *Whigs and Tories United,* London, 1714; *The Craftsman,* London, see references given *supra,* Note 18 to Ch. IV, p. 131; Anon., *The Case of Opposition stated, between the Craftsman and the People,* London, 1731; [Erskine, James], *The Fatal Consequences of Ministerial Influence,* London, 1736; Anon., *Britons Awake, and Look About You,* London, 1743, especially pp. 11-13; [Shebbeare, John], *Letters to the People of England,* Letters I to VI, London, 1755-56; [Marriott, Sir James], *Political Considerations,* London, 1762, especially pp. 33-37; Mortimer, Thomas, *The Elements of Commerce,* London, 1772, especially pp. 216-301; Tucker, Josiah, *A Treatise concerning Civil Government,* London, 1781, especially Part II.

p. 159, n. 63, IV.

Writers other than those cited who defended monopoly privileges against either or both charges—high prices and restriction of enterprise—follow in roughly chronological order:

Robinson, Henry, *England's Safety in Trades Encrease,* London, 1641, especially pp. 21-25; 45-46; Parker, Henry, *Of a Free Trade,* London, 1648, especially pp. 21-24; Charpentier, François, *A Treatise touching the East-Indian Trade,* London, 1676, an interesting item, a translation of a French book by an anonymous translator, who explains that it is important for Englishmen to read it; Anon., *The East-India-Trade a most Profitable Trade to the Kingdom,* London, 1677; Anon., *The Scheme of the Subsequent Discourse,* London, 1683; Anon., *Two Discourses concerning the Affairs of Scotland,* Edinburgh, 1698, especially pp. 10-18 of the first discourse; Davenant, Charles, *Discourses on the Public Revenues and on the Trade of England,* London, 1698 (in *Works,* ed. Sir Charles Whitworth, London, 1771, Vol. II, the fourth discourse of the second part) and *Reflections upon the Constitution and Management of the Trade to Africa,* London, 1709 (in *Works,* Vol. V, especially Chs. VI-VIII of Part I); Anon., *Some Short Remarks on Two Pamphlets,* [London, 1710]; Anon., *Some Observations, showing the Danger of losing the Trade of the Sugar Colonies,* London, 1714; Royal African Company of England, *The Case of the Royal African Company,* [London, 1720], the company's own statement of its arguments; [Hays, (?)], *Importance of effectually supporting the Royal African Company,* London, 1744; [Postlethwayt, Malachy], *The African Trade,* London, 1745; Anon., *The Present State of the British and French Trade to Africa and America,* London, 1745; [Postlethwayt, Malachy], *The National and Private Advantages of the African Trade,* London, 1746; Anon., *An Essay on the East India Trade, and its Importance to this Kingdom,* London, 1770; Mortimer, Thomas, *The Elements of Commerce,* London, 1772, especially pp. 143-147; [Dalrymple, Alexander], *A General View of the East India Company,* London, 1772; Campbell, John, *A Political Survey of Great Britain,* London, 1774, especially Ch. IV of Book V.

The attacks on the monopolies and companies, other than those cited above, follow in roughly chronological order:

Child, Sir Josiah, *A Treatise wherein is demonstrated that the East India Trade is the most National of all the Foreign Trades,* London, 1681, a very interesting item, for while the trade is defended, monopoly is roundly condemned, see pp. 2-3, also the same author's *Trade and the Interest of Money Considered,* London, 1669, Ch. III; [Petyt, William], *Britannia Languens,* London, 1680, especially pp. 133 et seq.; Cary, John, *An Essay on the State of England,* London, 1695, especially pp. 61-62 and *A Discourse concerning the East India Trade,* London, 1696, p. 10; Anon., *A True State of the Present Differences between the Royal African Company and the Separate Traders,* London, 1710; Wood, William, *A Survey of Trade,* London, 1719, argues for opening trades in the form of regulated companies so that anyone may enter, pp. 258-298; [Defoe, Daniel], *The Case Fairly Stated between the Turkey Company and the Italian Merchants,* London, 1720, especially pp. 30-32, 39-40; *The Craftsman,* issues in 1726 to 1728 (in the collection published in London, 1737, in fourteen volumes, Vol. I, pp. 25 et seq.; 62; 75 et seq.; Vol. II, 196 et seq.; Vol. III, pp. 201-207); Anon., *Some Considerations humbly offered upon the Bill . . . relating to the Trade between the Northern Colonies and the Sugar Islands,* [London, 1732]; Anon., *Considerations on the American Trade,* [London, 1739]; [Richardson, William], *Essay on the Causes of the Decline of the Foreign Trade,* London, 1744, especially pp. 40-54; Anon., *Considerations on the Advantage of Yielding up to Spain the un-expired Term of the Assiento Contract,* London, 1748; Anon., *Seasonable Observations on the Trade to Africa,* London, [1748]; Postlethwayt, Malachy, *Universal Dictionary of Trade and Commerce,* 4th ed., London, 1774 (first edition appeared Vol. I, 1751, Vol. II, 1755) under "Companies" quotes Sir Josiah Child to the effect that they have probably decreased trade, though in his other writings Postlethwayt defended companies, particularly the African company; Tucker, Josiah, *The Elements of Commerce and Theory of Taxes,* Bristol, 1755, pp. 82-92; Anon., *An Infallible Remedy for the High Prices of Provisions,* London, 1768, especially the first 30 pages; Anon., *Considerations and Remarks on the Present State of the Trade to Africa,* London, 1771.

p. 164, n. 70, IV.

Most of the writings dealing with the economic aspects of monopoly raised discussion of the political question discussed in the text, and for their views see the lists given in Note 63 above. However, it is worthwhile to list a few striking instances of the discussion of the political aspect of monopoly.

Some of the defenses of monopoly as a means of state control follow, in roughly chronological order:

Robinson, Henry, *England's Safety in Trades Encrease*, London, 1641, especially pp. 5-6, 18-20, 21-25, 45-46; Parker, Henry, *Of a Free Trade*, London, 1648, especially pp. 1-17; Fortrey, Samuel, *England's Interest and Improvement*, London, 1673 (in McCulloch, J. R., *Early English Tracts on Commerce*, London, 1856, pp. 210-249); Davenant, Charles, *Reflections upon the Constitution and Management of the Trade to Africa*, London, 1709 (in *Works*, ed. Whitworth, London, Vol. V); Anon., *Some Short Remarks on two Pamphlets recently printed*, [London, 1710]; Mortimer, Thomas, *The Elements of Commerce, Politics, and Finances*, London, 1772, especially pp. 143-147.

Some of the attacks upon monopolistic privilege, emphasizing its political aspects, follow in roughly chronological order:

Cary, John, *An Essay on the State of England*, Bristol, 1695, especially pp. 60-64, and *A Discourse concerning the East India Trade*, London, 1696, pp. 10 et seq.; [Toland, John], *The Art of Governing by Parties*, London, 1701; [L., J.], *A Letter to an M. P. shewing the Injustice and Pernicious Consequences of the Proposal lately made by the Old East India Company*, London, 1701; *The Craftsman*, issue of September 7, 1728 (in Vol. III of the collected issues, London, 1731-37, pp. 201-207); Anon., *The National Mirror*, London, 1771; Pownall, Thomas, *The Right, Interest and Duty of the State, as concerned in the Affairs of the East Indies*, London, 1773.

p. 167, n. 71, IV.

It is unnecessary to burden the text with citations to substantiate the general point stated, but some discussion and illustration of the lack of contact between the political theorists and the mercantilists may be stated here. The general conclusion stated in the text is based upon a considerable reading in the literature of the period.

During the period of the Commonwealth there was, of course, voluminous publication on both sides, and during this period one of the great classics of English political thought was published, Thomas Hobbes' *Leviathan* (1651). The arguments of many of the writers were frequently scriptural, citing holy writ and developing theological reasoning, and arriving at opposite conclusions, either justifying the Revolution, or defending divine right or the logical necessity of a monarchy. During this period—noting of course that the debate begins before 1640 and runs after 1660—the following mercantilist writings of consequence appeared, and paid no regard to these arguments:

Mun, Thomas, *England's Treasure by Forraign Trade,* 1664 (written about 1630); Malynes, Gerard de, *Consuetudo, vel Lex Mercatoria,* 1636; Maddison or Maddestone, Ralph, *Englands Looking In and Out,* 1640; Roberts, Lewis, *Treasure of Traffike,* 1641; Robinson, Henry, *England's Safety in Trades Encrease,* 1641; Parker, Henry, *Of a Free Trade,* 1648; S., W., *The Golden Fleece,* 1656; [Bland, John], *Trade Revived,* 1659. Others might be mentioned, but the striking feature of both the mercantilist tracts and what might be called the strictly political tracts is that each group of writers ignores the issues and arguments that concern the other.

The Revolution of 1689 was preceded by a long period in which fears of a Popish plot worried many of the pamphleteers. Any number of writers discuss the question of allegiance to the monarch in terms of a conflict between the Catholic and Protestant confessions. Then of course the flight of the last Stuart and the reign of William of Orange gave rise to many attacks upon and defenses of the Revolution. It is unnecessary to analyze the profuse publication of the time; it is sufficient to point out that Sir Robert Filmer's *Patriarca* appeared in 1680 (though it was written much earlier) and Locke's two treatises *Of Civil Government* were printed ten years later. As was the case in the period of the Commonwealth, mercantilist writings of some importance fall within this span of years and make no mention of the political issues, some of them being:

Anon., *The Ancient Trades Decayed, Repaired Again,* 1678; [Petyt, William], *Britannia Languens,* 1680; Child, Sir Josiah, *A Treatise wherein is demonstrated that the East India Trade is the most National of all Foreign Trades,* 1681; Barbon, Nicholas, *A Discourse of Trade,* 1690; North Dudley, *Discourses upon Trade,* 1691; Coke, Roger, *A Detection of the Court and State of England,* 1694; Anon., *Considerations requiring Greater Care for Trade in England,* 1695; Clement, Simon, *A Discourse of the General Notions of Money, Trade, and Exchanges,* 1695; Cary, John, *An Essay on the State of England,* 1695; Asgill, John, *Several Assertions Proved,* 1696; Pollexfen, John, *England and East India Inconsistent in their Manufactures,* 1697; Davenant, Charles, *An Essay upon the Probable Methods of making a People Gainers in the Balance of Trade,* 1699.

It is unnecessary to labor the point further; the above discussion was designed merely to illustrate and document the general conclusion stated in the text.

p. 169, n. 78, IV.

The passage in which Bolingbroke discusses trade, referred to in the text, follows. It is found in his *Works,* Dublin, 1793, Vol. III, pp. 102-104:

The situation of Great Britain, the character of her people, and the nature of her government, fit her to trade and commerce. Her climate and soil make them necessary to her well-being. By trade and commerce we grow a rich and powerful nation, and by their decay we are growing poor and impotent. As Trade and Commerce enrich, so they fortify our country. The sea is our barrier, ships are our fortresses, and the mariners, that trade and commerce alone can furnish, are the garrisons to defend them. . . .

The result of what has been said is, in general, that the wealth and power of all nations depending so much on their trade and commerce, and every nation being . . . in different circumstances of advantage and disadvantage in the pursuit of this common interest; a good government, and therefore the government of a Patriot King, will be directed constantly to make the most of every advantage that nature has given, or art can procure, towards the improvement of trade and commerce. . . . It results, in particular, that Great Britain might improve her wealth and power in a proportion superior to that of any nation who can be deemed her rival, if the advantages she has were as widely cultivated as they will be in the reign of a Patriot King.

One further remark may be made regarding the possible influence of divine right theory upon the mercantilists. Only a few of the great names have been referred to in the text; but a reading of a great many minor works reveals how thoroughly the conception of the analogy to the household and the argument of the common interest of king and people was embedded in the literature of the mercantilist period.

Index of Subjects

Absolute monarchy, incompatible with a national bank, 146; incompatible with trade, 146; injurious to public credit, 146; injurious to trade, 147; inferior to limited monarchy, 151

Administration, competence of taken for granted, 142; entrusted to individuals or companies, 184; *see also* Administrative agencies

Administrative agencies, *see* Council of Trade; Banks; Workhouses; Justices of peace; Privy Council; National administration

Agriculture, encouragement of, 7, 48-52; changes in organization of, 49; relation of to trade and wages, 51-52; improvement of waste lands, 105; connection of cheap subsistence and low wages, 105-106; connection with manufacture and foreign trade, 106; chronological list of mercantilist writers proposing programs for, 201-202

Alnager, 38; *see also* Weaving industry; Woolen industry

Apprenticeships, 90; *see also* Statute of Apprentices; Statute of Artificers

Aristocracy, 126

Balance of bargains, 22

Balance of power, between states, 120

Balance of trade, 87, 142, 179; general, 23-24, 27; chronological list of mercantilist writers dealing with, 197-199

Banks, 134, 141, 173; national, 41; security of under parliamentary government, 42; land bank schemes, 71; proposals for a national bank, 141; based on value of land, 141; national, chronological list of mercantilist writers advocating, 209, 219-220; land bank scheme, chronological list of mercantilist writers advocating, 209-210

Bank of England, 71

Board of Trade and Plantations, 7

Borrowing, state control of, 42

Bounties, 14, 25; on export of corn, 51, 105; criticisms of, 69; chronological list of mercantilist writers criticizing, 207-208

(British) East India Company, *see* East India Company (British)

Bullion, prohibition of export of, 85

Bullionist school, 22, 24, 43

Bureaucracy, *see* Administration; Council of Trade; Privy Council; Justices of peace; Workhouses; Banks

Canonist doctrine, paying of interest, 11

Capital, importance of to industry, 39; importance of, 43

Census, demands for, 89

Charles I, 51, 124

Church, relation to state, 166

Circulation, of money, 28, 102; *see also* Circulating medium; Money

Circulating medium, furnished by banks, 141; *see also* Circulation; Money

Citizen, duty to obey his government, 75; liberties of injured by monopoly, 161-162; *see also* Liberties of the subject

78-85, 120, 180; connection with rise of mercantilism, 4; growth of contributes to genesis of mercantilism, 7-8; regulation of manufacture, 10; rise of connected with mercantilism, 20; comparison of to a family household, 53, 55, 72-73, 126, 130, 140, 143, 173, 174, 226; presumption of right to regulate economic affairs, 86; justification of right to regulate economic affairs, 86; dangers of monopoly to, 159-165; policies of to secure balance in economic affairs, 180; mercantilist belief in broad powers criticized, 181; mercantilist failure to examine nature of, 183; mercantilist confidence in as it existed, 184; chronological list of mercantilist writers asserting power of, 210-211; importance of trade to, 225

Naturalization, Coke's views on, 64

Navigation acts, in Tudor period, 6; as embodiment of policy for shipping, 14, 179; arguments for, 56-59; political argument for, 57; economic argument for, 57; criticism of, 65; criticism of on economic grounds, 70; as weapon of rivalry between states, 117; chronological list of mercantilist writers advancing political argument for, 202-203; *see also* Shipping

Nazism, *see* Totalitarianism

New industries, encouragement of, 34, 83; subsidies for, 37; chronological list of mercantilist writers urging state encouragement of, 199-200; *see also* Infant industries; Manufactures; Monopoly

Order, importance of to state, 109, 110, 112, 121; importance of in community, 126, 180

Paper currency, advocates of as modification of mercantilist doctrine, 71

Parliament, 5, 7, 96, 103, 124, 128, 132, 143; relation to king, 128, 131, 144, 149, 173; function of to advise, 131; criticism of its legislation on trade, 137; function of to express popular assent, 144, 182; importance to public credit, 147; expresses popular agreement with king, 148; as means of reconciling king and people, 148, 149; compared to family council, 148; finance powers of, 149; union of with king, 150; function of in Coke's view, 151; cooperation with king, 153; as machinery of popular assent, 153-154; instrument of expressing popular consent, 154; corruption of elections by monopolies, 163; relation to king debated by political theorists, 165-167; relation to king in legal theory, 170-172; *see also* Constitution; King; "Mixt English constitution"; Monarchy

Parties, *see* Factions

Peace, pleas for, 115-116

People, *see* Population

Planned economy, 73-74, 120; mercantilist system as, 180; *see also* Economic planning

Political philosophers, *see* Political theorists

Political philosophy, mercantilists contact with, 124; little reference to by mercantilists, 165, 178; ignoring of issues of by mercantilists, 223-225

Political theorists, little citation of by mercantilists, 166-167, 174; little reference to mercantilist writers by, 166-167

Politics, interdependence of with economics, 121

Poor laws, 6, 17, 95; criticism of, 46

Index of Names and Books

v